Richard

The Maharajah has bitten off a White Elephant

The Maharajah has bitten off a White Elephant

Tales from a Gullible Traveller.

Richard Hunt

www.kingshampress.com

First published in 2013

By Aeneas Press [an imprint of Kingsham Press]

Oldbury Complex

Marsh Lane

Easthampnett

Chichester PO18 0JW

United Kingdom

Typeset in Minion

Printed and bound in the UK

ISBN: 978-1-904235-73-6

British Library Cataloguing in Publication Data

A catalogue record of this book is available from the British Library

Hunt, Richard

About the author.

Richard Hunt taught social history and ran the history and art programmes of Southampton University's Department of Adult Education for many years. Born in Burma, he spent his childhood in India as one of the last children of the British Raj. He renewed his affection for the country when, many years later, he was seconded to Madras (now Chennai) University. Back in England he hesitantly arranged a first group tour to India in 1984 and has been leading groups to most parts of India as well as other destinations ever since.

Acknowledgements.
With grateful thanks to Jill, my long-suffering wife, who accompanied me on all the journeys, taking care of the things I need and those I lose (including, sometimes, members of the group), remembering the things I forget, forgetting or at least forgiving the exasperations of some of the journeys and the mood-swings they engender. Without her, there would have been short-lived chaos and a swift end to the tours.

A very big thank-you, too, to all those who came with us, some once, some two or three times, some much more often. Clearly without them the journeys wouldn't have happened either, and while our travellers, what they got up to, how they got on with the country or with one-another provide much of the material in these pages, they are all - well, very nearly all - remembered with real affection. Many we count amongst our closest friends and many have said 'You really should write a book'. One of these was our friend and publisher, who has had many occasions to regret his advice.

CONTENTS

HOTELS

TRAINS

PROLOGUE

'I did enjoy that! It gave a real sense of India. You could feel you were really there.'

'I wish we were there.'

'Well, we keep talking about it; why don't we go?'

We'd all been sitting in the cinema, watching *Heat and Dust* - we had been reading the book and went to see the film as part of our *India* course - but afterwards as we stood on the pavement outside in the raw November drizzle, waiting for our coach, others joined in.

'Yes, I've been wanting to go all along.'

'And I wouldn't mind getting out of this horrible weather. When can we go?'

So we went, tentatively and completely inexperienced. And as India is so big, we went again, and then again and did not stop going.

That was how I found myself an *accidental* tour leader of trips to India; pushed into it by the people who came on the course. I was born next door, in Burma, and moved as a small child to India. Much later, my wife Jill and I spent several months working and travelling around the country. We became, quite slowly and after much discomfort, very attached to the country and its people. This led to a course, just called *India*, put on for adults by my university department after we returned. Of course I didn't know enough to teach it myself, but with lots of help from colleagues in all those abbreviated places - the BM, The V&A, SOAS (The School of Oriental and African Studies) - it went well. Lots of people wanted to attend, partly drawn by lectures no doubt, but also by the visits to museums, temples, concerts, restaurants and the cinema to see, among other films, *Heat and Dust*. Now they wanted me to arrange a visit. Jill advised against it. It was all very well travelling around India on our own, but looking after a group - and it seemed as if it would be a big group - was another matter. Could we cope? and would they get on, with us, with each other, with India?

It all began not such a very long time ago, but long enough it is a little sad to reflect, for this to be a *period* piece. Sad, as it means that those of us who took part are period pieces too. Those earlier journeys - starting in the very late 1970s, (although we continued and *continue* to make such journeys, perhaps into dotage) - were during a sort of 'in between' time in India's history; not the 'Old India' of the British Raj or 'Romantic India' of the Indian princes, and certainly not the booming modern India of today. After all, the

British left over 30 years before we started to visit (come to think of it, I was one rather small Britisher who left with the British, but went back) and the princes had become more or less absorbed into an Indian democracy. As the rather unfortunately titled (ex) Maharajah of Wankaner, a former princely state in Gujerat, said to us rather plaintively, conducting us round his vast but somewhat down-at-heel palace,

'My father was a king. Do you understand? A *king*! He ruled his country; but I … (a sad shake of the head) today… I am a mere *beggar*!' When we enquired what he begged *for*, he replied, 'For votes, my dear fellow, of course, for votes.' Sadly, the Maharajah, in attempting to use his status to join the state legislative assembly, was neither living in the past nor in the present; our guide put his finger on it, 'His highness is totally stuck-up in history.'

Our visits also came some time after India and also Nepal were discovered by young people in the '60s; by the time we arrived there, the hippy trail and the Beatles' dabbling with the Maharishi was old hat. Mind you, remnants of that culture, too, could still be found; strumming guitars on beaches in Goa; apple pie, pancakes and maple syrup in Kathmandu. I felt rather flattered when approached in middle age by a seedy money changer-cum-drug pedlar, whispering,

'Pssst… Change money?'

'No thank you.' To my chagrin I had been caught out in this way before and came off very much the poorer as a result of some very clever slight-of-hand conjuring.

'Pssst…' he continued, 'You want *hashish*?'

'Er, no, I don't think so.'

'You want *magic mushroom*?' I didn't know much about magic mushroom, so I asked,

'Magic mushroom? What will that do?'

'Oh, gentleman, it will make you feel good!' He looked into my face for a moment, adding, 'Make you look good!' He paused again, 'But only for six hours.'

The India we were visiting was feeling its way slowly towards modernity. The ill-fated Ghandis were still in and out of power - Madam Ghandi had already driven the naked hippies from the beaches of Goa, and stripped the princes of their privy purses and titles - and when she was out of power, another Prime Minister, the somewhat idiosyncratic Mr Moraji Desai, would cycle by after his morning constitutional drink of his own urine. *Be Indian -*

Buy Indian was a watchword then; if it could be made in India you could have it, if it wasn't, you went without. Often enough, even if it was, you still went without.

Much of India no longer goes without. She makes and exports a lot, to be sure, but imports a lot too: some of the most enticing images of Hindu gods and goddesses come from China - a brightly coloured plastic *Lord Shiva*, who lights up while a miniature Holy River Ganges literally flows from a rock pool at his feet - can sit on a shelf next to the Chinese flat-screen TV. People ride Chinese bicycles; the better-off ride Chinese motor-bikes. BMWs and Mercedes from Germany, and Jaguars and Landrovers, made in Britain but the company owned by Indians, are the status cars of the really wealthy. *Chanel* is now the only shop inside the old, but nowadays very plush, Imperial Hotel in Delhi where shops used to sell tourist tat.

Of course there are many more people, much bigger cities, more wealth, more and busier roads. But there are also more poor people, people in slums, people who, far from benefitting from the new roads, sometimes see their houses sliced in half in the frenzy of road-building or widening or straightening for the thousands of new cars that only others will drive. Prices of everything have rocketed making the poor poorer and the rich richer, and incidentally squeezing we middle-of-the-road visitors to India who used to so much enjoy the crumbling, rough-around-the edges best of Indian hospitality. We can't (unless seriously rich) afford or enjoy what has become the five-star plus, value-added luxury of hotel rooms, spas or gastro-fusion restaurants that tourism now seeks to provide for the 'high-end' market. At least that market is now very often *Indian*, whereas in the early days of our visits, to see an Indian in a mid-range, let alone top-range hotel, was very unusual. When Ron, a British *Indian* member of my group, who had left India in his youth and hadn't been back for forty years, attempted to change money in our hotel, he was refused. He was quite upset about it, so I asked the Indian cashier why.

'He is an Indian, sir. We only change money for hotel residents.'

'Well he may be an Indian, but he *is* a hotel resident; he is a member of my group.'

'Really, sir? May I look at the list? Do you have his passport details?'

In those days there was only Indian Airlines for domestic flights and there were still a lot of central government or state-run hotels. Nowadays, a host of private airlines compete for the growing market, and many of the government hotels have been sold off in the world-wide mania for competition and privatisation. A few concerns have escaped so far - it is still our dear Indian Railways which successfully conveys millions of passengers often to tiny, out-of-the-way (and not always profitable) places at very modest charges - but sadly many people are derogatory about government run institutions - schools, colleges, hospitals - which, like school children who are told they are inadequate by bad teachers, sometimes turn out to be inadequate. When complaining about some lackadaisical service to a hotel manager, it is so disappointing to hear the plea, 'But this is a government hotel, sir.'

Deep pockets of the old India remain, some of them deplorable such as caste and sex discrimination; there is still exploitation of the poor and weak: the Mahatma would be so disappointed. There are also aspects of old India that are deeply admirable, such as the warmth and generosity of ordinary, quite poor Indians. So often in our visits we have been pressed to have tea or snacks from the humblest villagers or households who least could afford it. Indian families, who always seem to be eating when travelling, invariably offer to share their meals. When we were stuck, unable to catch a flight, Jill and I were given not just a bed, but their *only* bed, by a young very junior airline clerk and his wife who took not so much pity on us, as an opportunity to welcome us to their country. Much later, during the Gulf War, we encountered a different welcome. We watched anxiously as the TV in our hotel announced that the ground forces were invading Iraq. Nevertheless, we went out and were returning to the hotel in auto-rickshaws - those vulnerable little motorised three wheelers - when we met, coming in the opposite direction, a big crowd demonstrating against the war and in favour of Saddam Hussein. Big portraits and angry bannrs were waved above the crowd shouting: *'Death to America', 'Death to Imperialism'*. Our nervous white imperialist faces were very evident and the atmosphere was tense. The drivers, also nervous, pulled over to let the crowd go by, surging past us on both sides. Jill and I were in the lead auto; two menacing heads poked under the canopy, their angry chanting turning to grins,

'Hello! How are you? Welcome, welcome to India. Why don't you come to my shop?'

'I have very nice paintings, would you like a cup of tea?' We looked back at the others behind us while the main crowd surged ahead, still chanting *'Death to America', 'Death to Britain'*. There was a crowd of well-wishers around each of our autos urging the occupants to visit their art studio, their shop, their restaurant.

India has achieved so much; there was *famine* in the late period of the British Raj, but with an almost four-fold increase in population since then,

India doesn't just feed, clothe and more-or-less house itself, she became a net exporter of food and cash crops. Of course there are still the sad neglected regions that attract little investment and few foreign tourists, or - like Rajasthan - are very popular with foreigners, but conceal much rural poverty and discrimination behind a façade of princely grandeur. It is to the India of the period that was catching up, or perhaps overtaking, that these memories relate. They may poke fun, for our journeys have given us much amusement as well as fascination; at their most frustrating, our trials have usually ended in collapsing in laughter at the sometimes incredible responses of the hotel staff, guides, drivers and so many others to our predicaments. Above all, our visits hold a deep affection for what that very accurate advertising slogan calls *'Incredible India'*.

And despite what you may think at first, these pages also record a deep affection for the people who travelled with us; without them we wouldn't have been able to go back again and again, and many have become our very close friends. Of the many hundreds, the only truly impossible were one-and-a-half. Both disliked everything about India and, their real crime, behaved rudely to Indians. To be fair they also disliked me and my mannr of leading tours. One, a German lady, complained that I failed to carry a tour-leader flag, and did not, as she demanded, introduce a rota to change our seats on the coach after every 100 kilometres. She accompanied her husband and berated him throughout the tour when she wasn't angrily *cleaning* India - yes cleaning! - she had brought the means with her! The half-a-person for whom we have little affection didn't have a husband to absorb her venom. She was so loathed by the group and all those we came into contact with, that she unfailingly soaked up all the animosity which might otherwise have flowed in my direction when things went wrong. In this sense, she was an *asset*, and I must confess that her extraordinary unpleasantness also gave some, not all of us, a few amusing moments. There was always a row over her meals; in a lovely little hotel where I knew many of the staff, one of the waiters came to me in tears.

'Oh Mr Richard, your lady is shouting and shouting. She is saying she must be having the yoghurt, but yoghurt is finished in the kitchen. But she is shouting, so I sent to the market for the yoghurt. Now she says she will not pay, but from my own pocket I have paid…'

'Don't worry my friend,' I reassured him, 'I will pay for the yoghurt. And remember one thing: that lady is staying in your hotel for four days; she is with me for twenty-six days…'

'Oh Mr Richard…' He put his arms round me and hugged me close.

Those who revealed their delight in India and Indian people probably come top of the list of 'favourites', many of whom made our trips so enjoyable through good humour and good companionship. You will meet some of them; the Raj Quartet who entertained without fail; the pithy Jacky and long-suffering David, who kept us amused in the darkest days; loyal and ever helpful Betty; Rosina, who just loved India so much; dear Jean, whose health preoccupied us... Some, however, you won't meet at all - at least not on a tour. Choosing who comes with us isn't normally an issue; we're seldom actually 'full' and it's usually just a matter of 'first come, first served'. But the first incident, the first of these bits and pieces drawn from several journeys and several places, reveals that some who join a tour can be a problem; in this case solved in a mysterious and macabre way.

GOING & COMING

BETTY'S DESK DRAWER

There had been a large and enthusiastic response to the suggestion during our *India* course that there would be a tour; quite a few people who were attending said they wanted to join, but what about their wives, or husbands? What about their friends? Or their relatives? Or others who had heard about the trip who had no connection with the course? I knew there were too many, but with almost no experience of such matters, I had little idea of what would be a reasonable number and no idea of how to say 'no.' The Indian agents had told me that our coach would have 35 seats, but had not said that the rear seats were very uncomfortable and bounced their passengers into the air over any bump; nor did they mention that the seats over wheel arches had no leg-room at all.

'Do not worry', came replies by fax - fax was the mode of communication in those days - 'more can come and we can accommodate also. We can send a car also. We can send minibus also.' Even I could see the difficulties of a convoy of vehicles and a big group of people in temples or mosques, so I cautiously considered around 25 as a suitable number, whereas wiser heads counselled 15. As you know, Jill had said that the whole idea was a bad one and that I would hate every minute.

One couple who wanted to join and who had terrified me for months had been *eliminated* in a horrific way. They had attended some of the *India* lectures and announced their intention of joining the trip. But in another over-ambitious course - modestly called *The Middle Ages* - a year earlier, they had proved themselves to be not just difficult, but downright menacing. *The Middle Ages* included a day's coach excursion to some local churches in Hampshire, a bishop's palace and some monastic sites. The only difficulties were, as with India later, that there were too many people attending and in this case a professor friend of mine, who had kindly suggested the idea, could not, or rather would not, lecture. It was not that he was incompetent or unwilling. No, far from it, but he had a slight stammer, and in a distinguished career had risen rapidly to a professorship without *ever lecturing*, but with a good deal of time for writing. To be fair, he wrote a special guide to the places we would visit on our day excursion, and he promised to be on hand to answer questions to one or two people at a time. But he said he could *not* address the group due to his stammer, and, though he would be present, jokingly suggested he may attend *incognito* in a false beard and dark glasses. I went along on the day to help, but the written notes had explained the arrangements - there would be a coach trip, a field guide with maps, plans, and points to look out for, with excellent explanations. There would be the opportunity to ask questions - altogether the day would be a jolly medieval mystery tour, but with *no lectures*.

So our couple had read what was offered, paid the fee and got on the coach - a 50 seater, by the way. But at the first church they raised an objection. Why was there no lecture? I explained again, suggesting we all go through the notes together, look at the things we were meant to look at, after which there could be questions. They objected. I glanced at the professor - silent and staying at the back of the group. He was unmoved. The couple demanded that lectures should be given. I invited them to look at the excellent booklet. They complained loudly, denounced the whole idea and demanded the coach return them to Southampton. The other 40 or so people now protested that they wished to continue with the tour and certainly would not allow their coach to go back with these two. I informed the irate couple that we would certainly refund their fee, but regretfully they would have to find their own way back - perhaps a bus or a taxi? By now everyone was angry; the couple, the group, the professor (who now had no hint of a stammer), the coach driver - and we were late. We drove away leaving the irate couple on the pavement by a bus stop outside the church, shouting that this was not the last I would hear about it.

And indeed it was not. They phoned my boss; they wrote to the chairman of our board of studies; they repeatedly phoned and wrote to the Vice Chancellor. I was called to be interviewed. The reverberations went on for months. And then they joined the India course and wanted to join my three-week tour to India.

'I'm afraid it's full with a waiting list' - I was replying to an angry telephone call.

'No it's not. Someone told me that you still have places.'

'I can't imagine who told you that.'

'Never mind who told me. The tour has only just been advertised and priority must go to those of us on the course. And I know perfectly well that you've accepted some who have nothing to do with the course' (true).

'Er, well, some people booked very early, and some want to travel with husbands or…'

'Nonsense. Let me tell you this, if you don't put us down on your list there'll be trouble…'

I failed to inform them of the next meeting of those planning to travel, but they turned up. To start the meeting I offered a light snack of *samosas* - those delicious Indian savoury pastries - made by a Sikh lady I knew. She charged me 12p each for them - the same price as her little shop, but I didn't know how many I would sell, so I bought 50 and offered them to the group, nicely warmed on plates, for 15p each. A potential profit of £1.50. The irate man immediately spotted my greed:

'These are 12p in the shops, why are they 15p here?'

'Well, I had to go to get them, and have no idea how many…'

'It's disgraceful. What kind of set up is this? And why weren't we informed of this meeting?'

The meeting was not a great success. I could hardly bring myself to explain the things I needed to explain. The mood was chilly. I only sold 15 *samosas*. What was I to do? The irate man and his equally irate woman were clearly insisting on joining the tour. Jill told me they could not come as they would ruin it for everyone. Others told me they wouldn't come if the couple did. Should I write to them or telephone? Should I find a solicitor? Jill advised no action but certainly I was not to send them any of the documents that I was sending the others. Then, to mix metaphors, fate stepped in and played a horrible hand. He *died, yes died*! I heard no more from them for a few weeks and someone told me he had died. The poor man was only in his 40's - a research chemist in a hospital laboratory. Caught a virus and died. And I heard no more from his partner.

Betty was a secretary in my department and was coming with us to India. She had helped me serve the *samosas* at the awful meeting and knew all about my difficulties with this couple. I was often in her office and one day after the sad news, she casually remarked that she was not altogether surprised by events. I was looking down in to her desk drawer - a plentiful supply of rubbers, glue, prit-stick and a surprising amount of blue-tack apparently moulded into strange shapes, some with pins and paper-clips sticking to them. Betty had a bit of a reputation among the other office girls for rather esoteric practices - fortune telling, or even, according to some, casting spells. Sometimes, exasperated by colleagues, I would grumble to her about my frustrations. She would often reassure me with vague offers of help:

'Oh don't worry about him, we can sort that out.'

'Yes' she told me now, 'I was very impressed with that lecture on Hindu gods the other week. Ever so interesting. Especially that *Ganesh* - the elephant one. He's the remover of obstacles. I didn't know that. Really useful, removing obstacles. But I'm a great believer in old proverbs - you know - about lots of ways of skinning a cat…'

JEAN'S BAG

On that first morning Jill and I drove from our home to the university, where I plannd to leave the car. It was very early, about six am, and as we approached the familiar landmarks on this dark March morning, I recognized a solitary figure lit by the headlights and dim street lighting, standing at a bus stop opposite the main library building. A long raincoat, a headscarf covered in a plastic rain hood, a walking stick and a mountain of baggage. It was a surprisingly mild morning with no sign of rain, and across the road, near the entrance to the library I saw some of the group gathered in the dim lights of more street lighting. All were sensibly dressed, but at a glance it was clearly a group going off on some kind of adventure: gaily coloured parkas, light coloured trousers, even sun hats and camera cases. On the ground were piles of luggage, but again it displayed a sense of adventure - rucksacks and brightly coloured bags as well as suitcases.

We waved to the solitary figure and tooted the horn at the group, who waved back cheerily. I dropped off our own luggage with Jill and drove around the corner to my exclusive parking place. A Citroen Dyane is a very narrow, small car, and I habitually parked in a place where only my car would fit. As I walked back towards the group I saw that the coach had arrived and was parked just 150 yards away, around the corner from the bus stop where the solitary figure still stood. Jill was talking to some members of the group across the road but headed towards me as I came up to the bus stop. The figure in the rain hood was still there.

'Jean! It's you! Are you waiting for a bus?' A weak joke on my part.

'Of course I'm not, I'm coming with you.'

'I know, I know, Jean. Just joking. Why don't you join the others? They're all over there…'

'How can I? I can't go over there. I can't carry all this luggage, and I can't leave it.'

Careful pre-departure notes had tried to encourage minimum luggage. I had made the point at an earlier meeting when one lady had complained that she needed more saying,

'But surely, India is a country where one can have one's luggage carried for one.'

I couldn't resist replying, 'True, but one has to be careful where one's luggage is carried to. And before we get there and when we return we will have to carry our own.' And here was Jean, stranded 50 yards from the others with luggage she could not carry.

'Let me help you', I offered. By now Jill had crossed the road as she evidently wanted to ask me something. However Jean's luggage now drew her attention, and she had heard her plaintive comment. She hissed at me,

'I've told you. Do not start carrying other people's luggage. They'll expect…' We had our own which was very modest, but were carrying a few extra items in case emergencies arose.

'Not that one!' cried Jean. 'I've got to keep that one. I have to keep it with me all the time.'

I had tried to lift one of her bags, but immediately put it down. It must have weighed more than our entire luggage.

'Goodness, Jean, what do you have in there?' I was astonished both by the bag and her possessive grab as I had attempted to take it.

'It's my medicines. I have to have them with me all the time. It's got to travel with me. I may need it any time.'

'D'you mean in the 'plane? With you, in the 'plane?' Jill was sounding incredulous.

'Yes, I have to have them with me.'

'But will they let you?' I asked. 'Isn't it a bit big and heavy for the cabin?

'They'll have to. It's my medicines. It has to be with me. I told you before, when I told you I had to have an outside seat. Have you got me an outside seat?

There was a half-remembered telephone conversation held many weeks earlier:

'I must have an outside seat on the aeroplane'

'An outside seat? I don't quite understand.'

'An outside seat - on the aeroplane. I can't be inside.'

'Not inside?'

'It's my leg. I must put it outside'

Now here was Jean and her leg and her luggage, and in particular her medicine bag. And Jill was standing beside me, her stance recognizable. Exasperation was near.

'Shall we join the others?' Her tone matched her stance. It took the three of us to lift Jean's luggage to the rear of the coach, but she refused to allow her medicines to be loaded into the luggage hold, resolutely standing beside the large and heavy bag while the others joined us. I was the last to board the coach, heaving up the bag which was just narrow enough to be pushed between the rows of seats. It made the journey to the airport standing in the aisle beside me, with Jean sitting just behind.

Boarding the aircraft had also offered a few disquieting moments - some slightly disturbing snatches of conversation were overheard while the group rearranged their seating or their luggage on the aircraft. Jackie, who had only quite recently been married to David - not their first marriage and not her second - was heard to say quite loudly,

'David, do take your hand off my knee.' David, never keen to join the tour and only there on the instructions of his recently acquired wife, looked embarrassed and crestfallen.

Within a few moments of this, Ingrid, a lady in her 60's who had divorced twice ('I only wanted one of them for money and the other for sex, and they were both useless,' was her whispered but widely heard statement at one of our preliminary gatherings), and was now 'between men,' uttered another loud stage whisper as she leaned across to Val, and was heard by everyone within a radius of 10 seats,

'Did you bring any condoms?' This elicited an astonished gasp from some members of our group and some very stern looks in my direction from two ladies, not of our group, as I happened to be standing nearby with a clipboard and had just been talking to Ingrid.

At Heathrow the medicine bag must have been overlooked by the check-in staff. In answer to the question 'How many pieces of check-in luggage?' Jean had not proffered that her 'cabin' bag was her heaviest piece of luggage and it had not been examined or weighed. With others to help her she had managed to get it through the security checks and on to the aircraft without challenge. On board, Jean, now in her outside seat, was clutching her large medicine suitcase in the aisle beside her, while a stewardess was attempting to wrestle it from her.

'…but Madam, it cannot remain in the aisle, it must not…'

'I must have it with me. I told them…'

'…but Madam it must not block…'

'I may have to take some pills at any time. And I must…'

'I will help you Madam. Allow me.' I backed away from the tug of war that followed.

LAND THE PLANE

I never fully understand why we were using Air France to reach Delhi. Our agent in England had told me, I suppose, that despite having to change planes in Paris the times were not so bad and the price was pretty good. But a delayed flight from London to Paris and a very fraught and nearly missed connection had not put us in a very good mood. Neverthless, we relaxed when we got on the Delhi flight - it left more or less on time, leaving us with an easy connection to Kathmandu, our starting point for the next tour .

It was perhaps a couple of hours before reaching Delhi when I noticed the very smartly dressed Italian lady, sitting in front of me, reach down a large, bright pink vanity case from the overhead locker and make her way down the aisle on her high heels. She was wearing quite a lot of make-up and her elaborate hair-do was just a little dishevelled - mind you, we were all dishevelled after a night on the plane. She was gone quite some 20 minutes or half-an-hour, and on her way back was transformed. She had changed some clothes, rearranged her hair, redone the make-up and was shaking her fingers to dry the newly applied bright red nail varnish. She sat down carefully so as to not disturb her hair or crease the clothes.

But after another quarter of an hour there was an announcement from an evidently angry captain - first in rapid-fire French, and then slower and equally angry English.

'Laydeez an' Gentlemen, zis eez your Captain. In one an' alf ower we were landing in *Delhi*, but we 'av 'ere zat ze *fog*, she 'as come to Delhi, and now we must go to *Karachi*.' The word Karachi was spat out with venom.

'We must wait in Karachi until ze fog av deezapear from Delhi. So zer weel be some delays. But now, we go to Karachi.'

There were sighs of dismay from all round us; from our group there were grunts, moans and a cry of 'Oh Christ!'

But from the Italian group in front, already quite boisterous, there were some very demonstrative cries, and as those who understood either the French or English announcements translated for those who did not, the noise grew to *fortissimo*. The Italian lady, who understood the announcement later than most stood up, waving her hands, calling,

'Noa, Noa. We goa to Daily. Whya we goa to Karachi?'

Air France stewards and stewardesses circulated through the cabin, presumably to allay fears as questions were asked about the length of delays, times of arrival and flight connections. The plane turned around, we did go to Karachi and during the descent to the airport we were told to stay in our seats,

'Until ze fog as deezapear from Delhi. Zen, when zey inform us, we will go to Delhi.'

We landed and moved about in the aircraft, wondering when we would leave. Naturally the members of our group wanted to know from me how much time we would have before our flight to Kathmandu. This diversion meant at least two or three hours delay and we would certainly be cutting it fine. After less than an hour came another announcement.

'Laydeez an' Gentlemen. Eet ees good news! Ze fog in Delhi, she 'as gone and now we can depart for Delhi. Pleeze return to your seat and fasten your seat-belts…' and when we were airborne a rather more cheerful Captain was able to tell us,

'Ze flying time to Delhi eez two hou-er and our estimated time of arrival ees…'

A little later our elegant lady, who had evidently become a little dishevelled once more, returned to the lavatory with her vanity case. Some time later she reappeared with her *coiffure* teased back into an acceptable shape, her face re-done. But within another 20 minutes we heard another crackling loudspeaker outburst of French, followed by a pause and then

'Bouef! Ca'alors. Zees ees incroyable… Zees ees totally beyond my experience… Laydeez and Gentlemen, we are informed zat ze fog, she 'as come back to Delhi! Yez, ze fog, she 'as come back. So we mus' go back also! We mus' go back to Karachi!'

The whole aircraft erupted. People were standing, waving their arms. The morning sun was streaming through the cabin windows; people were leaning over, looking down, shouting,

'Fog? Fog? No fog. I can see the land.'

The Italian lady could be heard above the excited babble,

'Karachi? Karachi? Noa Karachi! I mussa goa to Daily! Noa Karachi!' She had pushed her way to a window and was leaning over the others sitting there.

'I canna see Daily. Look, look, there is Daily. Landa the plane, I canna see it! Landa the plane.' A stewardess came to calm her and she subsided into her arms, sobbing, her mascara slightly trickling onto her cheek, her hair awry, whimpering gently, 'Whera is fog? No fog… Daily…'

But it was to Karachi we went once more, with a sullen and resentful plane load of passengers and no-one, perhaps, more sullen and resentful than the Captain. And there was worse news to come: we were told that in Karachi we would disembark while the plane was refuelled, cleaned and made ready, and that we would be given breakfast. How long we would wait was not made clear but I knew that our well plannd and leisurely connection in Delhi airport had already disappeared. Meantime, the visit to Karachi was not a success. There was certainly no sign of fog here as we left the aircraft in hot sunshine. Surrounded by surly armed guards, as we stepped on Pakistan tarmac we were handed dog-eared and stained cards that read *TRANSIT* and boarded the very battered coaches to take us to the terminal. More heavily armed military shepherded us inside to a gloomy grey dining hall and lined up along the walls to stare at us while we sat at the long, completely bare, wooden trestle tables, awaiting breakfast. The scene was that of a black and white prison movie.

Breakfast comprised some trays with glasses of luke-warm what may have been Coca Cola and plates of dry biscuits, which were placed on the tables in silence by the scruffiest of waiters in grey baggy shirts and trousers. We had the feeling that Karachi airport was quite used to receiving rejects from fog-bound Delhi, and did so with resentment and a minimum of courtesy. The 'breakfast' caused minor protests in Italian, French, English and Hindi-English with much hand waving and table thumping. People attempted to go to the lavatories but came back grimacing and shaking their heads. Our Italian lady, all the time clutching her pink vanity case, remained pointedly aloof, her face theatrically held high, close to tears, but perhaps unaware of the smudged mascara.

Almost three hours later, when we had been informed that we would be beginning our descent into Delhi, the lady once more attended to her toilet, emerging from the lavatory refreshed and remade, but tight-lipped. We finally saw her at the luggage carousel retrieving, with the help of her compatriots, her two very large suitcases that matched the pink vanity case. We never learned whether the Italians had missed a connection or were merely late into Delhi. We were certainly late: we were nine hours late. We had been travelling for very nearly 24 hours, had certainly missed our connection and had no idea of what arrangements, if any, had been made for our onward journey to Kathmandu.

But to leave you not knowing what happened would be unfair. We did get to Kathmandu, but how and what happened when we arrived is another story.

THE GENERAL STRIKE

I said 'how' we arrived is another story, but in truth 'how' they did it we never knew. Our Indian agents, responsible for all our 'ground' arrangements, which also meant 'in the air' arrangements after reaching Delhi, had worked wonders. On learning of our long-delayed arrival, whether by pleading, cajoling, or bribing - perhaps all three - they managed to secure our seats on the last flight to Kathmandu that day. We only knew about this after the usual crush and chaos of an arrival; the jostling in immigration queues, the scramble for trolleys, the anxiety about whether luggage would appear. But yes! There were our agents, holding up a sign board, calling urgently,

'Welcome, welcome, but you must hurry. Please! Our flight is in less than one hour and we must rush for the check-in.'

And by golly we did rush, a team of porters seizing the trolleys and moving at a speed it was difficult to keep up. Rush, rush, push, push, and by some miracle, on to a plane to Kathmandu the same day as we arrived in Delhi over nine hours late.

We were met at Kathmandu airport by a party of very smiley Nepalese gentlemen in their little colourful caps, *namastaying* politely and offering us garlands and even small bouquets of flowers. But our sense of relief at arriving and the charm of the greeting were rather diminished when we learned we had arrived at the time of a *general strike*. Our new guide's demeanour also changed when he whispered to me that this may present problems as it would be unsafe - indeed dangerous - if we moved outside our hotel.

'You will kindly inform to your guests?'

'Me? Why don't you inform to our guests? They won't mind too much just now as they are all exhausted by the terrible journey - did you know we have been to Karachi? Twice? - but they won't be too pleased if they have come all this way to stay in a hotel. How long is this likely to go on?'

'We are not very sure. Tomorrow is day of strike, but already shops have closed, police and army are on streets, demonstrations have started. Maybe after tomorrow everything will be OK? But maybe only. Maybe some more days.'

Somehow this unwelcome news was transmitted to the group.

'Christ almighty!'

'Now they tell us!'

'If they knew, why did they send us here? Why didn't we stay in Delhi?'

'Or not come at all?'

'What the hell are we supposed to do? I didn't sign up for all this discomfort to see the inside of a hotel!'

But in reality we were too tired to pursue the matter; what we wanted was a decent bed. Some made the effort to go to dinner, most did not. As we all know, no matter how tired, a combination of travel, jet-lag, and in my case anxiety does not always help towards a good night's sleep. And going to bed early often means waking early. So a rather despondent group drifted in to breakfast. Comparing how much or how long they had slept soon turned to 'What next?'

'Have you found out what's happening?'

'Surely they don't think we can sit around here all day?'

Unfortunately I had only found out what was not happening. The hotel staff seemed very edgy, and the reception people would only say we should not go outside as the hotel could not be 'reponsible' - for what?

'You're not on strike,' said someone to one of the waiters at breakfast. 'If you're not on strike, how do you know others will be?'

'It is strike, madam. We are not on strike, but politicians are saying there is strike. Maybe there will be much shouting and marching and we do not want guests to be hurt.'

Some of us gathered in the foyer, looking across the garden to the road. It all looked very quiet, with very little traffic. A few, led by Betty, who was of the opinion that nothing as insignificant as a general strike should be allowed to interfere with her holiday, wandered as far as the hotel gates, which were closed. They reported back:

'Nothing happening at all.'

'No-one there.'

'Don't know what all the fuss is about.'

'Why can't we just go out under our own steam?' Our guide had impressed on me that not only was it unsafe, but the company could not provide transport for our sightseeing. I felt I'd better make a show of going to the gate and seeing for myself. I spoke to the hotel gatekeeper in his little sentry box,

'I see the gate is closed.'

'Yes, sir, it is strike.'

'I see. It looks very quiet outside. You are not on strike, I see.'

'No sir, I am on duty.'

'What is your duty?'

'I am *chaukidar*, sir, I am watch-man.'

'Is it your duty to keep the gate closed?'

'Oh yes, sir.'

'What if I need to go out? Can you open it?'

'Oh yes sir.'

More of the group had gathered in the foyer, talking to the front-office manager.

'Excuse me, sir, your group is saying they wish to go out, but it is general strike.'

'Yes, I know.'

'But if they are going out of hotel we cannot take responsibility…' I turned to the group,

'Now, ladies and gentlemen, you heard what this gentleman says - if we go out they can't take responsibility.'

'Wouldn't make any difference if they could!' Clearly Betty had been instilling a fighting spirit into the others. 'We certainly can't sit about here all day!'

'Well, I can,' said David, 'I have no wish to be caught up in a riot!'

'If there's a riot we can come back,' retorted Betty.

Over half the group decided to walk the half-mile or so into the city centre to at least look around; a rendezvous was arranged for departure, we met and set off. The friendly *chaukidar* saluted, opened the gate and we stepped out into Kathmandu. We could immediately see that the situation had changed. There was still no traffic, but at intervals of perhaps every ten yards stood or squatted a soldier; they all looked small and oddly dressed and several were smoking. Most had flat-looking helmets, some berets, some the traditional civilian woven caps; most were wearing what we assumed were flack-jackets, but these seemed to have been made from yellow corrugated cardboard. However, most of them leaned, shouldered, or propped a *rifle* against the wall- long, old-fashioned rifles, some with bayonets fixed, some with worn old webbing straps hanging down. Betty, striding along at the front of our group turned to the others:

'Don't they look sweet! Just like little toy soldiers. Just like my horrid brother's toy soldiers. I feel I could go "Stamp, Stamp, Stamp!"

'Please don't!' we called back.

Passing along the street, the shutters on the shops were down and the small roadside stalls were covered in plastic sheets. An occasional cyclist or motor bike passed. But as we approached, one of the cyclists called out cheerily,

'Hello! What is your country?' Another man, standing nearby called,

'Here is my shop. Why don't you come to my shop? Come and look!' and whipped off the plastic cover of his small low stall on the pavement. There was an array of jewellery - rings, bracelets, necklaces, some ornaments, perfume bottles… A neighbouring stall holder spotted us and uncovered his wares - almost identical - and within a few minutes a shop shutter was being raised with that familiar chattering noise and the owner calling for us to have a look. There were more clattering shutters going up on both sides of the street. More and more stall-holders were uncovering their wares: embroidered bags, tee-shirts and scarves were being waved; postcards, stamps and wooden trays were pushed under our noses; little bells were being rung to attract our attention. The bargaining and money changing began. Val, who had already whispered to me that George, her new man, who was with her on this tour for the first time, may agree to become engaged, nudged me excitedly. George was in deep negotiation with a stall holder who held up a tray of very inexpensive rings.

'Darling George!' she said.

We didn't reach the town centre. There was so much purchasing en route that we returned to the hotel after less than two hours, flushed with success. We had gone out against orders, the shops had opened, some of us had our postcards and stamps as well as all mannr of exciting gifts for the unwary back home, Val was engaged, and the holiday had begun. When we returned to the hotel for lunch our guide was there, calling excitedly,

'It is OK, it is OK! No more strike! Strike is over!'

We knew it was, and I felt a pang of guilt at having contributed to the breaking of the General Strike.

OLD BOMBAY AIRPORT

Bombay was renamed Mumbai some years ago, but, back in the days when it was Bombay, the airport - especially at two am - was beyond imagination. Many of our tours into the south or centre of India meant we went via Bombay airport; we had come to know it well. First there was the smell. Not altogether unpleasant, but a heavy, slightly *sweet warm* smell. There may have been the scent of exotic flowers - jasmine perhaps - or spices. But there was also the smell of stale urine, although not the same beer-based stale urine of the urinals of old-fashioned British pubs. Then there was a faint farmyard tint in the air and perhaps bodily odour, but the overall effect was strangely exciting as well as mildly repulsive: we had certainly arrived in a foreign place. On this occasion the smell grew more pronounced on the rather ancient airport bus waiting to transfer us to the terminal, where I suspect that the crush of bodies and hand baggage contributed.

Of course, the smell was associated with the heat. After the air-conditioned cabin, it met us as we stepped out onto the stairway down to the tarmac. 2am is the cool time in most places. In Bombay it was usually around 27 degrees, but it had been nine degrees in Heathrow and perhaps 19 during the flight. Many of the Indian passengers who had been wearing woollens, quilted jackets, mufflers and, in two rather ostentatious cases, knitted balaclava helmets when they boarded the flight in London, now seemed taken aback and some of these items were removed walking down the stairway and on to the waiting buses. Our waiting bus filled up and continued to fill.

'Kindly move, sir.' The remark was directed to me by a large seated Indian lady who overflowed her seat, and whose thigh had been inadvertently brushed by my knee in the press of bodies.

'Madam, if only I could…' I had lifted one foot off the ground to try to comply with her request, but now I had nowhere to put it down except on someone's bag or another foot. The coach jerked to start, causing all the strap-hanging passengers to sway together, and my knee to press once more against the thigh of the seated lady. In this way we lurched the short distance to the terminal, disembarked from the coach and made our way inside. It was much as I remembered from the last visit - dimly lit, smelly, grubby, crowded, with long queues and lengthy procedures for passport and immigration control. There seemed to be more light outside the building with arc lights, flashing lights from aircraft and headlights from vehicles. Inside, some but not all the fly-blown strip lights were working.

A knot of some of our group were waiting at the first bend in the corridors under signs saying '*Transfers*', '*Transit Passengers*', '*Baggage Reclaim*', '*Lost Property*', '*Latrine*', '*Passport Control*', and many more. A group of us - a bit later off the plane - caught up with the earlier arrivals.

'Where do we go?'

'Which way are we…?'

'Thank goodness that's over, I do hope…'

'What a funny smell'

'I hope it's not going to be this hot…'

'Ingrid has gone to the loo. She's left her bags with me.'

We made our way together, following signs for '*Immigration*' and '*Baggage Reclaim*'. The light was too poor for some of our group who were attempting to fill in the immigration forms that had been handed out to most but not all on the plane. Now those who had failed to find or failed to complete the forms attempted to do so.

'What do we put down for "address in India"?'

'Where did you get that? Do we all need one of those?'

'What's this Visa number? Where do we get that?'

'Look, it's here - in the passport.'

'Where are we going? It says on this form we have to put down where…'

'Do we have to put down how much money?'

'It says here we do…'

'What about this video camera? It says here…'

At the Immigration check, two overhead large black and yellow signs divided us: '*Indian Nationals*' in one queue, '*Foreigners*' in another. There were people from our group in both queues. David held back looking puzzled.

'I say, where should I go?' he asked.

'Well, in this one' I offered,

'But it says *foreigners*',

'Don't be so silly,' from Jacky.

We were on the way to reclaim our baggage, where more silliness awaited us.

THE BAGGAGE HALL

The slow, slow process of form filling and queueing, and then scrutiny and stamping and finally flourishing retrieved passports went on. Finally, after perhaps three-quarters of an hour had passed, some of us began to enter the baggage reclaim hall. This was the most astonishing of all, and I saw my group members recoil in horror as they entered the Hieronymous Bosch painting of the *Last Judgment*. The baggage hall was vast, dimly lit. In the centre were several silent and still carousel machines, each surrounded by mountains of luggage with passengers and more uniformed staff pushing and pulling at trolleys and baggage. One of the carousels started up and clattered loudly and slowly. One enormous parcel went round. It was covered in sack-cloth, partly stitched with string and had lots of blue writing in crayon - some in English, some in Hindi. One entire side had burst open and smaller sack-cloth parcels had fallen out. It was watched by many pairs of eyes, but no-one touched it. The other machines remained still.

Over against the wall, opposite the carousels, luggage was everywhere in huge piles, sometimes approaching the ceiling of the large, hangar-like building. There were suitcases, certainly, many of them encased in 'dust-proof' canvas wrappers, but also huge cardboard boxes, tin trunks, wooden crates, sacks and, most of all, *bundles* of every desciption - some were only the size of a fridge, others seemed the size of motor cars. Many were split open, with the contents - more bundles - spilling out. Swarms of people - some in grubby uniforms - were climbing up the piles and pulling and pushing at the bundles, which tumbled down spilling more of their contents: cooking pots, electric fans, clothing, odd shoes, childrens' toys.

Some of the staff - police perhaps - looked very strange. Navy blue military style 'side hats', navy shirts stiffly-starched, very voluminous khaki shorts, navy woollen stockings neatly turned over at the knee but *without feet*, and leather sandals. They carried sticks and walked about occasionally shouting or poking at someone, and sometimes blowing whistles. Fans whirled overhead. Ladies in saris were bent double, sweeping with one-handled, soft, wispy brooms. They swept the litter and the dust to and fro, from one to another, with the dust climbing and whirling under the fans in the dim light.

'How on earth will we ever find..?'

'Christ, is our stuff among that lot?'

'Which carousel is ours…?'

'Where do we get trolleys?'

Some had found trolleys, but were wrestling with wheels that didn't turn or would only move one way. Four men in dirty grey uniforms could be seen - pushing, shoving, kicking - a long line of trolleys from the far end of the hall. A stampede in their direction and the line was attacked and dismembered, but all done with smiles and much head-shaking. A few of our group joined in with the stampede and were met with:

'Kindly allow me madam. You are most welcome. Please tell me your name?'

'You are very elderly. Let me assist you. How many years exactly?'

Now another carousel started up and slowly moved round making a terrific clattering sound. Nothing appeared on it, so they both clattered round at very slow speed with just the original broken bundle. A new battered cardboard box appeared and the crowd surged towards it, as far as the crush and litter allowed there to be a surge. Then a large plastic shapeless bundle appeared, but nothing much that looked like the luggage that people normally take on an aircraft. Some of our group, together with a large number of passengers stood looking in disbelief; some attempted to push trolleys nearer to the empty carousels. Then, in the gloom, I saw a bunch of perhaps twenty men in grubby and varied uniforms - khaki, once-white, blue - were swarming over another growing pile of luggage between the two moving carousels. Luggage had been appearing through the hatch, but before it could start its journey, they snatched it and threw it onto the pile.

'Wait here', I yelled at a few of the group nearby and moved towards the hatch as fast as people and trolleys allowed. Getting nearer, I was sure I glimpsed a bag with one of our distinctive yellow labels being snatched at by one of the uniformed men. Indeed I did, but as I got there I found another of our labels on the floor. I picked it up; it was Jean's.

'Here, what are you doing with our luggage?' I cried in desperation. I saw several more of our labels in the pile now three or four bags deep.

'We are off-loaders, we must off load all baggages…'

'But why? We are looking for our luggage.'

'Are you Tour Leader of Travel Club? Are you Mr Hunt? Are you with the Travel Club?' A man, smartly suited, wearing an identification badge with his photo smiled at me. I had hardly noticed him in his dark suit, but he had been there giving instructions to the uniformed staff. 'I am Balusubramanian, from the travel agency, but you can call me Balu. My name is very difficult for you, no?'

'Well, yes. But what is happening? Some of our luggage is in this pile, and my group is over there…'

'I am so happy to meet you. Do not worry. It is my job. We will collect all your luggage for you. Do you have the luggage tags?'

Luggage tags? What luggage tags? Then I remembered: of course, Jill had the luggage tags. We'd been given them in Heathrow. Where was Jill? And then I remembered Jill also had all the hand luggage and all the group and, no doubt, all Jean's bags …

'Yes, yes, I'll get them for you.' I looked across the clattering carousels, saw some of the group on the far side and picked my way across. 'Have you seen Jill?' I asked Betty as I got near the group.

'Yes, she's gone back to help Jean. There was some problem over her bag, or visa or something. Look she's left me with all this stuff. I think some of it is Jean's.'

But then I saw them: Jill with a heavy bag, Jean with a stick. Neither looked pleased. I tried to sound enthusiastic.

'Ah, good, our man is here to meet us and he's dealing with the luggage. Do you have the baggage tags they gave us at Heathrow?'

Jean broke in, 'It's just that I had it filled in the other way - for the going out, I mean, and they made me do it all over again.'

'Yes, yes' said Jill. 'All right, you're in now. It doesn't matter. Yes, the luggage tags - here, they're all stuck on to our plane ticket.'

'Good, can I have them? Our man…'

'No, I'll take them. They are on the air ticket and if you lose that… I'll take them. Where is he? You stay here with Jean, and Betty's somewhere with our bags. You stay with this lot; I'll take them. Which one is he?'

So I stayed with Jean and the bags and the group, explaining that our luggage was being looked after, and if we all stayed together the bags would be collected and we could all leave. The group looked apprehensive, some quite alarmed. Some voiced their apprehension and alarm, others drifted to the lavatories.

'Didn't you say we change money here?' someone asked. Christ! I had forgotten the money. In the dim distant corner of the hall were two neon-lit cubicles with illuminated signs: 'Bank of Maharashtra' said one; 'Bank of…' said the other, but I could not make out the name.

'Oh, er yes, that would save some time. If some of you would like to go over there and change your money, that's where we will all meet.'

'I'll have to stay here, David's gone off to the loo.'

'So have several others. I've got Ian and Betty's bags.'

A procession of our people, laden with hand luggage, some of it piled in trolleys, now pushed and stumbled past and round the crowd, - reversing, bumping, apologizing - towards the bank kiosks. I went with them, leaving a rearguard of toilet-watchers waiting behind. I turned and ran back to them.

'Oh yes, if Jill is looking for me, tell her I'm over with the others near the banks over there.'

A queue had formed at each kiosk. Our members joined the queues. Those who were undecided began to check:

'Which one do we go to?'

'How much shall I change?'

'Is it better to change Travellers Cheques or cash?'

'Will it be a better rate here than in a real bank?'

'What about at the hotel?'

But then…

'We're missing one bag.' This in a very different tone was spoken emphatically into my ear. Jill was at my elbow, with a very concerned looking Mr Balusubramanian behind her.

'Oh Christ, really? Are you…'

'Of course we're sure,' hissed Jill, 'We've 27 tags and 26 bags. The 26 labelled bags are all there. And, of course, we have no idea who's is missing. All we have is a number - no name.'

'Kindly ask your group to identify each and every baggages,' said Mr Balusubramanian in a resigned but kindly voice. 'I will ask staff to unload the trolleys, so that they can easily identify. Don't worry, but we must search the unidentified luggage to find the … will it be a suitcase? or a …'

I thought of, and indeed glanced back to the piles of broken, spilling, tumbling detritus we had encountered on entering this place. Already sweating, my head began to swim. Someone said,

'Look out, I think he's going to faint'

'Quite green…'

'Here give him some water…'

So I drank and poured some into my hand and splashed it around my face and over my neck. I bent over dripping and felt for a hanky in my pocket. Something else was there, and with the hanky I pulled out the yellow luggage label I had found on the floor.

'Jean', I gasped, 'Can you please tell this nice man what this label was on? I found it on the floor.'

IDENTIFY YOUR LUGGAGES

This time we were trying to get *on* a plane. We were nearly there, with tickets and boarding cards, just waiting for the flight to be called - a domestic flight to Hyderabad. I heard several of our group members calling:

'He's here.'

'Over here.'

'That's him, over there…'

'Are you the tour leader with this British group?' An insistent, urgent voice and a tugging at my elbow.

'This way please, come this way. Hurry please.' A deep foreboding - one of the group was lost, or ill, or had been arrested? But no.

'Come with me please. You must identify your baggage of British group. This way please. Please show your boarding card.' He pushed me to the front of the queue, thrust the card into the hands of the attendant and returned the stub to me. He then pushed open the glass door into the half-light beyond. Once again I was confronted by piles of luggage. Some was loaded onto trolleys, but most spread out on the concrete floor. There, in the gloom I was asked to identify our group's luggage.

Although there was a great deal of luggage, there, by the greatest good fortune, quite near me on the tarmac, were our bags. I could see their yellow luggage labels supplied by our agents back in England. I went over to make sure. Yes! Black lettering on one side of the yellow label, and there, on the back was the name of one of our group. Next to the bag was another with the same label, and another, and another. But there were also boxes, bundles, other cases and plastic sacks. Then I saw another yellow label, further along the line, and another.

'Yes, yes!' almost overcome with relief. 'Yes, these are ours, yes, there's another.'

'You have identified the baggages of your group?'

'Yes, look, I've…'

'What is the total number of baggages? You have the baggage tags?'

'Er, its 27. My wife has the tags, she's…'

'Very good, you have identified your baggages. Now you must return, coaches are here for boarding.'

As I was led back to the door leading to the departure lounge, it opened and people pushed their way past me, part walking, part running, some carrying, some wheeling cases and rushing on to a waiting coach. I peered through the door and saw a cluster of the group waving frantically to me. Someone was waving something.

'Can I go back inside? My group is there. Something is…'

'Kindly board the coach. You have your boarding card, yes? Then you can go also.'

'But…' There was no way I could get inside with the crush of people coming out. Before long two of the group members struggled out.

'It's OK,' said Ian breathlessly. 'It's OK. Jill has sorted it out. She's got a new one.'

'A new one?'

'Yes, Jean. It was Jean wasn't it,' he was talking to Betty.

'Oh Christ.'

'No, no, it's OK. It is now. She lost her boarding card. But Jill and that other Betty sorted it out. I don't know if they found it or got her a new one, or what.'

It wasn't OK at all. I knew it wouldn't be. Jill was once again left with our luggage and the group and now a missing boarding card. More and more of the group had passed through the door. Some clustered around me near the door; others marched ahead to the waiting coaches.

'She had it all the time…' said someone rushing past me.

'I'm not surprised she couldn't find it. How many bags has she got, for Christ's sake?' I heard but did not see the irritated Jacky sweep by. Jill came into sight, struggling with her arms and shoulders laden.

'Is everything all right?'

'No it is not. You must tell her,' not so quietly. 'I've already told you, you must tell her. I'm not going through that again. You must make it perfectly clear to all of them that they are responsible for their own luggage, their own tickets and their own fucking boarding cards. They all came bleating to me: "Where is he? She's lost her card and why isn't he here to see to things?" I told them you had been called to see to their luggage and you can't be in two places at once.'

We bundled onto the coach and then off, and then up the steps into the aircraft. Once again the pushing and struggling with hand luggage, and finding the right seat and the right row, and who was sitting with whom and why are we on our own all the way back here? The overhead lockers were full by the time we found our seats, so there was the rearranging and pushing. And all the time I was trying to locate and count - not easy as the plane was very full. Surely we must all have found our way here? This was our last flight for a considerable time. Pray God we would all arrive together. Slowly most people subsided into seats, clicking seat belts and shuffling with magazines and papers. Indian music was playing softly and attractive Indian girls in *sarees* walked up and down, closing lockers, adjusting seats to upright and checking belts. Turning my head as best I could, I saw several of the group already fast asleep. Some read, others dozed; we all waited. But we did not move. Ten minutes, fifteen minutes, twenty minutes passed. Then there came a loud voice from someone moving towards the rear of the 'plane.

'Where is tour leader of British group?' I saw a man approaching, wearing a security pass, holding a clipboard. He looked familiar. He repeated more loudly:

'Where is tour leader of British group?'

I sank lower in my seat, but several British voices called out:

'He's back there.'

'He's over here.'

'Er, here,' I muttered. What was wrong? I raised my finger just a little.

'You are tour leader? You have identification?' He sounded angry, flustered.

'Well, er, I have a passport. Jill, do you have my passport.'

'Please come immediately, you must get down from aircraft.'

'What for? What has happened? Is all my group not here?'

'Group? group? I do not know about group. I am baggage in-charge. You have identified all wrong baggages for group.'

'But…'

'Come, sir. You must recheck all baggages.'

So with head bowed I rose from my seat, blushing and embarrassed, climbed over Jill, who said nothing, and followed the in-charge towards the front of the aircraft.

'The flight is delayed, sir, because you have identified all wrong baggages.'

'But I saw…'

'See, here, are these baggages of your group?' About a dozen rather familiar bags were lined up under the wing of the aircraft. There were yellow labels, and I was beginning to recognize some of the colours and adornments of the bags.

'Well, er, yes, it does look as…'

'Please check all tag numbers and identify each and every item.' I walked along the short line and saw that they did indeed all belong to us.

'Yes, yes, all these. But where are the others? There should be 27.'

'Those you identified previously are loaded. These you failed to identify.'

'But I couldn't see them all. It was rather dark and there was a great deal… I saw some and assumed…'

'You must identify each and every one. Only then can they be loaded. I asked you if you had done this thing and you said "yes".

'Well, I'm very sorry, but I saw our luggage and assumed that…OK, yes, these are all ours. Can they be loaded now?' A contemptuous grunt and -

'Kindly go on board aircraft. We are now suffering additional delay of 40 minutes on this flight.'

The walk back to my seat was uncomfortable: crew, passengers, group members looked hostile and suspicious.

'What's happened?'

'Is everything all right?'

'Is my bag…?'

'Yes, yes, it's all perfectly all right. Just some little mishap.' I caught a glimpse of Jean and it occurred to me that I had said 'Yes' to all the bags on the tarmac. They all had yellow labels and our names. What if another tag had fallen off? Jean had seen me.

'They said I couldn't bring my bag on, but I told them…'

'Yes, Jean dear,' Cynthia was sitting beside her. 'I suggested we use the term 'emergency medical supplies.' They seemed to think that would be in order, so poor Jean was allowed to bring her bags. Several people helped her. Betty was so kind, and I was a little weighed down myself.'

'And so was Jean,' from Betty sitting next to Cynthia. 'Jean what have you got in there? I could hardly lift the bag. Mine was heavy enough, but that's mostly scotch - that's my medicine. Is yours the same?

YOUR FLIGHT IS CANCELLED

My suspicions began when our agent asked *me* to check the departure time of our flight home to London. As we arrived at the airport we could see a large crowd of people clustered around one of those tiny windows with metal grills on the *outside* of the building. Our man said the group should stay on the coach, but that he and I should get down and I should go to this window.

'That is where you must check your GF (Gulf Air) flight', he said, pointing to the crowd at the window. There was now a distinct nervousness in his voice.

'Why? You've reconfirmed our tickets. What is there to check?'

'Ok, ok, please stay on coach. I will check-up.' He got off and I could see him worming his way to the window.

'What's happening? Do we get down?' The group was soon aware that something was amiss.

'Oh, it's all right.' I sounded cheerful. 'He's only gone to reconfirm everything, we're just waiting to find out…'

But find out what? After about five minutes he was back.

'Your Gulf flight is cancelled!' he sounded surprised, but of course he already knew.

'Gulf Airways has totally cancelled the flight Bombay to Muscat.' He was heard by several of the group and the alarm spread rapidly.

'Cancelled! He said our flight is cancelled!'

'What?'

'Oh Christ!'

'What on earth..?'

What on earth indeed. I had no idea.

'What do you mean cancelled?' I spoke harshly to the agent. 'How can it be cancelled? We have OK confirmed seats. What do you mean?'

'Gulf Air has cancelled your flight I am telling you. They say they will try to get you on another.'

'Another? What other? When is there another flight? What do you mean "try"?'

'After some time, they are telling. Now you have to go to some hotel.'

'Some hotel?'

'They are saying all Gulf passengers with onward connection are going to Leela Hotel. First they are saying Centaur, but Centaur is some distance and

Leela is nearby only. Also Centaur has very unsanitary reputation and Leela is new hotel...'

Others crowded round: 'What's all this about going to a hotel? We're supposed to be flying to England. I've got an appointment …'

'Don't worry,' said our man, trying to talk quietly to me. 'After some time they will tell us what is happening.' Then, very quietly he added, 'Just now they are saying that *seven* of our passengers can go to Abu Dhabi.'

'*Seven people*? *Seven people*? We are 27 people. What do they mean seven people? Our tickets are for London via Muscat! What has Abu Dhabi got to do with it?'

The group joined in: 'What the hell is happening?'

'We've got tickets for God's sake! What's wrong with them?'

I caught Jill's eye. It meant 'do something'.

'OK', I began, 'Er, it seems there's a delay. I know we've all got proper tickets, but the airline has cancelled this flight we were going on and is going to arrange another. Meantime we have to go to a hotel and wait to see…' Luckily no-one seemed to have overheard the 'seven people' exchange, but even so the group continued:

'Oh Christ, I knew…'

'How can they do that?'

'Bloody Gulf, I should have known…'

'Don't worry,' I said, extremely worried. 'They will have to re-schedule our flight. It may mean a short delay, but…'

'How short? I've a man coming to collect us from Heathrow…'

'And I've a meeting with the solicitor…'

We made the short journey to the very grand Leela Kempinsky hotel - very much grander than anywhere we had stayed on the entire tour. It was a big, new, glitzy place, but not-at-all glamorously located between building sites and slums. Nowadays, of course, Bombay-cum-Mumbai has expanded far beyond the airport, and new 'cities' have sprung up and continue to grow for many miles in all directions, accompanied by more building sites and slums. But in the 1980s this process was not so far advanced and the new and very five star Leela Kempinski was an airport hotel was on the fringe of the city. Stepping inside the hotel and leaving the grim surroundings outside was, in some ways, a relief from the anxieties of whether we were flying to England or not. In the vast marble, cool, flamboyant entrance lobby we were offered clean, chilled hand towels and pink welcome drinks with straws, and we occupied sumptuous sofas and chairs. We, however, did not match the surroundings: we looked like a group of refugees, tired, hot and nervous, clutching all mannr of bags and parcels that comprised our hand luggage.

People sat on the sumptuous chairs and sofas in the lobby, went to the loo, peered at the coffee shop and the various shop windows offering jewellery, carpets, clothing, books… There was no sign of the agent and, in those days before the arrival of the mobile phone, half an hour became forty minutes and then an hour (the time was now very noticeable - it was 2.30, the same time that we should have been checking in for our flight to London). One of the reception staff approached me to say that Gulf Air would provide the buffet lunch which was set out in the dining room. We all moved there rapidly and I had taken one spoonful of the quite good mulligatawny soup when the agent approached, indicating that he wanted a private word.

'Well, what's the news?'

'They are saying that now *eleven* can go to Abu Dhabi. Maybe to Doha…' But then he was gone and I was left with trying to answer the unanswerable questions.

This time there was a telephone call: I picked up the receiver in the hotel lobby.

'Now there is very good news; seventeen are already confirmed and others have very good chance on wait-list.'

'How do you mean "Good chance"?' I demanded.

'Oh, very good. Do not worry, my superior says no need to worry as Gulf will definitely work out.'

'That's all very well, but do we even know which flight we are going on?'

'Yes, yes, GF will fly to Doha, and then there will be change to Abu Dhabi.'

'What? *Doha*? No-one said anything about Doha *and* Abu Dhabi. That means another change. We booked a London flight via Muscat. Now we are being told *Doha and Abu Dhabi*. What are the flight times? When is this Doha flight?'

'It is 23.10 this evening. You must be at the check-in before 20.10. If you will excuse me, I must take my leave. As soon as we have more information I will definitely contact you.'

It was the middle of the afternoon. Somehow I had to explain to people that we would all stay at the hotel until eight in the evening and then some, but possibly not all, would fly by a convoluted route to London. The hotel was being quite helpful: they could provide us with three rooms and offered to supply extra towels for washing and changing.

Jill and I tried to find the various knots of people in the lobby, or in the bookshop, or those wandering out to look at the rather magnificent pool which was overshadowed by the scaffolding of another high rise building rather too close. To the first group I said, 'Well, I'm sorry to disappoint some of you, but it seems very likely that we will *all* be setting off for home tonight. They haven't confirmed the final timings, except we leave the hotel at eight this evening for a flight at about eleven. Apparently we are flying to Doha and then changing for Abu Dhabi…' Even this short announcement was punctuated with,

'Where?'

'Where the hell's Doha?'

'Changing again?'

'When does that mean we'll get home?'

There was a certain amount of diving into the main baggage under a net in the main lobby to retrieve swimming costumes, and the group was once more scattered: some to the rooms, some in the shops, some at the swimming pool. Jill and I decided to take our hand luggage to the pool and did get into the water, but we were interrupted at about half past four by the hotel pool man, who called me to say there was a telephone message at the kiosk. I went, dripping, to take the call.

'Hello, this is Ashok, I am GM from Tripidi Travels. How are you?' It was difficult to hear as there was much shouting and laughing and splashing from the pool where a group of our ladies, together with Tom, the only man, were playing at 'synchronised swimming', or rather 'synchronised poses' while standing on one leg.

'Who? Sorry, I can't hear you very well. Who is speaking?'

'This is Ashok this side, sir, from Tripidi Travels; I am the manager of your agency here in Bombay only. I am speaking from the International Airport.' This was one of the rare occasions when 'only' was appropriate. They were indeed our agents in Bombay only - appointed by our main agents in Delhi. And perhaps for the last and only time.

'What is the news on our flight?'

'Yes, yes, it is good news! It is very good news. All tickets are confirmed; all members of your group can take flight this evening. I think you already know they will fly first to Doha.'

'Yes, I was informed. This is *not* good news, this is very *bad* news: we were due to change only once at Muscat - the same as on our flight out to India. That is what we booked…'

'Yes, yes, but Muscat flight is cancelled. Therefore you must fly to Doha.'

'And then?'

A pause - 'Then from Doha you must fly to Abu Dhabi.'

'And then?'

A longer pause - 'Then from Abu Dhabi you must fly to Paris.'

'*PARIS*?'

'Yes, Paris. Paris France.'

PLUS ONE AND PLUS ONE IS PLUS TWO

'*PARIS*? *Paris*? Why are we flying to Paris? We are supposed to be flying to London. Why would we fly to Paris?' I was on the phone to the agent for the umpteenth time that day.

'Yes, yes, from Paris you will be flying to London only.'

'But why Paris? Is there no direct Gulf flight to London?'

'Yes, yes, but from Muscat only, or Bahrain. But the Muscat flight is totally cancelled and your Bombay flight arrives too late for Bahrain…'

'Dear God! Does Gulf fly from Paris to London?'

'Er, no sir. Then you will fly by Air France.'

'Air France? Christ almighty. When will we be flying by Air France? More to the point when will we be arriving in London?'

'Just a moment, sir, I will check just now.' There was an ominous pause. 'Your flight arrives in London Heathrow at 09.40.'

09.40? That didn't seem to be at all too bad. The connections must be pretty good…

'Well, that is not so bad. We are flying at eleven this evening and arriving at 09.40?' Even with a direct flight the time from Bombay to London is about nine hours, and with our original flight schedule with one change the journey was about eleven hours. So, allowing for the time difference, this rearrangement seemed remarkably good.

'Yes, sir, you will arrive in London on Tuesday at 09.40. It is plus two.'

'Plus two? What is plus two?'

'It means plus one and plus one. So it is plus two. Tonight your flight will arrive in Doha is plus one; and the flight arriving in Paris is plus one. That is plus two.'

A horrible realisation was dawning. 'What is plus one?' I asked very slowly. He was explaining elementary arithmetics to a child.

'Plus one is one day after. It means next day arrival.'

'So what is plus two?'

'Plus two is two day after. It means arrival after two days. So you arrive Tuesday only.'

'TUESDAY. You say Tuesday ONLY. Are you saying we leave here today - Sunday - and arrive on TUESDAY?'

'Yes, yes, your connection is for plus two. Don't worry, we have arranged everything. Is OK? Luckily we could arrange with GF and AF. So the coach will pick you up at 8pm. Is it OK?'

Jill had come out of the pool and was standing beside me dripping and holding a towel. She was silent.

'You heard?'

'I did. How can they do this? I told you not to use these awful cheap airlines…'

'The flight was cancelled, for Christ's sake. Any flight could have been cancelled. They weren't particularly cheap and the BA times were awful. These were a lot better…'

'Well they're not now. There's going to be a revolt. I wouldn't break the news until you have to.'

The frolicking in the pool was continuing. Betty and Cythia, and even Molly had joined in what looked like a game of up-to-your-neck-in-water line-dancing. Hugo and Alwyn were asleep lying under an umbrella; some were reading. It looked a normal, relaxed holiday group on a Sunday afternoon. My day, which had started so well overlooking the Kerala beach, had collapsed, but there was no urgency to alarm the others that they wouldn't arrive home until Tuesday. I fended off the inevitable questions with 'I hope to have it all clear by dinner, but rest assured we will all be going home whether we want to or not!' Mr Ashok phoned me again to give the flight numbers and timings of our various flights, with their respective plus ones or plus twos. It all looked terrible: there was almost three hours' wait in Doha, nearly five in Abu Dhabi and two hours' in Paris. The tickets would all be handed to me this evening on our way to the airport. I wrote all this down on the pad beside the phone in the hotel lobby, luckily with no one to overhear the conversation or to see my face, and stuck the paper in my pocket. This, as many have pointed out to me, is unwise, as pieces of paper, often with vital information, seem to disappear from my pockets. Jill usually takes care to look after important information, but I failed to hand over this one. But it didn't matter: the broad, unpleasant outline was in my head.

We went to the dining room quite punctually at six-thirty, to find several of the group already sitting down eating, or helping themselves to the buffet in the centre of the room. There were some other European-looking people there, as well as a few Indian families with children, but most of the group already at our large table were those who had stayed inside the hotel for the afternoon: Jacky & David were there with Jean, and to my surprise Ian and Betty 2 were sitting with them. As we stood in the door of the restaurant some of the pool group came along.

'Well?' said Betty, 'is everything sorted out? I wouldn't have minded another day or two of this place rather than going back to sort out you lot in the office.'

Jill butted in, 'Let's go and look at this buffet, it all looks very grand and it will be the last decent meal we have until we get home.'

It was very good, and as we were among the earliest diners the food was mostly hot and fresh. A choice of soups, salads, lovely grilled fish…

'I hear we are going to Paris,' said Ian loudly, as we carried our plates over to the table. The hostility was very evident. 'Is that right?'

'Er, yes, I'm afraid we are. Er, I've only just found out. I was going to tell everyone after…'

'Well we found out ourselves and it was an unpleasant piece of news, I can tell you. We were talking to a German couple - they're over there with their friends. They're going on the same flight. Seems they're going to visit their daughter in England on the way home. Why the hell are we going to Paris?'

It appeared that there had been a handful of people booked on the Muscat flight who had also been transferred to the Leela Kempinsky hotel. Some were flying to Germany, but this particular couple were first going to England. Most of those for Muscat were Indian migrant workers, on leave from their jobs in the Middle East. Presumably Gulf Air had treated them less generously, as they had certainly not been seen at our hotel, and presumably had no onward connections outside the Gulf countries. It was just my luck that the German couple should let the cat out of the bag - and to Ian of all people - before I screwed up the courage to tell the group myself. The food on my plate now looked less appetising, but Cynthia was sitting next to me and she, together with half the long table, had heard Ian's announcement.

'Isn't this just marvellous!' she said, beaming at her plate. 'It's just what we want to set us up for our journey into the night!'

'I'm not feeling all that hungry,' I said, 'I'm afraid I've some bad news to tell everyone about the delay…'

'Oh, do you mean we are *orf* to Paris?' she smiled. 'Oh, yes, Ian and Betty have been telling everyone, but really, please don't worry at all. It's not your fault in the least, and we shall simply soldier on and get there in the end.'

In the end, breaking the news, not only about Paris but about the plus one and plus one, came as a surprise to very few.

YOGA IN THE AIR AND ON THE GROUND

The flight from Bombay to Doha takes about four hours. We had departed before midnight and most of the Indian passengers were soon fast asleep. A few of our own people were also asleep, but to my astonishment, looking behind me in the plane after an hour or so, a few rows back there were some legs waving in the air. I recognized these legs from the brightly coloured trousers, some covered in elephant patterns. There were about six legs, belonging to perhaps four people, and they were pointed more or less upright, moving slowly in a vaguely circular pattern with the feet and toes pointing as if in inverted ballet 'pointes' towards the ceiling. I knew the origin of this curious spectacle: two or three times during our tour, several of the group had attended rather brief yoga classes offered by some of the hotels. On at least one occasion this had been conducted beside a swimming pool and indeed, as we had been there, Jill and I had been persuaded to join in. The rather charming young female instructor had patted my stomach and mentioned 'four months?' while attempting one of the yoga exercises. I had not been a keen participant, but the 'synchronised swimming' and line dancing we had seen in the pool had all been part of these exercise regimes which the select few had taken up from time to time. Now the enthusiasts were clearly using the boredom of the flight to practice some of the movements, albeit in a rather haphazard and certainly restricted way. They were certainly demonstrating a considerable degree of flexibility in raising their bottoms with their hands, with their legs in the air above their heads. Our Indian neighbours on the plane may have found this rather indecorous, and it certainly presented an unusual spectacle to the cabin staff as they passed up and down the plane. Nothing was said however, and the yoga did not last for long. Indeed, our sleep, reading or yoga was soon interrupted by an unusual breakfast which was difficult to identify, but was possibly a spicy omelette, served an hour or so before we reached Doha. I may add, though, that however beneficial to health and well-being, the leg waving regime did have an unfortunate sequel.

Doha airport is, I suppose, similar to other airports in the Middle East. We arrived in the dark, of course, but the arrival hall was brightly lit, with lots of white marble, some fountains playing, mirrors, moving advertising displays and a considerable number of armed guards. We transit passengers were shepherded to a waiting area, which had adequate but not very comfortable seating, and it was clear that it was not going to be easy to while away three hours or so. There was certainly no alcohol available, we had eaten 'breakfast' on the plane, and there was just a small coffee shop selling nuts and confectionary. Paperbacks had been circulating among the group for the past two weeks or more and, as Jacky rather unkindly said, 'I'm fed up with trying to read other peoples' appalling choice of books.' It was during this period of boredom, while some tried to read, talk, or even doze off, that perhaps four or five of the yoga party, led by Catherine and Val wandered off to explore more of the airport. They were gone quite some time, and it was rather disturbing to look up to see them all trooping back together, walking rather quickly, accompanied by two male and two female armed guards.

'We've been chucked out!' called Catherine when still 20 yards away. There was a note of almost triumph in her voice. The rest of us looked up startled, but Catherine was interrupted by a flow of rapid and rather angry Arabic from all the guards who gesticulated, pointing very determinedly to some empty chairs. Most of the group sat down at once, clearly intimidated, but Catherine and Val were still standing, starting to explain what had happened to those of us nearest to them. The guards became more abrupt, and even more peremptory rapid-fire Arabic poured out, especially from the female guards. There was more pointing and the two miscreants did as they were told and sat down. We were all very curious to find out what had been going on, and they were equally keen to tell us, but only when the guards moved a short distance away did they begin.

'Well, we only wanted to find a place a little bit out of the way.'

'It was Val who found the place -it was ideal - a lovely quiet room with mats already set out on the floor…'

The penny dropped soon enough and to my embarrassment the ringleaders were rather proud of themselves and of being ejected when found rolling around on their backs, legs in the air, *in the prayer room*. The guards were looking on, unamused, as I tried to quell the growing splutters of laughter from the group. The guards took no further action, but I felt we had had a narrow escape. We had completed the first leg of our journey home.

But now an airport official came looking for me. That dreaded call of 'Tour leader, where is tour leader?' rang out and he was accompanied by yet another guard. Oh God! What now? The rest of the group rather too eagerly pointed me out. The official was in a suit, with a clipboard and an identity card hung around his neck. Was that the bulge of a revolver under his arm?

'Oh Christ! What's this?' cried David. 'Surely they're not going to arrest us…'

'Complimentary breakfast,' came the curt staccato reply. 'Your group can go to restaurant. These staff members will show you the way.' He pointed to the group of guards.

'I'm not leaving here,' cried Ian. 'You don't know where they'll be taking us. Could be because of those stupid women…'

'The prisoner ate another hearty breakfast,' joked Tom. 'I wouldn't mind another breakfast; didn't care too much for whatever it was they gave us on the plane.'

On the plane breakfast had been served at about two o'clock in the morning. It was now about five am, and this breakfast turned out to be rather good - fried eggs with excellent thinly cut chips. Strangely, most of the group fell on it like locusts, some of us eating more out of relief than hunger.

[illegible]

PARIS FRANCE

As you know, we had no intention of going to Paris. We were supposed to go home, which meant London. Paris had been thrown in as an unwelcome extra. But we had plenty of time to get used to the idea and after flying from India, and all round the Middle East, Paris was so near. Just a short hop across the Channl and we would be home.

How was it then, that Paris should prove so very difficult? We got off the plane to be met by an Air France official holding up a placard marked 'Londres/London'. Several of our group were already gathered round him, pointing to me as I arrived.

'You take ze flight to London? Yez? Ze Gulf Hair 'as requested ze seats to London, yes?'

'Er, yes. Thank goodness. Where do we go?'

'You must go to ze transeet, and from zer, zey will deerect you.'

'Good, thank you. What about our luggage? Do we collect our luggage?'

'Do you mean ze baggage? Ze baggage ees wiz you?'

'Well, I suppose it's come to Paris. We only have luggage tags to Paris. We came on this flight from Abu Dhabi…

'Zen of course. First you must collect ze baggage, zen you go to ze transeet. 'Ere I av your cards for ze transeet. Zis eez your ID number you must show at transeet.'

'But to collect our baggage do we have to go through immigration?'

'You must show zem ze transeet. I av told you, you are in transeet.'

In transit, but needing to collect our baggage? I was confused, tired and totally unclear as to what to do. But we dutifully dragged or carried our handbags along long corridors, down escalators and were at last stopped at the queue for immigration by another official with 'Transit Passengers' on a placard. He examined my ID number and explained that we had to wait till the other passengers had retrieved their bags and then by-pass the immigration to collect our baggage. Through a glass screen we could see some of our yellow labels going around on the luggage carousel. Another wait, the passengers collecting luggage dispersed and eventually the carousel stopped.

'Now you can bring your baggages, but please 'urry, as you av to chek een.'

'Check in? But we are in transit. Why do we have to check in.'

'You are een transeet, but your baggages, zey are not een transeet. You av to check in ze baggages.'

Some of the baggages were piled up on the floor, others were on the carousel. But after much checking and re-checking one was missing. Tom, by coincidence very often the last to receive his meal at table, had a bag missing. A few cardboard boxes and a battered bag remained unclaimed, but they were not Tom's.

'Well, that's about the final straw!' He was red-faced. 'How is it that it's always me..? What the hell am I supposed to do next?'

'Let's just make sure it isn't round the back of this bloody carousel.' I was also thinking it the final straw. I grabbed our official who had been waiting to take us to 'check-in', who pointed me to the small lost property kiosk.

'We seem to have a bag missing from the Gulf Air flight GF 720.'

'Where is eet coming from, zis flight?'

'Well, from Bombay, but that flight number is from Abu Dhabi. It was loaded in Bombay, but we had transfers in Doha and Abu Dhabi.'

'Doha and Abu Dhabi?

'Yes, that's right, we changed in Doha and then Abu Dhabi. But the bags were booked through to Paris.'

'My God! And Paris, iz zis ze final destination?'

'No it's not. We are in transit to London. You know we are in transit for London!'

'London? Boef! Ow can you be in transeet when you are looking for your baggage? It could be anywhere! What kind of baggage. You must contact the airline. Gulf as an office, but now is too early…'

But by an incredible stroke of luck I could see, on the floor behind the pessimistic official, a sporty looking bag with the familiar label.

'Excuse me! There - on the floor behind you. I think I can see the bag.'

'What bag? There are many bags.' Indeed there were, on racks, on the floor, many parcels, suitcases of every shape and size.

'No, there, on the floor, with a yellow label.'

'Zis one? I do not know zis one.' He turned to a colleague and they rattled some French together.

'Thees one is not you carousel. Anozer one and iz not reclaimed.'

'Well it's ours. Can I have it please. We are in a hurry and have to go to transit.'

'First you cannot go to transeet wiz your baggages, and also you cannot reclaim your baggage wizout ze form and also your identity.'

'Oh Christ! We are in a hurry. I will bring the owner.'

'You are not ze owner? Zen you cannot reclaim ze baggages.'

I ran the length of the baggage hall to the waiting group and a fuming Tom. 'I've found it, ' I was breathing hard. 'I've found it. But you have to come to identify it. Show them your passport.'

'Where the hell was it?'

Spluttering with displeasure, Tom filled in forms describing the bag that was now on the counter in front of him: his name, his passport details and flight numbers of all the flights we had taken. The minutes ticked away.

Our earlier official now strolled up, rather casually, saying. 'Eef you do not come immediately, you wheel miss ze flight. First you have to check in ze baggages. Now you av all your baggages?'

We had all our baggages, but we had to move at some speed. Not all our group were capable of moving at some speed, so some of us, pushing trolleys, raced along trying to keep up with the official marching ahead of us talking into his walkie-talkie. He turned to me.

'It is London, yes?' I nodded agreement. 'You weel be on *two flight* to London.'

'How do you mean "two flight"? Who will be on two flight?'

'Gulf 'az cancelled your flight and you are re-routed? Is zees correct?' It certainly was correct. 'Air France cannot take all ze group on one flight, but we av anozer one after 40 minutes. But we must 'urry because ze first flight, it has already completed check-in and security.'

'Do you mean *we* are travelling on two flights? Our group? Do you mean we have to split into two flights? I don't believe...'

'Yes, exactly, zay must be in two flights. Please 'urry.'

Jill caught up with me. 'Is there much further to go? Jean and a few others are struggling and if this keeps up we'll have a heart attack on our hands. What's the great rush? Surely...'

'It seems that the flight has already completed security and they are waiting for us.'

'Well you'd better inform them exactly what is happening. They all want to know...'

'Believe me, they won't want to know. It's awful - I'll tell you but now we have to check in if we're to catch the first flight.' We were now both pushing

trolleys, trying to keep up with the walkie-talkie man who was striding ahead.
'First flight? What do you mean first flight? How many flights are there? We're only going to London - we can't change on the way to London.'
'Sshh!' I warned.

It seemed a long way to the check in, but I got there well ahead of those struggling to keep up. Our walkie-talkie man now had several other officials with him and one of them immediately demanded,
'Ow many baggages do you 'av? Ow many for the check-in baggages?'
'Well I don't know exactly. We are 27 in the group, and some of them have two bags and…'
'Never mind! All ze baggages must go on the next 'plane and eleven passengers must travel on zis first plane. Give me eleven transit cards, and I give you eleven boarding cards. They must go immediately to the gate. It is gate 26.'

'Which eleven?' I had no idea what he meant us to do. 'And what about their baggage? 'Surely,' I said, 'Zey must travel wiz zeir baggages?' I was falling into the French idiom.
'Please send eleven of your group now,' he retorted, 'Or zey will miss ze plane. We av no time to send their baggages, and we av no space for their baggages. And if zey miss zis one, then 'oo knows when we have space on anozer one. We av only 16 more seats on ze next one. All the baggages will come on the next one.'

It never did become clear to me why, but my task now was to send eleven of our group on to a plane, without their baggage. The others would follow with everyone's baggage. I had naively thought that no baggage could be transported without the passengers on the same plane, but apparently this was not to be the case. No doubt Air France, in partnership with Gulf Air, was attempting to shift passengers they had not expected from Paris to London, and protocols of security were being waived.

The group were mostly collected behind me listening, but hardly understanding or believing what they were hearing. It was time to explain.

'I think most of you have heard what's going on. It seems that eleven of us have to get on a plane that is leaving for London immediately, but the rest of us will have to get on the next one, which is 40 minutes later.' There was a howl of rage, protest, disbelief and anguish.

'My God, after what we've been through?'

'This is just ridiculous.'

'Surely you can do something?'

'I must get on the earlier flight; I have to get to work and we're already…'

Of course, there was more disturbing news to impart:

'I'm afraid it won't make any difference which plane we go in, as all our luggage is coming on the later plane. So those who go on the first will just have to wait for the second plane to arrive. I know it sounds ridiculous, but if we don't accept this, we'll have to wait until an afternoon flight, and there's no guarantee we'll get on that. Anyway they've issued the tickets now, so I'm afraid we'll just have to accept it.'

The next outburst was a little less ferocious, as most people saw the inevitability of the arrangement. But there was still considerable resentment.

'Did you know about this?'

'What a complete cock-up.'

'Look,' I said, 'We've got to be quick. I think most passengers are already on board. Will those whose names I call out please go immediately to gate number 6. As you see, all the bags are here and are going to be checked in on the next flight, and we'll all meet up in Heathrow.' I started to read out the names and hand out the cards: 'Ian and Betty, Jacky and David, Tom, Molly, Catherine… Jill…Oh Christ! I've just seen that *our* fucking cards are with this lot! Oh *fuck*! Oh excuse me! I'm so sorry… But that means I'll have to be in the first group.'

Cynthia was her usual helpful self. 'No, no, Richard, that is a very sensible solution. You will be in the first group and will be able to gather everyone together for when we arrive. Betty and I will remain behind and ensure all the luggage is sent on to the plane. Don't worry about it. We are, after all, in the hands of Air France, and we shall manage very well.'

The eleven cards for this flight were distributed and the officials were hurrying us away from the others and the pile of bags. I just had time to thrust the other batch of boarding cards for the later flight into Betty's outstretched hands before following the first group through a door in a glass screen heading for the departure gates. But then I could hear a loud thumping and could see Val and Betty were banging on the other side of the glass, mouths making exaggerated movements which I couldn't hear, and gesticulating.

'What's the matter?' I tried to shout to them. The glass screen did not reach the ceiling, but was about ten feet high. Cynthia was with them, waving a boarding card at me and calling.

'What's the matter?' I repeated. Again, Betty was waving and shouting.

'There aren't enough. I gave them out but she hasn't got one,' shouted Betty. She has a loud clear voice, and, though distant and muffled I could just make it out, helped by Cynthia who was holding a boarding card against the glass and pointing at it.

'Who hasn't got one?' I shouted back, quite mystified. The advance guard of 11 minus me were walking away and I shouted 'STOP! Please look at your boarding cards carefully. Has anyone got the wrong card, or too many cards?

It was my fault. I had given what I thought were two cards to Molly - one for Jean - but Jean was not in the advance party, and Molly had not noticed there were two. Now I had Jean's boarding card on the wrong side of the screen.

'Throw it over,' suggested Molly.

'Don't be ridiculous,' said Jacky. 'Can't you take it back?' But it meant going the wrong way through security and another official stopped me.

'Throw it over,' called several of our group on my side, and I could hear from the other side of the screen more calls to 'Throw it over.'

Now it is not easy to throw a boarding card over a high glass screen in full view of several dozen passengers. Three times I tried, jumping as high as I could. But each time it fell, fluttering back on my side of the screen. I tried flicking it, as I had learned to do with playing cards and cigarette cards while at school. I tried folding it into a paper dart and flying it over. At first it looked as if this would be successful and, as there was now quite a large crowd watching, there was a cheer. But paper darts have a mind of their own and a way of turning in a circle and flying back towards the thrower, and as the dart soared upwards and turned away from the screen the crowd's cheer turned into a moan. Eventually our irate official marched up to me, seized the card from my hand and, without a word, walked back through security, opened the glass door in the screen and handed it to the waiting Betty.

'For you, ze flight iz delayed!' he hissed at me. 'Ze pilot perhaps must lose 'is take-off. Beouf!'

We eleven caught our flight, which took off twenty-five minutes late, and an hour and a half later, with another breakfast - the fourth on this long and circuitous journey - and some, but very little sleep, landed at Heathrow. It was soon after ten o'clock in the morning. We were exhausted, and we now had to wait for the others and our luggage. The immigration queue was slow, and the man at the counter unsmiling and unwelcoming. We slowly made our way to the baggage reclaim area, where the other passengers from our flight stood collecting their luggage from the carousel, but we did not. The only place to sit in the baggage hall without baggage is on a trolley, so I pushed mine to a display screen showing 'Arrivals', watching anxiously for the next Air France flight. It showed 'Delayed.'

A BLEEDIN' YO-YO

Now, the question was, would our coach turn up to meet us? This is always a matter of some concern when leaving an airport, and while there has usually been no problem, occasionally our driver or guide or agent has been late. But this time there were many reasons to fear the worst. We were arriving on the wrong day; at the wrong time; on the wrong airline; at the wrong terminal. In Bombay, when we first heard the news of our delayed and diverted flight, and again in Paris, I had given the ground staff the contact details of the coach company that had brought us to Heathrow, and of the taxi firm that was due to collect Ian and Betty who were staying with their daughter. I had been reassured that messages would be sent and that we would be met from the correct flight. Could it possibly work? We had been travelling for over 36 hours from the time we left our hotel on Kovalam beach - a journey that was originally to have taken perhaps 18 hours. How could our coach driver be here to find us?

We hadn't yet felt the cold, but now, walking with the others through the 'Nothing to Declare' channl I did feel cold - and anxious. I searched among the throng of greeters for a placard with anything I could recognise. No! Nothing! Jill and I left the others in a huddle with their trolleys and walked up and down the line of greeters, even asking some if they knew anything of a coach for Southampton. For 20 minutes we searched without any real hope. Then Betty found me and pulled me forward. Standing, not with the others, but at the back of the arrivals area, I saw a man reading a newspaper. Betty had apparently looked over his shoulder and seen, upside down, a placard with the rather terse message 'HUNT SOUTHAMPTON'. Thank God! I nearly fell into his arms with relief. He was unmoved by my emotional greeting.

'Oh, you're 'ere. Thank Gawd. I dunno what the car-parking's gonna be like, chief. I've been up and down here like a bleedin' yo-yo. First you was on this bleedin' flight, then you was on that.'

'Well, thank you very much, but we are here now and I am delighted you are too. I'm so relieved - we've had a terrible journey. I think it's pretty miraculous you knew where and when to find us!'

'Too right, Chief. I am bleeding miraculous. 'An' I 'ope your lot will show the customary miraculous appreciation… Bleedin 'Ell! Are all them trolleys your lot?'

'Er, yes, I'm afraid… Oh, I'm also looking out for a taxi for two of my people. I don't suppose you know anything about that do you?'

'Me? Naw, I don't chief. But then, this place has been like bleedin' Piccadilly Circus. Bleedin' flights delayed, bleedin' flights cancelled, bleedin' changin' this an' that. How's a bleedin' driver supposed to do his bleedin' job? I arsk you?'

But Ian had found his driver; Betty had seen them and came rushing over to let me know. At eleven in the morning, Cynthia assured me, she could easily catch a train and a connection to Cambridge. More farewells and we followed our bleedin' driver, pushing our bleedin' trolleys into the bleedin' cold of a March morning. The contrast with India couldn't have been sharper - the warmth of the welcome and hospitality, against the indifference - even resentment of our English driver.

'You'll 'ave to wait here while I fetch the coach. It'll take about ten minutes if the bleedin' traffic lets me. 'Ang on 'ere.' So we did, huddled and shivering on the pavement, while other passengers, some departing, others arriving, moved past us in a continuous flow. Ours was an almost silent group who handed the luggage to the now more silent driver - only an occasional grunt and 'Bleedin' ell! What have you got in here, missus?' - as he heaved our bags into the hold and we climbed into what now appeared a very luxurious coach indeed - very much more luxurious than anything we had encountered in the past three weeks. It was a remarkably smooth road as we left the airport, and strangely quiet despite the congestion of traffic. The inside of the coach was warm; the seats were clean and large and plush; there was almost no jostling and pushing of hand luggage into racks too small to take it. When I looked round after a few minutes half the group was asleep, and I guess I must have been asleep myself very soon - a blissful two hours of sleep, with only occasional waking moments.

We stopped where we had started our journey, near the library of the University. In contrast to the cold dark early morning of our departure, our return was in the afternoon in watery sunshine. Our driver's mood had not lifted, even when, as he applied the handbrake he spoke over the microphone, 'Right, then, ladies an' gents, we're here. Though 'ow I was supposed to find you with all that chopping and changing, I dunno. Now, if you would like to show your appreciation, I 'ave placed this tin…'

Some people had friends or relatives collecting them; others had phoned for taxis while we were in the airport. I was hoping that our car was still parked in its customary place around the corner and that, after three weeks, it would start. With more hugs and farewells and promises of reunions to come, we started to disperse. Jean, however, told us she was going by bus, so Jill and I carried her luggage over to the bus stop and gave her good-bye hugs. She stood rather forlornly, as on the day of departure, with raincoat, rain hood, hand bags and a mountain of baggage. But at that moment Tom rushed up to say that he had offered her a lift home in his car, and that his wife was waiting beside the coach. Jean had forgotten this offer, so the three of us carried everything back again.

Several letters and cards arrived from members of the group over the next couple of weeks. One of them was from Cynthia - a lovely long appreciative letter. And then some days later the phone rang; it was Cynthia's warm and cheerful voice,

'Cynthia, how lovely to hear from you.'

'Richard my dear, I do hope you received my letter?' I had, of course, and had sent a circular letter to everyone thanking them for their co-operation and friendship, reminding them of a reunion we were planning, and mentioning tentative plans for another trip to India the following year.

'And Jill? How is darling Jill? It was such a wonderful experience! I have received my photographs - some of them rather pleasing - and showed them to several friends. Now, Richard, I know I was a trial to you, but could you bear it if I were to join you on your next tour? And may I bring my sister-in-law? She was so envious of our adventures together…'

THE RAJ QUARTET

A FEW WORDS ABOUT THE RAJ QUARTET

I think I should explain that our Raj Quartet was not like others you may have come across. It was not four novels set in India; it wasn't a group of four musicians or a composition in four parts with an Indian theme. No, our Raj Quartet was simply four ladies who knew each other very well, and who accompanied us on a series of journeys to India. Of course, it wasn't just a matter of any four ladies. To have a quartet you do need four; but to have a Raj Quartet you must have four of the right sort. This may lead you to think that these ladies would have been brought up in the India of the British Raj? But this was not the case. Certainly all four were of an age that they might have been - they were all born long before the end of the Raj in 1947 - but none were brought up in India. Perhaps the members of some family connection had served with the Raj? Well yes, but this did not really make any of our four into ladies of the Raj. In any case, which well-connected family did not have someone who served out in India? But surely, you say, they must be connected in some way with India? Well, yes, but the only real connection was that they travelled there several times, long after the Raj had ended. No, it was more a question of who they were, their style, their mannrisms, and how they responded when they were there. They became affectionately called the Raj Quartet by their travelling companions, and even came to call themselves members of the Raj Quartet.

And, you will rightfully insist, members of a quartet must have some connection with one another. Just so: a quartet can hardly function without the frequent interaction that a polished performance requires. Not necessarily a conscious rehearsal, you understand, but a familiarity that ensures smooth verbal entrances and exits. Well, our quartet had certainly known each other for a very long time: they came from the same social milieu of landed families, famous schools, society balls and debutantes. Coincidentally, two had married the brothers of the other two. In more recent years, when some were widowed, they had travelled together, but not, so far, to India.

Each member of a *Raj* Quartet must also carry an air, a confidence, a certain style that the term suggests. Not the same, of course – they each had a very distinctive mannr - but a sense of belonging to an age, with a certain breeding, a bearing, a demeanour which could place them in a period, and in a social position where they could comfortably have held their own - whether in the Poonah Club *in* the days of the Raj, or a ball at the Ritz, or as in one case long, long after the Raj had ceased to exist, in the private drawing room of the (still) English Secretary of the Tollygunge Club in Calcutta where our group had been invited for drinks. There we visitors were introduced rather grandly to one of the guests - 'the dowager Maharani of Cooch Bihar'. Although wearing a sari and heavy jewellery, this lady appeared remarkably English and was, we learned, originally from Essex, with heavily drawn and rather ginger eyebrows and Essex accent that revealed her origins. We learned that she had attracted the attentions of the Maharajah many years before, when he had spied her in the chorus of the Gaiety Theatre. Now Cynthia, one of the members of our Raj Quartet was heard to murmur - not sufficiently *sotto voce* -

'Ah yes, (pause) Cooch Bihar (another pause). Cooch Bihar. Much reduced, if I recall. A very minor state …'

Cooch Bihar, it should be said, was far from being a minor state in its day, but it had long since ceased to be a state at all: its territories absorbed into the province of Assam; its grandiose Italianate palaces now dilapidated and empty, anachronisms, some of which were uncomfortably attempting to be a museum, or perhaps a hotel, or government offices. But the murmured rebuke spoke volumes - of unfortunate marriages, dissolute life-styles, past excesses. Indeed, on passing through Cooch Bihar many years after the interlude at the Tollygunge, a group of us called at what had become a rather sad museum. As always in these places on the walls there were many portraits – oil paintings and black-and-white photos - of Maharajas and their wives, of princes and princesses, of visiting dignitaries, of the King Emperor and Queen Mary. But none resembled the lady in the Tollygunge Club. I asked a very respectful museum attendant, who had already told us that his father worked there while it was still a palace, 'I don't see any pictures of the English Maharani? Wasn't there an English Maharani?'

A rather awkard silence followed as the attendant hung his head, but after a few moments he muttered, 'But sir, she is not spoken of.'

Now, in the 21st Century, it is increasingly difficult to find even one candidate for a Raj Quartet. Reminiscing over dinner while on a tour in a hill station, or an atmospheric old colonial hotel, people remark:

'What marvellous characters, they don't make 'em like that any more.'

Of course they do; we have met many, but the passage of time means that while the characters are with us, their numbers are declining and the sense of period is passing.

The Quartet, though not at that time a Raj Quartet, had been formed many years before. All four women had shared a London flat in the war and all, to my undying astonishment, served in some secretive department of the War Office. The connections were strengthened: Lucy married Cynthia's brother; Ann married Lydia's brother. Class, family connection and background had undoubtedly brought them together even before the war-time posting and all this, together with friendship and affection, ensured that the Quartet would make its appearances in the war time and post-war upper class social world from which they came. They would meet at country houses, at London flats, dancing at the Ritz, at family marriages and funerals, at the Aldeburgh Festival as soon as it was formed in the late '40s, at each other's homes and in adventures abroad. Years later a family connection had taken them to Indo-China, but not, so far, to India.

Even in the 1980s our Raj Quartet took some time to coalesce. At first there was just one: Cynthia came alone, or rather she joined the rest of us on one of our early tours to India. There was no indication then that there may be more to follow, but the following year she was joined by her sister-in-law, Lucy, on the next tour. A year later, with the addition of their old friends Ann and Lydia, the Quartet was formed. It was only to present its full and rather glorious appearance to the rest of us over a period of some three years in which all four toured north India, the south and the east. After these, it assembled for a few special and sometimes private occasions – a luncheon party, a lecture, a museum visit. And then advancing years and some frailty meant that first one, then another could not join our tours. Our Quartet was reduced to a Trio; sometimes a Duo; and finally with Cynthia as a Solo traveller once more.

We are of course concerned with the members of the Raj Quartet, but inevitably with their fellow travellers, too. Some of these appear retrospectively to play the part of a chorus, sometimes a discordant chorus it must be admitted; but many others played prominent roles – even leading roles - from time to time. And while the rest of the cast were gathering on that cold dark morning before we set off on this first journey to the South, through the window of the coach that was parked around the corner I saw the solitary figure of Cynthia, the founder and, sadly, the surviving traveller of the Quartet. How strange then, that our first encounter should result in *losing* Cynthia.

LOSING CYNTHIA

There had been plenty of cause for concern long before this, but it was on the second leg of the flight, long past the point of no return, that the trouble began in earnest.

'What? What do you mean Cynthia's not on the plane? How can she be not on the plane?'

'I tell you she's not. Betty was sitting next to her but she's not seen her since we stopped in Muscat. And nor has anyone else.' I can tell you by now I was feeling not just the customary anxiety, but real panic.

'Well, she must be. She must be somewhere. She must be in the loo.'

'What, for two hours?'

'I knew something like this would happen. I said from the beginning that it was not a good idea, but you wouldn't have it.'

She was quite right: she - she being my dear wife, Jill - had said from the beginning that it was not a good idea, and while there had been plenty of reasons in the planning stages to see that it was not a good idea, I had persisted. Once begun, the plan had rolled forward with a momentum of its own. There were all those who had been so enthusiastic about going on the tour; there were the travel agents in India and at home who naturally wanted it to go ahead and played down the difficulties; there were my friends and contacts in India who were eager to help. It would be awful to let them all down, and I - in truth both of us, Jill and I - were keen to return to India. Despite the discomforts and frustrations we had spent several fascinating months there.

'But why must we take a whole bunch of people to look after?' she had asked. 'Yes, of course it would be interesting to go back, but for heaven's sake it's difficult enough getting about without worrying about a whole lot of other people. You'll hate it, and I will hate it more than you.'

'Well, it's too late to be going on about that now. We're on our way and there's no going back.'

'Unless, of course, you have to go back - back to Muscat to find her! We're not even half-way there and you say you have lost one of them!'

A few hours earlier it had all started quite smoothly. We had been assembling for our departure. There she was:

'Er, hello, you must be Lady Cynthia? I'm Richard, we've…' It had to be Cynthia: I knew all the others and they all knew each other from previous gatherings. While I had gone over to take some of my stuff to the waiting coach, they were chatting in small groups around the piles of luggage just around the corner. But Cynthia was already sitting alone on the coach as I climbed the steps.

'Ah yes, how *do* you do. Please, *do* call me Cynthia. I am so very pleased to meet you at long last.' I instantly recalled the voice from several telephone conversations - how could I not? It was a very distinctive, even startling voice. It was polished and mellow, rich in upper-class vowels and pauses; it was almost a caricature of an upper class voice in the very grandest of grand mannrs. But it was warm and humorous. She spoke again.

'Ah yes, may I call you Richard? Professor… oh dear, I have become so bad at names, um Professor - your professor - he told me *so* much about you and I was *so* excited. It is *too* kind of you to allow me to join you. After all, I have been quite unable to attend any of your lectures. Cambridge is so very far *orf*… I'm afraid I shall be the total duffer in the group…'

The professor was Paul, my boss. He had not been able to tell me much about Cynthia. He had met her at some small drinks party in Cambridge, and in the chit-chat she had expressed a long felt desire to revisit India - a place to which she had briefly accompanied her husband years before. Paul had told her that one of his staff was arranging a trip to India as part of a course for adults. He rang to tell me that this rather grand elderly lady had expressed an interest in joining the tour and may contact me. Within a day or two she did ring and I heard her extraordinary voice for the first time. She told me how she had longed to go to India ever since a small child - several of her friends had been born there; some boarding school chums had parents out there and some of her relatives had served there. In the '50s her husband was invited to an academic conference in Delhi and Cynthia had gone too, but they had little time to catch more than fleeting glimpses of some of the great monuments of Delhi before returning to Cambridge.

We had talked some more, I had sent Cynthia some details in the post, we became good friends over the 'phone, she decided to join us, and here she was. Now I could match a face to the voice - a pretty, lively face, with bright eyes, surrounded by a cloud of curly white hair. But we couldn't talk on the coach for long. The other members of the group started to climb aboard and there was a good deal of chattering and calling out of greetings as small hand bags were pushed into overhead racks, and people pushing past me as I stood talking to Cynthia. I introduced her to Betty as she pushed her way down the aisle with her bags. It had been arranged that Cynthia and Betty would share a room on the tour as neither wanted to pay the extra for a single room. They had not met, but had often spoken together by 'phone, and Betty, a secretary in my department, had told me how well they got on together and that sharing would be no problem.

'We both like a drink you see, so we will get on famously.'

I had warned both of them that sharing with a stranger was fraught with dangers, especially for a tour of three weeks, and wasn't convinced that drink would form a sufficient bond. Betty was very much a personality in her own right, also with quite a 'posh' accent, clear in diction and could clearly hold her own. She was also jolly, very amusing and entertaining, so I was hoping for the best. But I might tell you that there had been a 'sharing incident' a year or so before on another tour, a week-long trip to Venice we had organized for another of our courses. Here the rancour on the part of one lady, who had agreed to share a room as she 'seldom slept and so wouldn't mind in the least' and very evident distress on the part of another who 'had been in the Women's Land Army as a girl and could share with anyone,' had made it seem like a month. I was left to cope with the fury of the first, who after the first night in the hotel had shouted at me that she,

'Could not stand that woman's snoring and had not slept at all', and the other sobbing into my arms saying,

'I'm so sorry, I'm so sorry, I had no idea, and she was so very beastly.' We had only solved the problem by extracting the snoring lady from the hotel and installing her in a flat in Venice where our guest lecturer was staying, but the fury and the distress had not been assuaged and the trip was certainly tainted for everyone else. I urged Betty, who I had known for some years, and who was now to share with Cynthia, to confess if she snored, smoked or to admit to any other nasty habits.

'Drink' she owned up immediately, and had told Cynthia who was apparently relieved and delighted.

Now, on the coach, they greeted each other as old friends, and I left Betty to squeeze in beside Cynthia while I tried to get off the bus and look for my wife Jill and our luggage, and attend to the needs of some other, rather more demanding travellers.

From that early start I lost track of Cynthia. Our coach reached Heathrow, where we unloaded our luggage and trundled it to the check-in counter of Gulf Air. There was a good deal of confusion here as people demanded the things that people demand: seats with leg-room; seats in the aisle; seats by the window; seats with their friend; near the front; near the back; not at the back; not by the loos. Luggage was weighed and disappeared, tickets, passports and visas examined, boarding cards distributed. Our group then scattered: *en route* to the security check several went via the lavatories; then, after the security check they were scattered in the departure lounge - drinking coffee, in the lavatories, book stall, camera shop and above all, the duty-free. Indeed, it was at the duty-free that I met up again with Cynthia and Betty. Our flight had already been called, and I was trying to see if anyone was left behind. I caught sight of them in the queue to pay for their purchases.

'Oh, hello there, the flight was called you know. Everyone else has already…'

'Yes, we did hear,' began Betty, 'but Cynthia thought she better just go back for a bit more.'

'Oh dear, I am *so* sorry. Are we holding you up? I shall not be a moment. I thought it may be wiser to ensure…' Cynthia, now at the cash-desk, was struggling with her hand-bag, her boarding card, her ticket and passport, trying to pay the lady, but muddling her documents in her hurry.

'Can I help?' I offered, 'Can I hold...'

'Oh Richard, you are *too* kind, but…'

'Well we need to go, can I carry this bag for you?' There was quite a large leather bag at her feet. 'You seem to have quite a bit to look after.'

Betty also looked quite laden, so I stooped to pick up Cynthia's bag, but could hardly believe its weight! It made me stumble forward and almost drop it. It had not been fastened, and as I half-dropped and half-put it down, so the bag tipped forward and two bottles of scotch, in their protective plastic sleeves, skidded on to the carpet.

'Oh, I'm sorry,' I said, I'll just…'

Picking them up, I put them back into the bag with another bottle that had not escaped.

'Kindly be seated, sir, you are causing obstruction.' Was I? A steely eyed, well-spoken, polite Arab stewardess said I was, so I sat. After take-off, when it was too late to check that everyone was on board, I walked around and, with a sense of relief, located everyone. I spoke to several, but Cynthia was deep in conversation with a very animated Betty. A couple of hours later, on another walk round after a meal had been served, both were soundly asleep; one head lolling forward, the other back with an open mouth. Their meal trays were still in front of them, with several empty small wine bottles of the kind they serve on planes, and several empty miniatures of spirits on each tray. I felt a deepening anxiety, but put the flicker of misapprehension to one side. This was on our first flight - Gulf Air to Abu Dhabi, via Muscat. It evidently was not the 'dry flight' that some members of the group had warned when I announced it would be a Middle-Eastern airline.

As we were descending to Muscat the cabin announcement explained that those of us continuing to Abu Dhabi would remain on the plane, while those leaving for Muscat would disembark. As more passengers would join us would those continuing to Abu Dhabi kindly remain in their seats. Then there were the usual rather inaudible messages about remaining seated until the aircraft came to a complete stop, being careful of overhead lockers, taking all belongings, etc., etc. I did not have time to talk to Cynthia again during the short time on the ground, as Jean wanted to discuss her medical conditions and requirements and there was hardly time to hear about Ian and Betty's dietary arrangements. This Betty, by the way, was not the sharing-with-Cynthia Betty. Not at all! This Betty was Ian's wife, who we had better call Betty 2 as we may meet her later. After about half an hour we took off again for the short flight to Abu Dhabi and when the 'Fasten Seat-Belt' sign was switched off, I walked round the plane. *Cynthia was not in her seat*; Betty had an empty seat beside her.

'Is Cynthia in the loo?' I asked.

'I don't know. I haven't seen her for a while. She got up to walk around when we were on the ground and I haven't seen her since.' Betty was always calm and collected at work, but now she sounded uneasy.

'I assumed she had gone to the loo, or found someone else to talk to, or sat in another seat…'

'Ladies and gentlemen, this is your captain,' came the announcement, 'We will shortly be commencing our descent to Abu Dhabi airport. Kindly return to your seat and fasten your safety belt.'

'Please sit down sir, we will be landing shortly,' from the stewardess. So I sat down in Cynthia's seat next to Betty. I was quite a long way from my own seat beside Jill, and I could see there was a food trolley in the way, so I sat down in Cynthia's seat. Anxiety was now acute. Where was Cynthia? Had I lost one of the group? Before even arriving? How? Everyone had received written instructions in various pre-departure documents *and* the itinerary: the flight would touch down at Muscat, but we wouldn't get off until Abu Dhabi, where we would change planes for Bombay. I had also told everyone, and so had the pilot's announcement.

The plane landed and I struggled the wrong way, against the flow of people struggling with their bags, to get back to my own seat, and Jill who was wrestling alone with our hand luggage.

'Where the hell have you been?' Jill demanded. 'I've been struggling with all this…'

'Er, well, I was looking for Cynthia, but she doesn't seem to be on the plane. And there had followed the conversation you heard earlier.

But the queue was moving down the plane and we had to shuffle along and get off. There was no Cynthia as we did so, nor on our bus waiting to take us to the terminal. But then, there were several bus-loads of passengers - she must be among the others? Tension grew as I counted everyone at the transfer desk inside. The cool, air-conditioned gleaming marble of Abu Dhabi airport did little to calm me down, and my whispered questioning of the others managed to spread alarm among the group. Cynthia was *not* there and she was the only one missing. I looked around for someone I could ask, but the others had all been waved through and were disappearing down a corridor. I nervously stayed behind, and was just blurting out my fears to an uncomprehending uniformed official when - thank God - Cynthia appeared through a glass door from the opposite direction, hurrying along, clutching her rather heavy hand luggage and looking rather red in the face. I felt an overwhelming sense of relief.

'Ah, Cynthia, there you are - I was so worried about you. I couldn't find you. Here let me help…'

'Oh, Richard, I am so *frightfully* sorry. Oh dear. You see, I had left these bags by my first seat and had to wait until everyone got *orf* before I could… I am so frightfully sorry…'

'Your first seat?' I was genuinely mystified.

'Well, yes, afterwards it was all rather a rush and they gave me another seat. It was so fortunate that I had my book-mark with me…'

'Your book-mark?'

'Well, you see…'

'Oh, look,' I interrupted, 'everyone's going, perhaps we should go through to join the others.'

We were now the only ones at the transfer desk apart from a few disinterested staff.

'Do you have your ticket?' I asked.

'Yes, I do. Now I do. That was the problem, I only had my bookmark, you see.'

I didn't see; but now we had to move, and I was no longer anxious about Cynthia, merely mystified, relieved, but with my heart still thumping. I was conscious that my hanging back with Cynthia was going to cause friction: I had no hand luggage with me, it had been with Jill, who did not really know where I was and she had been left in sole charge of the group - something I had promised her would not happen. And there was the next leg of the journey to worry about. So with some fumbling in one and then another of Cynthia's bags, the required ticket was produced, exchanged for a boarding card, and we could join the others. Betty and Jill had done their best to calm the group and explain what was happening. But the explanations had aggravated concerns about the disappearance of the tour leader, who was supposed to lead, not disappear. There were a few calming voices, but overwhelmingly I heard:

'And what kind of a tour leader loses someone on an aeroplane?'

'And we were telling him about how we can't eat that Indian stuff…'

'And I was telling him that I had the wrong seat and should have…'

'And I was telling him that we must find a pharmacy… and he just disappeared'

'Are we to get on this plane? Are you absolutely sure?'

'They haven't given me the right boarding card. I was sitting with my friend and now…'

'I hope they give us a better meal; the last one was dreadful…'

'We didn't know what we were supposed to do! Even your wife looked worried, so how do you think…'

It was some time before the mystery of Cynthia's disappearance and the bookmark was revealed. Betty learned the truth during the next flight to Bombay, but was sworn to secrecy lest I should think that Cynthia was a batty old woman who would be a liability throughout the tour. When the confession came, some days later, Betty and Cynthia came to me together (rather like two naughty schoolgirls). The explanation was simple enough. Betty began: Cynthia had clearly not taken in the travel agent's flight itinerary; she had been absent from our preliminary meetings (far away in Cambridge) when the flight schedule was discussed; she had slept through the announcement on the plane. The words 'disembark', Muscat' and 'Abu Dhabi' had been heard when the plane was on the ground, but what with the passengers standing up and opening lockers and a slight natural haziness, aggravated by a mainly liquid lunch, had all somehow caused Cynthia to move along with the passengers getting off the aircraft. She had thought, for reasons never fully explained, that she would be getting back on the same one, so left her bags in the overhead locker and under her seat. Cynthia, gaining in confidence, took up the story.

'You see, I was under the impression that everyone got *orf*, so I followed down the steps and then I was on a coach, and before I knew what was happening we were whisked *orf* and arrived at this building. But now I appeared to be the only European - everyone else appeared to be ladies completely swathed in black, or gentlemen dressed in white. Then they all disappeared so I sat down to read my book. Everyone else had *gorn*. The next thing I knew I was surrounded by fierce looking men with guns, some of them shouting "Ticket! Ticket!". Someone snatched my book and leafed through it, and that was when my book-mark fell to the floor. I was rather *crorss* as they had *lorst* my place, and I find that if that happens I have to read a great deal of what I've read before. Don't you find that? I find that I don't quite know what I *have* read before... Then some fierce *ladies* in uniform came and started patting and prodding at me, pushing me into another room and telling me to take my clothes *orf*. " *Orf! orf!*", they shouted, pulling at my clothes. And "Bag! bag!" but I said, "No bag - bag still on *aer-o-plane*. Kindly return my book - look you have *lorst* my place."

'There was a great deal of shouting - no doubt in Arabic - from outside the room, and one lady left me. I had only removed my cardigan so I put it on again and went out too. A man held my book and the bookmark. "No ticket, no ticket" they shouted, so I said "No, but you have my bookmark."

'What is bookmark? Book is OK - no is illegal book, no gun in book, no drug. What is bookmark?'

I told him: 'The bookmark, my dear good man, is my *boarding card* for the *aeroplane*.'

'Thank *heavens*, Richard, I had it with me. I *do* believe I should be in an Omani gaol to this day! I swore Betty to secrecy, as I feared you would send me home as a foolish old lady.'

'But what happened next?' I asked. 'Where did you go? I looked for you on the plane but...'

'Ah, yes. Well, you see, they led me out to a car, pushed me inside and drove me *orf* across the airfield. Of course, I did not know where they were taking me. I was rather terrified as I feared they may be taking me *orf* to gaol! I did tell them that I was with friends and should rejoin them, but no one seemed to understand. I had guards with me all the way, even until we were inside.

'Inside?' Inside where?' I was confused but caught up in the drama.

'Inside the *aeroplane*! They positively bundled me up the steps and inside the *aeroplane*! One was holding my book and my bookmark. They whisked me into a frightfully comfortable seat near the front and a charming steward asked if I would like a drink. Well, I had a small brandy to recover and fell fast asleep. I was quite exhausted…'

I had certainly overlooked the possibility of Cynthia travelling in the First Class cabin, and now felt rather foolish. But there was also a small sense of achievement; I had arrived in the departure lounge of Abu Dhabi with all the group members including Cynthia. The aircraft was waiting at the docking berth to receive us, and the next stop would be Bombay.

LUCY'S ELEPHANT

We didn't know about Lucy's elephant until much later that day. We were staying in a jungle camp that offered a variety of activities and we had been split up into small groups to take part. The keen bird-spotters had gone off on a nature walk; some had gone in jeeps to a distant part of the park to continue the search for wild animals - hopefully rhinos or even the always elusive tiger; a few of us had spent a really uncomfortable afternoon trying to sit in dug-out canoes too narrow for western backsides, drifting - certainly not paddling - mainly sideways down the river, seeing the occasional bird or tortoise and not much else. It was only when we got back from this, sore and rather grumpy, that we were told about Lucy.

'Didn't you know?'

'She's been quite badly hurt.'

'Who has? What's happened?'

'It's Lucy! She's fallen off her elephant!'

'Christ! What's happened?'

She hadn't fallen off an elephant, but it was a rather serious accident. It seems she and a few others had, at the last minute, been offered another elephant ride even though we'd earlier been told we had 'used up' our allocation of elephant rides. As elephants walk almost silently through the jungle, the chances of spotting animals is much better than roaring about in jeeps, so the rides are very popular. Lucy had loved riding on hers and had become very fond of this particular elephant, so when she was offered the chance of one last ride, she was delighted. Usually four people would ride high up in the howdah, with the mahout sitting lower down on the neck of the animal, but on this occasion there were only three tourists, and Lucy had a front seat.

Now part of forest conservation consisted of burning the old brown tall grass to encourage new growth - food for the deer and other grazing animals - but unfortunately the mahout had chosen to drive his elephant near or through the bush fire (we never learned which), searching for a rhino. The animal had taken fright and ran in panic through the trees, with the mahout unable to control her. Poor Lucy, sitting high up in front, had taken the full force of being knocked against low branches. We learned most of this, blurted out by an excited but very sympathetic group of our people, as we made our way hurriedly to the cabin that Lucy and Cynthia were sharing.

Inside we found Lucy lying on her bed, with cold towels wrapped around ice pressed against her legs and a bandage across her face. Cynthia was in attendance, and so were two American doctors, members of another tour group, who had befriended us a day or two before.

'Oh my goodness, Lucy! Oh dear! What has happened?' Jill and I were both alarmed at her appearance.

'Ah, Richard, you are too kind. Unfortunately my elephant did not care for…'

'Lucy, darling,' said Cynthia, 'Do try not to talk. You see,' she said, turning to us, 'Poor Lucy has had a nasty shock. I'm afraid her legs are rather bruised and there is a tiny cut *acrorss* her nose. No don't worry about it, darling… but she is in considerable pain and I fear she may not be immediately mobile.'

Cynthia was trying to be reassuring, but managing to alarm us even more. I turned to the two doctors who we had come to know quite well.

'What do you think? Have you had a chance to have a look at her?'

Al, the tall thin psychiatrist spoke quite confidently. 'Oh, I guess she's doing just fine - there's nothing broken that we can tell, but she's goin' to need a lotta rest.'

His short fat friend, Frank, a gynaecologist, joined in. 'She most certainly is. Cynthia tells us you are moving on in the morning. Well. I guess this lady is not.'

'Oh dear, that means…'

'Yeah! That means she stays, and I guess a plane to fly her out. She sure can't make it over these roads.'

'A *plane*? Christ! How do we get a plane?'

The roads to the jungle camp had been dreadful - we had arrived in jeeps travelling along river beds and rough tracks for several miles. But what was the solution?

'These gentlemen have been perfectly marvellous,' broke in Cynthia. 'But what I wish to enquire is whether my dear sister-in-law should be allowed Scotch whisky?'

The doctors cheered up noticeably. Frank spoke first. 'I definitely prescribe Scotch whisky!'

His colleague agreed, 'And I can definitely recommend lot of Scotch. As a matter of fact, I can recommend we all have a lot of Scotch.'

'A splendid idea,' chimed in Cynthia. 'Now, do we have enough glasses…'

So, for half an hour or so the six of us: Lucy sipping through a straw, Cynthia, our two medical advisers, Jill and I drank Scotch to ease Lucy's condition.

The doctors did much more: they raided the camp kitchen for any remaining ice, packing it around her legs, they cleaned and dressed her poor wounded face, and it was they who knew about the procedures for getting a light aircraft from Kathmandu to collect Lucy and Cynthia, who elected to stay with her. Before the plane could come for them, Jill and I rather reluctantly set off with the rest of our group on the appalling bumpy road to continue our tour to Pokhara, arranging to meet up with Lucy and Cynthia in Kathmandu on our return in a few days.

We did manage to keep in touch with Cynthia by phoning their hotel, and by the time we met again Lucy had made a very good recovery, though much of her face was a purply-green and she was walking very carefully with a stick. In the airport waiting to fly home, Cynthia, sitting next to her, was heard to enquire, 'Lucy darling, did you happen to see my suitcase go by on the trolley?'

'No, Cynthia dear, I did not observe it *en passant*.'

A week or so after our return to England Lucy phoned me.

'Ah, Richard, this is Lucy. Is this an inconvenient moment? I am so sorry to trouble you further after all the disturbance I caused you.'

'Oh Lucy, I'm just so pleased to hear you. I must ask - how are you feeling?'

'Well, to tell the truth, Richard dear, although quite active - I can get about you know - I must confess to still feeling somewhat *piano*.' (Piano was delivered very slowly with the emphasis on the aa.)

'I'm not at all surprised, after all… But tell me have you had a proper check-up? And we must deal with the insurance claim.'

'Yes indeed, that was one purpose in telephoning you today. You see, I have consulted with my doctor and we have been puzzled as to how we may describe my little mishap on the insurance form. We have decided to write down 'ELEPHANT CRASH'.

We had, of course, expressed our thanks to our American friends for all the help they had given Lucy, but they dismissed this lightly.

'It was nothing,' said the psychiatrist, Al, 'Now, if I had *talked* to that lady and let her *talk* to me that would have been *professional*. Then I could charge!'

'And if I had delivered her baby,' said the gynaecologist, 'That would have been a *miracle* and I could really charge.'

'You are right,' replied Al, 'Talking has never been properly appreciated. I was staying with a bunch of hippy kids in California, mostly smoking grass, and they asked for my help.'

'So you can help with drug counselling?' I asked.

'No, not so much. Actually it was their cat needed help. It had got torn in some barbed wire and needed stitching up, and the kids said "Hey, Doc, fix the cat!" But I said I'm not that kind of Doc. I can talk to the cat! But the cat is wild, it won't listen to me! I can't get near it! It will tear me to pieces. The kids said "Don't worry Doc, we can fix that, you just stitch it up. So they rolled some joints and smoked like crazy and blew the smoke in the cat's nose. And you know what, after a few minutes that cat was lying back, stoned. We stitched it up…'

'And if it comes to thanks', said his friend, 'It is us who should be thanking you. All the time we have been with you we have not been with the Prof. You know what I mean!'

We did know what he meant. A few days before the accident a group of us had been chatting and joking at the bar before dinner. Our two friends, who we had not met till then, came over to join us.

'What are you guys doing? You seem to be having a good time!'

I'm not sure that all of us were having a good time. After bumping our way to the camp earlier in the day, one of our members, a recently retired accountant, had suddenly fainted, falling forward into his soup as we sat at lunch. The soup woke him up, but there was some consternation, especially from his wife, but not from Alwyn, an intrepid much older lady, who had left her even older husband behind, Youth Hostelling in Scotland, and who muttered audibly, 'What a wimpish thing to do! I do hope we're not having much of that kind of behaviour!'

'Are you not having a good time?' someone asked of the Americans.

'I guess we are, but if you don't mind, we'd like to join you over here. The Prof - that's him sitting down there with those three guys - it's his tour - he's trying to hold a meeting. But we'd prefer to drink with you.'

'Yeah,' joined his fat friend, 'I feel kinda guilty as he wants us to have a meet, but he's not doing so good.'

'I do *not* feel guilty,' said his friend, 'In my line it is not *professiona*l for *me* to feel guilty - I let him (pointing to his friend) feel guilty. In any case the Prof wants to talk RHINO.'

'He should talk Rhino. Why not? This is a Rhino tour.'

'I know it's a Rhino tour, but I don't walk to talk rhino when I should be having a drink. Say what, if you guys just ease over and listen up for a few minutes you can hear them talk Rhino.'

The Prof and his three companions were sitting in deck chairs in front of a camp fire quite nearby, so a few of us 'eased over' a little nearer to over-hear. The prof was handing round some papers.

'OK,' he said, speaking slowly and deliberately (his voice was strikingly similar to that of Woody Allan at its most plaintif), 'So you've got the check-sheets. Now we all saw the rhino this morning in the river, and we have to note his behaviour. So, on the check-sheet can you give a tick in the column if the rhino was taking a bath, or was he having a wallow?'

We returned to our two new friends leaning on the bar.

'See!' they grunted in unison.

We learned that whereas we had made the very uncomfortable journey to the camp by jeep, the American group had rafted down the Trisuli river, and in some places had white water rafted in rubber boats. I was genuinely interested: would this be a better way to reach the jungle for a future tour? I asked how the trip had been.

Tall lean Al said, 'It was good, I liked it a lot.'

Short fat Frank said, 'And I did not.'

'Oh dear,' I said, 'Why was that?'

'Well, do you know what a hot-dog is? Do you have hot-dogs in your country?' We nodded.

'Well, you know a hot-dog is a sausage in a bun, but do you know that if you bite on a hot-dog wrong, the sausage can jump right out of the bun?' We were intrigued.

'Well, let me tell you, coming down that goddam river, the goddam boat whooshed past some rocks and spat me out. The raft was the bun and I was that sausage!'

Sad to say, the next morning we had a minor altercation with the American professor. We were all due to go out on elephant back to search for wild life - we were excited at the prospect of seeing rhinos, maybe a sloth bear - and were queuing up with the American group to get on the elephants. We had all been asked to wear dark or jungle colours and to remain silent when in the jungle, so were rather surprised to hear the Prof say to two of our ladies, next in line.

'No, I'm sorry you can't come on these elephants. These are our elephants.'

'But we were told there are four on each elephant… which are your elephants? There are two more places…'

'No, I'm sorry. It's just my group on these elephants because we are having a Rhino Seminar.'

'A what? A seminar? On an elephant?'

But we did let them go without our ladies, who waited, and we watched our two American friends wave wanly as they trundled away. Later, I asked Frank, 'You said you didn't like the white-water rafting - how was the elephant?'

'Huh,' he replied dourly, 'Rafts don't fart!'

CYNTHIA'S CORF

All four of them were sitting together in the back row of the lecture when I first saw them. Of course we knew Cynthia and Lucy from previous Indian tours, but for this next one their chums Ann and Lydia were joining us and it was at this one-day event - some lectures on India - that we would meet them for the first time. Three had arranged to come some distance to stay with Lucy - who lived not so far away - to attend the day, but mainly to meet me and some of the others who would be on the trip.

I didn't see them when they first arrived: I was being told off by a senior colleague who was annoyed that the Indian lectures were being held in the largest of our teaching rooms. He held a regular series of Saturday lectures on 'Branch lines of Hampshire Steam Railways' or some such title, and usually used this big room for his slide projector, laying out maps and so forth. However, his audience was just ten people, whereas for my rather obscure day on 'Forts and Palaces of Rajasthan' there was a recruitment of over 50. We needed the big room to fit them all in, so he was obliged to use a much smaller room, and he and his enthusiastic railway buffs were pretty cross about it.

'How the hell have you got that crowd to come to a subject like… what is it? And where the hell is Rajasthan anyway?'

So it was only when the lecture was about to start that I got to the room to introduce the speaker and take a seat at the back. The four of them were there, just two or three seats away from me. The lecturer had switched on her first slide and was about to start. As you know, Cynthia had a very distinctive voice in the grand mannr. She leaned across:

'Richard, my dear, how lovely to see you. Now, I believe you have not met…'

Half the audience turned round in surprise.

'Hello Cynthia,' I whispered, 'Sshh…I'll meet them later, the lecture's started…'

'Of Course,' said Cynthia, smiling. The other three were waving and nodding.

My friend Wendy, giving the lectures that day, had spoken for about ten minutes, and was just pausing for a moment when a voice - supposedly hushed, but not at all hushed - boomed across to me, louder, and if possible, even grander than Cynthia.

'We are so looking forward to this tour!' The word tour was pronounced as two syllables '*too-ar*'. Ann was leaning forward and smiling at me. I wasn't focussed and did not understand that I was being addressed at first. I looked across, puzzled.

'Our *too-ar*,' she explained, 'We are absolutely thrilled to be coming.' The whole audience was turning back to see what was happening.

'Oh, good,' I whispered back and tried to signal to Wendy to carry on. She did, and we reached the coffee interval without further incident.

At coffee we were properly introduced. Of course I had been told all about them by Cynthia who had asked if they may join the tour, but I had not seen them before. Ann and Lydia were sisters-in-law and close friends of Cynthia and Lucy. Ann of the booming voice was immaculately dressed, with careful make-up, elegant hair-style, with an amused glint in her eye; Lydia, was a tall and striking woman, equally grand in mannr and accent, but who told me she was a social worker, and was very evidently the wisest as well as the oldest of the quartet.

We chatted for a while, others who I knew came up and were introduced, and we all went back into the lecture room for the second part of the day. Shortly before the break for lunch, poor Cynthia started coughing, which she tried hard to control, holding a hanky over her mouth. The coughing went on for some time, and grew worse. I looked over to Cynthia and could see she was really struggling, so I slipped out of the room to the coffee bar next door and brought her a glass of water. She took several sips, but after a few more minutes, the coughing started again - rather more loudly, with some spluttering - to the point that she started to her feet to make her way out of the room, trying to apologise to those sitting near her.

'Oh dear… I am so very sorry… please excuse…'

As I was nearer the door, I went out with her to see if I could help; we went together to the coffee bar, where the girls were preparing for lunch.

'I'm… frightfully… sorry,' said Cynthia, between coughs and splutters, 'I seem to have… the most frightful *corrff*.' Cynthia's grand mannr voice and accent was somewhat distorted.

The girls who work in the coffee bar knew me very well; I saw them most days of the week, but now they were both puzzled and looked at me for explanation.

'You what?'

'What'd she say?'

'I'm terribly… sorry… I appear to have a frightful *corrff*.'

The girls were no nearer understanding. 'What is she on about?'

I couldn't help a bit of teasing, 'You know very well what she's on about. This lady's got a frightful *corrff*! Now Cynthia, would you like some more water, or a coffee, perhaps.'

Cynthia, still choking, did not follow the exchange, and asked, 'No, no coffee thank you. Do you, by any chance, have such a thing as a *jujube*?'

Now I knew what a jujube is (or was). It was a word my mother used for a soft chewy lozenge when I was a small child. But I hadn't heard the word for 30 or 40 years.

'A what?'

'You heard! This poor lady asked if you have a *jujube*.'

''Wass she on about? 'Ere, Richard, are you having us on?'

'He is, he's 'aving us on. This has got to be a set-up.'

The nearest thing our coffee bar had to a jujube was a Polo Mint, which seemed to cure Cynthia's choking fit by the time the others came out to lunch. There was much animated conversation over the lunch break. I heard the quartet's voices relating stories to an enthralled group of the audience; lots of people, including the coffee-bar staff asked me who they were.

Back in the lecture room only three of the quartet were present. Ann was missing. As the lecture started I pointed to her empty chair, with a raised eyebrow to the other three. It was Lucy who answered. Luckily, Lucy had a much quieter voice than the others.

'Ann will join us shortly,' she whispered, 'She felt obliged to help those dear young ladies with the washing up.'

'Yes,' joined in Lydia, 'She feels a certain social obligation, which is quite at odds with her political views - quite extraordinary.'

There is just one other matter I should clear up. For several of our later journeys with the Raj Quartet, there was a fifth, honorary member. He was Malcolm, who had met the Quartet on some previous holidays before I came to know them, and it was they who introduced him to me. They had told me that, sadly, that year they would be unable to come to the summer party that we normally held for the people joining our tours, but asked if they could come to lunch (they called it luncheon) on another day and could they bring their friend Malcolm, too.

So they came for lunch, Cynthia, Lucy, Ann and Lydia, and they brought Malcolm. He was a shy, gentleman, retired for some years, who had never married, but looked after his mother into old age. He was obviously very fond of the Quartet, if somewhat overwhelmed by them, and had clearly been brought to lunch as a potential candidate for our next tour. The conversation about India began with Ann.

'Richard, where shall you take us on our next adventure?' At that time the decision had not been made, but we were thinking about eastern India, so there followed a discussion of the merits of Calcutta, Orissa, Darjeeling... They became quite excited and Ann directed the conversation once more.

'That sounds perfectly entrancing!' she turned to Malcolm, who had been very quiet, and said,

'Malcolm, you must come too.' She turned back to Jill and me.

'Yes, Malcolm must come too. You see, Malcolm has a hair-dryer - we all borrow it.'

Malcolm was useful for more than his hair-dryer. The Quartet used him unscrupulously as their fetcher and carrier - very often of their Scotch whisky, but sometimes of their luggage - their guardian of unwanted items and their messenger; but always treated him with great affection. And Malcolm looked after them with devotion, enjoying every moment. When, at the end of the eastern tour, he stayed on a little longer than the Quartet who departed early, he appeared both bereft by the separation and at the same time hugely relieved of the burden of responsibility.

ANN'S KNICKERS AND LYDIA'S BRA

It is perhaps surprising that reference should be made to the underwear of the elderly and genteel members of the Raj Quartet, but it was they who brought the matter up on more than one occasion. It was Ann who explained her predicament at one of our gatherings:

'You see, Richard, I can only afford to accompany you on your *tou-ars*, by plying my needle.'

Now, if this was true, I was a bit surprised both by Ann's apparent shortage of money and that she actually earned some. It was difficult to think of her in a dressmakers or milliners shop. Her husband had been a grandee of the City and they had homes in London and a country estate. She had once responded to a criticism by the group when I had taken people to look at an interesting Indian house that was supposed to be empty but appeared to be occupied. Someone in the group had said:

'Really, we can't just walk in! These people are living here. How would you like it if a crowd of perfect strangers came wandering about in your house?'

'Oh, my dear,' Ann had replied, 'I am *perfectly* used to it. My house is open to the public.' This, we discovered later, was true, the house being a Jacobean mansion and estate.

Going back to the subject of Ann's need to earn money, Cynthia added

'Ann is a wonderful needlewoman. And a baker! And an artist too!'

'Really? asked someone, 'What do you make?'

'Cakes,' replied Ann. 'I do make rather good cakes. That, too is why I may accompany you on your *tou-ars*. My husband Charles does not care to travel, but he cannot be without my cakes. So before each *tou-ar*, I make him his cakes, which are served to him each day by our dear house-keeper.'

'And do you sell cakes?' We were quite intrigued.

'No longer. I used to sell wedding cakes, but no longer. No, I have turned my attention to *découpage*, and make very beautiful trays and decorated boxes. They sell in Knightsbridge boutiques.'

'And needlework? You said you have to ply your needle?'

'I do. I used to make wedding dresses,' explained Ann, 'They were absolutely beautiful and so much in demand. But really, it has become too much for me. Quite recently I had to prepare for my nephew's wedding.'

'Oh dear, was there too much to do?'

'Well yes. It was a great success, but I fear it will be my last. In addition to the dresses for the bride and the bridesmaids, a little boy was to be a page, so I asked him how he would like to be dressed. He said he wished to be a farmer, like his father' - his father, I may say, farmed most of Northumberland - 'so I decided to dress him as a farmer - in a suit of green velvet, with velvet knickerbockers and buckle shoes. He looked marvellous. No, now I only make hand-made knickers - the most exquisite French knickers in the finest silk, trimmed with real Brussels lace. They can only be afforded by German tarts!'

As often happened when Ann related a story, a crowd had gathered round. Among them was Ethel who was enthralled. She came from a different background to Ann.

'Cor, how wonderful! I don't suppose you could make any for me? No I don't suppose so, my bum's too big!' Ann looked, but with almost closed eyes. She did not reply.

She went on to tell us that she had taken up needlework at a young age. 'I found it necessary, do you see, to have my needle about me to deal with emergencies. You young people (we were all in our 60s or 70s) are all too young to remember, but in *our* young days, after we were liberated from the corset but before the arrival of the suspender belt, our silk stockings were attached to our knickers by those curious buttons and fastenings. Well, that was all very well, but with the increasingly energetic dances that came in, it was not so much the stockings that came down, but the *knickers were orften pulled orf as well*! Not infrequently my knickers were round my ankles, and I found I was much in demand in the ladies' cloakroom of The Ritz helping my friends to replace their elastic!'

On quite a different occasion, our group was gathering for a drink. We were in a hotel room in Madras on the first evening of a tour. Not all the members had met, so we got together a few nibbles and invited everyone to bring some of their duty-free and meet together before dinner. This was the second tour on which all four members of the Raj Quartet were present, and there had been some doubt as to whether they would all join.

Lydia had phoned me at home some months before.

'Richard, do tell me, I am concerned about the climate in southern India, will it be too hot?' They had been together with us in the north the year before and it had been quite cool in Rajasthan.

'Well, it will be hotter than last year. On the other hand, we'll be there at the coolest time of the year for south India - it will start to get warmer in February.'

'I see. And I have one more concern. The food in the north did not altogether agree with me. Those interminable Indian buffets. Shall we be obliged once again to eat from *cauldrons* of filth?'

I thought this was a bit harsh, but we talked some more and Lydia decided to join. She was sharing a room with Cynthia and they were drinking with the others in our room.

'Lydia, would you like some of these nibbles? Nothing spicy here.' I remembered the cauldrons of filth and avoided offering Lydia the Bombay mix; just some crisps and nuts.

'No, I certainly could not have anything to eat.'

'Oh dear, are you not feeling well?'

'I am perfectly well, but may not eat a single thing.'

'Oh dear, we'll be going in for dinner quite soon. Won't you be going to dinner?'

'I may take dinner, but would first have to adjust my dress. At present, if I ate a single morsel I fear I may burst!'

'Good heavens, what's happened?' There was a pause.

'Well you see, *I have washed my bra*!'

I didn't see at all.

'Er, I don't quite see how…'

'Yes, I have washed my bra, and now, if I ate anything at all I should burst. To attend your drinks party I felt I should be properly dressed, but my bra was wet.' I was no nearer understanding and beginning to feel I should not press the matter.

'I did not feel I could wear the bra that was still wet, you see, and searching my suitcase, found I had failed to bring another, nor did I consider it altogether appropriate to appear bra-less. So Cynthia has kindly allowed me to borrow one of hers. We are not the same shape, you may have observed. So for the moment I may not eat.'

LUCY'S LOO AT THE AJIT BHAWAN

It was earlier in the tour that Ann brought up the subject of the Ajit Bhawan. She was in conversation with other members of the group when she saw me.

'Ah, Richard, there you are. We were speaking of the *tou-ar*. I see that when we reach the city of Jodhpur we shall stay at the Ajit Bhawan.' It was a statement rather than a question, but the question hung in the air with Ann's customary quizzical raised eye-brow.

'Yes, that's right.' I said, 'Do you know it?'. A theatrical pause was followed by,

'I do.' This in a low, emphatic, slightly menacing tone.

'Really? I didn't know you'd been before. Didn't you like it? We thought it was rather nice when we went there to have a look. Don't you think it has charm?'

Another pause, and then in the same tone, 'Strictly limited.'

On earlier trips to India, Jill and I had stayed at some pretty awful hotels. We weren't young back-packers, but had very limited budgets and often stayed in the government run 'tourist bungalows' that now seem to have disappeared. They were usually adequate, but not much more, and sometimes rather less. But we had seen much better hotels, sometimes eaten there, occasionally swam there, and quite often shamelessly used their loos and washrooms. We had visited the Ajit Bhawan Palace while staying very uncomfortably in Jodhpur, and thought it rather lovely. It was a small 'palace' built for a younger brother of the Maharajah of Jodhpur as a modest 'town house', with a large garden. In common with many of the princes in Rajasthan - major and minor, including the elder brother, whose own vast palace was the largest, grandest and gloomiest of palace hotels - the owner of the Ajit Bhawan had converted it to a hotel, with bedrooms built in the garden in a rather charming 'village ethnic' style. Parts of the palace were still occupied by the owner; public areas were still decorated with hunting trophies, old black and white and sepia photographs of Indian princes and tiger shoots. We had met the owner - a handsome, distinguished gentleman, with the traditional upturned moustache of the Rajput grandees - who acted every inch the patrician and still liked to use the title *Maharaj*. We were enquiring about bringing a group the following year.

'Certainly, my dear good fellow. We shall be delighted to welcome you to my house, and I will be only too pleased to conduct you on my village safari personally.' This village safari - a tour by jeep through some of the villages in what still appeared to be his personal fiefdom - promised to be a highlight of our tour.

When our group arrived at the hotel after a long and tiring journey he came to greet us.

'Good evening, ladies and gentleman, welcome, welcome to my house.' He sounded impressive and looked impressive: as well as the stately moustache he wore Jodhpur trousers, a long silk shirt and embroidered waistcoat.

'You are travelling with Mr Hunt, an old friend of the family' (we had met just the once), 'Please feel at home, be at home, make yourselves at home.'

'How nice,' muttered David *sotto voce* at the back of the group, 'A home, a home *with bills*.'

'Yes,' continued the Maharaj, 'My staff members are here to respond to your slightest wish. You have only to raise one finger and your needs will be attended to.'

We dispersed to our rooms, which I still think *were* charming: round thatched 'huts' decorated with the local durry cotton rugs, block-printed bedspreads, but with very hard beds and uncertain plumbing. Dining was in the open air - tables arranged around bonfires and a buffet arrangement of large clay pots of food keeping hot on wood fires. The picturesque scene was again presided over by the Maharaj.

'Yes, here is your dinner. Typical Rajasthan food. Help yourselves. Please enjoy.'

David, married to Jacky, and not at all fond of Indian food, asked,

'Er, excuse me, is there a menu?'

'A menu? A menu? You ask for a menu? Do you think this is a hotel?'

'Well, I just…'

At that moment another member of the group spoke up,

'Excuse me, there are mosquitos in our room… there's a big hole in the mesh over the window…'

'A hole? A hole? Do not worry. I will immediately post a guard!'

By and large I enjoyed our stay at the Ajit Bhawan, but not everyone did. The hard beds were a major issue especially for Ann, who even carried her own lace pillow on tour, but also for the others. Several had slept or not slept very badly and the complaint was put to our host, who liked to invite comment but was not able to hear criticism.

'I'm sorry, but my bed was so hard I couldn't sleep at all.'

'Ah, the inconvenience is regretted. I fear the reason is the heavy monsoon.'

'The monsoon? What has the monsoon got to do with it? I'm talking about a hard bed!'

'Yes, you see the monsoon came rather late and affects the mattresses. As yet we have not had an opportunity to fluff them up.'

'Fluff them up? What do you mean "fluff them up"? Fluff what up?'

'The mattresses. You see our traditional Rajasthani mattresses are made from kapok. They become rather compressed during the monsoon, and each year we fluff them up, but this year...'

Later someone said, 'He really has an answer for everything, but I don't believe a word of it.' None of us believed a word of it, but some years later I read somewhere about an Indian caste - a rather lowly caste - of mattress fluffers, who did just that! Their unenviable task in life is to take out the kapok from old mattresses, fluff it up, and stuff it back in.

Our host did not endear himself to everyone when, on our departure for his 'village safari', he announced that he would be driving one of *three* jeeps:

'Do not worry, at each stop I will be with you to explain everything. But as we drive through the villages, you will observe the love and devotion of my people.'

'Really?' asked Lydia rather provocatively and then, 'Love and affection for whom?' carefully enunciated in her slow, grand delivery. There was a long look from the Maharaj, but no response.

At our first village halt a number of villagers came forward to greet the Maharaj; the women, mostly veiled by holding the edge of their saris across the face, stood decorously in the background, *namastaying* with their hands held high together, but bowing their heads. The men, though, came forward; some merely touching the fore-head with one hand and then bowing down to touch his shoe, a few *kneeling down* and *lowering their fore-heads to touch his shoe.* All this was gracefully acknowledged and we were shown the villagers - veiled ladies (married), unveiled ladies (unmarried), the potter's family at work, the black-smith. In the village we were first shown the well. The questions came thick and fast.

'Why is the well so far from the houses? They have to carry it all the way...'

There had been some unsuccessful attempts to lift the very heavy clay water pots full of water. Our host nonchalantly offered, 'The ladies should have some necessary exercise.'

At the school we noticed there were relatively few girls and not many older boys. Lydia was probing once more, 'I understand that Rajasthan has one of the lowest literacy rates in India. Why is this so?' Again the Maharaj had an explanation.

'These children will be farmers, like their parents, so what is the use of so much schooling? Of course some parents wish their children to go, so for some years they can go. But naturally girls cannot be at the school when they reach the age of being dicey…'

'Dicey? What do you mean "dicey"?'

'When a girl becomes dicey she naturally cannot be allowed to go about with boys in the school. She must remain at home, helping until she is married…'

The final straw came when a grandfather brought a tearful little girl before us. She was clearly in pain from an eye infection, and terrified of us and of the Maharaj. Without a word, our host took a tube of some ointment from his pocket, rubbed some on his finger, pulled the child to him and rather forcefully rubbed the ointment into the swollen reddened eye.

'What was that for?' The little girl had run off, screaming.

'She has eye infection; I have given her treatment.'

'Are there any proper medical facilities for these people?' Lydia's slow menacing delivery once again was directed to him. She was clearly the ring-leader of this unappreciative audience. He smiled graciously, 'I am standing before you.'

On our last evening at the Ajit Bhawan, Ann approached me before dinner.

'Richard, I should inform you that there has been an unfortunate *incident*.'

'Oh dear, what's happened?'

'Yes, it might have become a *catastrophe*, but fortunately it has been averted. Thank heavens for dear Bill and Hazel.'

'Goodness! What was it?' Bill and Hazel, two of our group, were standing with us.

'Yes, dear Lucy (Lucy and Ann were sharing one of the 'village huts') was about to descend upon the lavatory when, without any action on her part, it flushed *boiling water*! Our bathroom was quite awash!'

'Good heavens! That could have been very nasty! Is Lucy all right? How on earth…?'

'Fortunately she is, but it was most unexpected, as at no time during our stay has the water in the bath or basin been remotely tepid.'

Hot water, or the lack of hot water, had been another issue with most of the group, but I merely asked, 'What about the bathroom? Is it still flooded?'

'No, but thanks only to Bill and Hazel. They saved us from a disaster. They have been simply marvellous.'

Bill was standing listening and grinning widely. He was a retired sailor, married to the rather dour but kindly Hazel.

'Cor, I should say. There was a right ol' kerfuffle going on next door, an' we could hear these two carrying on…'

'Dear Bill! He heard our cries of distress.'

'I should say,' joined in Hazel. 'We went in there and you should have seen the place - water everywhere and *steaming* it was. I helped them mop it up.'

'Not before I could stop the lav from pouring water, you couldn't. I 'ad to shut it off. Luckily I ' appened to 'ave a jubilee clip in my pocket.'

'Our hero!' exclaimed Lucy.

SUMMER SANDS

Unusually, there had been a certain enmity growing long before we reached Summer Sands. Once again, I had allowed the group to grow too big: some had asked if their friends could join, others had asked me if they could be squeezed in at the last minute. Despite the lessons of travelling with groups that were too big for comfort, I had not learned to say 'no' and allowed the numbers to rise into the higher 20's. They included the full Raj Quartet, accompanied by a favourite niece and by the faithful Malcolm. From quite early in the tour there had been rumblings of unease partly caused by the group size. Two or three people started 'bagging' seats on the coach by going aboard even before breakfast and placing bags or coats, the equivalent of sun-lounger towels, on the favoured seats near the front. This had produced a reaction of disapproval voiced in particular by Ann and Lydia of the Quartet. As their voices were far from *sotto voce*, most people heard unguarded comments about 'extraordinary inappropriate behaviour.' This had put the culprits at some distance and in turn had produced rather unjust murmurings about a 'clique', unjust as the members of the Quartet had never intentionally excluded anyone from their circle. Indeed, as properly brought up ladies, they had always been careful to mix with the whole group and include everyone in conversation, and had often invited others to join them at their drinks parties.

Another faction had grown up around the forceful and outspoken Rosanna - an entertaining story-teller (she told us she had appeared in a TV documentary with the appealing title of *Older Lesbians*) but with a very short temper. She gathered round her a small group of women - mainly divorced or separated - who could give vent to their disappointment or dissatisfaction with men in her sympathetic company. This group rather avoided the Quartet, who were mostly widowed, and evidently disapproved of their privileged upbringing and their reliance on the obliging Malcolm as the fetcher and carrier of their luggage and whisky. Rosanna's use of forthright and sometimes foul-mouthed language also put her and her circle at a distance from the RQ who responded with mild rebukes '…hardly necessary…' that spoke volumes.

I may say that not many tourists visited Mangalore in those days. We were there as I had some friends in a local college who were arranging 'off the beaten track' activities for us, which would make an unusual and, I thought, especially interesting end to the tour. We were due to see farms, a school, hospitals, a dance programme… My friends had selected Summer Sands as our hotel (there wasn't much choice), but the first impressions were not good. We were a little late and no doubt tired, but had enjoyed a thrilling, totally unscheduled stop to join in a temple festival donation of jewellery to a goddess. This buoyant mood was dimmed by the decidedly scruffy, faded and partly broken sign announcing the hotel. Summer Sands appeared to be idyllically situated on a palm-fringed beach, but the gardens were unkempt, litter was strewn about and an old car with no wheels was rusting near the run-down hotel reception. The owner-cum-manager-cum-receptionist was defensive from the start.

'Welcome to Summer Sands. We are a family hotel. We are not five star.' There was an ominous silence from our group.

'No,' he went on, 'this is a homely place.' There were several mutters of

'Not my home, it isn't.'

'We have reserved our best rooms for your group,' he told us. They may have been the best rooms but they were not good. We were scattered around the quite extensive grounds in bungalows, with three or four bedrooms in each. The bathrooms were grim, with broken tiles, decaying doors and grey-looking towels. Beds and bed linen didn't look too bad, but there was an immediate incident when Charles, next door to us, thrust his hand behind his bed-head to switch on a lamp. He got a very large, long and very painful splinter under his finger-nail from the peeling veneer of the bed. The poor chap was very brave, especially when Norman, a retired dentist, produced a medical kit, cut away part of the nail and extracted the splinter. Someone had a miniature of brandy which was offered to Charles. Norman, however, who had gone rather pale, snatched the brandy and drained the bottle.

'I need it more than he does. I've never done an extraction quite like that.'

Charles, Norman and their wives agreed that the place was rather grim but seemed quite resigned. However, the first intimation of serious revolt came soon after. I met Rosanna walking back from the beach.

'You can't think we're going to stay here? I couldn't face the room so just walked down to the sea. There were kids *shitting on the sand*! You can't seriously expect us to stay here? The place is a fucking *dump*!'

It was dusk. We had spent a good part of the day - except our temple festival stop - driving on mainly bad roads. We were booked to stay here for four nights as the finale of the tour. During much walking to and from the reception trying to improve this or that disappointment, I met others who also voiced complaints.

'The place really is quite neglected.'

'The pillows are just awful.'

'The loo doesn't work.' But overwhelmingly,

'Isn't there anywhere else we can stay? Four nights is a bit much!' Although Summer Sands was very disappointing, Jill and I had stayed in much worse places, and anyway there wasn't an alternative. I decided to visit each of the rooms, apologise for the accommodation and tell them about the really interesting programme of visits that were lined up for us by the staff in a local college. From some I received a tolerant response, from others - especially the woman-faction - a tight-lipped hostility, from the Raj Quartet a warm and cheering sympathy, saying that, of course it was not palatial, but quite acceptable. They did warn me, though, that a 'Round Robin' was circulating, asking that I remove the group to heaven knows where. This, they said, was quite out of the question, and had refused to have anything to do with such a document.

Before the evening meal, my friend from the college called to see me. He wanted to discuss the visits next day and was mystified when I blurted out that the group was not happy with Summer Sands. By almost any Indian standards we were staying in luxury! His enthusiasm for the visits buoyed me up a bit, but I was feeling exhausted, acutely anxious and down-right miserable. It was with much trepidation that Jill and I made our way over to dinner to confront the group. It was served in the garden, and in the darkness, with just some lanterns for light, it looked attractive and the general scruffiness of the place was hidden. The factions were very evidently sitting table by table: the expanded Quartet quite near to my left, the malcontents to the right, the neutrals or near-neutrals between. We were the last to arrive; where should we sit?

Ann's loud and ostentatiously raised voice boomed towards us - slow and deliberately intended for general consumption.

'Richard - and dear Jill - we just want to let you know that we are having a perfectly *wonderful* time!' The other tables fell silent. I felt a genuine surge of relief and gratitude.

'Oh Ann,' I spoke without thinking. 'I think I must give you a kiss!' A cheek was proffered. Cynthia beamed and held up her face.

'I, too, should like a kiss.'

Lucy was not to be outdone.

'And I, too, should like a kiss.'

Lydia, older and wiser, was looking determinedly across at the tables, and

I followed her gaze. Some of those at the neutral tables smiled wryly at the kissing performance, but just a little further off, and definitely within earshot, sat the malcontents. There were theatrically dark and ominous looks and Lydia spoke again without removing her gaze from them.

'Richard, I fear that this is most unwise…'

YOU TOADY

As you know, Calcutta is called Kolkata nowadays, but not by everyone, and not when we were there. We were staying in great luxury at the Oberoi Grand Hotel. Still very grand, it was the early flag-ship of the Oberoi hotels, which had opened in the '30s as the fashionable hotel, ballroom and meeting place of the one-time capital of the British Raj. The hotel was lovely - so lovely that we stayed there three times during our tour - at the beginning, on our return from the state of Orissa, and again after a visit to some foothills of the Himalayas for a last few days before flying back to England. The Raj Quartet had accompanied our group to eastern India, but sadly had to fly home early due to other commitments, missing our visits to Darjeeling and Sikkim. I was concerned about how well they would cope on their own, but they reassured me that I had nothing to worry about. We said goodbye to them in the Grand, leaving them to catch their flight home later that morning.

I suppose I should have suspected that all was not well with the Quartet's return when the rest of us had *such* a difficult time leaving Calcutta a week later. Our group members were all packed up, getting ready to leave the Grand Hotel, just as the Quartet had been when we last saw them, when I got a call from British Airways informing me that our flight was cancelled. There was to be no BA flight from Calcutta to London via Delhi. Instead the BA flight would start in Delhi and we would have to take an Indian domestic flight to Delhi. It was now too late to connect, so, they informed me we would spend the night in Delhi airport to take the next BA flight to London.

I had carefully chosen BA for this tour as there was a direct flight to Calcutta with just a short stop in Delhi in each direction. It had worked perfectly well on the way out but, we now learned, was not going to on the return. I had sixteen people with me, many of whom had important reasons for not being delayed, and all of whom had made arrangements for getting home from Heathrow and none of whom were prepared to spend a night in an airport. After some years of arranging these tours I had some experience of delays and cancellations, and was aware of the need to show myself to be assertive - to BA, but especially to my group members.

'And you tell me that you propose to have us stay the night in *Delhi airport*? Why should we stay in the *airport*? As you are delaying us for over 24 hours you can put us up in a hotel.'

'But sir…'

'But nothing. There are early domestic flights to Delhi that will easily connect with the BA flight. I suggest you overnight us here, in the hotel, and we catch the early flight tomorrow morning. Alternatively you fly us to Delhi this evening and provide overnight accommodation in Delhi.'

'But sir…'

My bluff worked, and after much argument with our local agents and BA staff in Calcutta and Delhi about whether there would be a hotel or no hotel, which hotel and which meals, we stayed on in the Oberoi Grand for another night, dining in their splendid restaurant at BA's expense. We all pretended to be very angry at the delay, whereas we greatly enjoyed another night of luxury, a further opportunity to see more of Calcutta, and the triumph of making BA pay.

It was several days after our return that Lucy, perhaps the least demonstrative of the Raj Quartet, telephoned.

'I thought I should inform you, Richard, my dear, that we were not at all well treated by British Airways on our return from India. It is my opinion, and that of the other members of the Quartet, that they behaved rather disgracefully.'

'Oh Lord. Did you have trouble as well? I'm so sorry.'

'I fear it was dreadfully mis-managed. They cancelled our flight!'

'Your flight? Your flight too? My goodness, they did the same to us. I am sorry. I know you all had to get back. It must have been very inconvenient.'

'Indeed it was, but it was rather more than inconvenient. It was frightfully uncomfortable, and, we felt, somewhat uncaring.'

Uncomfortable? Uncaring? I was now worried; our experience was certainly not uncomfortable. I thought back to the jolly final meal we all had in the smart restaurant of the Grand.

'Yes, Richard, we were hoping that you may have a word with the people at British Airways. Lydia's brother was chairman of the old BOAC, but she thinks that he may have little influence now. The others felt you may seek some kind of recompense on our behalf. Even an apology would be appreciated.'

The matter was evidently serious; I have never known any member of the Quartet to complain about anything before.

'What ever happened Lucy? Our flight was cancelled at the last minute, but we stayed on at the Grand for another night…'

'Really? I fear we did not! The people at British Airways told us that we should be flown to Delhi, met there, taken to the international airport and be well looked after. But we were not. We felt we had been abandoned…'

'Oh dear, oh dear, I am so sorry. I was a bit worried when we all went off and left you...'

'In no way were you to blame, Richard dear. No, our discomfort was due entirely to the lack of care by the staff of British Airways.'

'But what happened? We were quite well looked after, but, come to think of it, only after we insisted. At first they said we should spend the night *in the airport*, but of course that was out of the question.'

'Oh, in that case, perhaps we have ourselves to blame. We did not challenge their altered plans. None-the-less, they promised that we would be met and cared for, and we were not.'

I learned that BA had arranged to fly the Quartet to Delhi by another airline in the evening of the day we left them; they were told they would be met and transported from the domestic airport and provided with accommodation. They had not been met, but had to manage their own luggage and find a taxi to transport them. They were not offered accommodation, nor any food before their flight to London late next morning, spending a terrible night on hard plastic chairs in Delhi airport, reliant on the cafeteria.

I wrote several letters to the chairman of BA in London, with copies to Delhi and Calcutta; I telephoned several times, mentioning that considerable compensation was due to these four elderly ladies. I did receive a rather ill-written apology, and during one of the phone conversations someone mentioned the possibility of offering them a complementary flight. I suggested they discuss the matter directly with the ladies in question, but I doubted whether a flight would be acceptable. Possibly a case of champagne for each, or a case of fine single malt whisky would be more appropriate?

Some months later the Quartet came to one of our pre-departure gatherings for another tour. I had already learned that BA, far from sending champagne or whisky, had sent each of them a *bouquet of flowers* by way of compensation. This was discussed at our lunch party.

'It really was quite disgraceful,' said Ann. 'And when we heard how you were treated so much better I really was quite *crorse*. Not about your treatment, of course, but it was so *unfair*. Such a shame, Richard, you were not there to defend *us*.'

'Yes, I'm so sorry, I was rather worried when we left...'

'We did have the luxury of our rooms in Calcutta before departing to the airport,' said Cynthia. 'The hotel manager was perfectly charming and said we could stay until six in the evening, and at no extra charge. So very kind.'

'But it became rather expensive, Cynthia darling,' joined in Lucy. 'If you recall, we did consume the entire contents of the mini-bars in each of our rooms… The hotel charges were rather *corstly*.'

'And as for flowers, how they had the cheek to send flowers I do not know.' Lydia still seemed outraged. 'I very nearly sent them back. I cannot recall a more uncomfortable night, and they could have so easily sent us to an hotel.'

'But the flowers were so very nice,' offered Cynthia. 'It really was a lovely big bunch of flowers! And they lasted so well - over two weeks, I think.'

'Well, I wrote back, saying that it was an insult,' retorted Lydia.

'Oh, did you really?' said Cynthia, 'I wrote back thanking them, and saying how lovely the flowers were.'

Lydia retorted sharply, 'You toady!'

CYNTHIA'S POLICEMAN

I should mention straight away that Cynthia was not in trouble with her policeman, she was just seeking help. The problem was that on almost our last day of the tour - a day when people were at leisure to relax, go shopping, visit a gallery or whatever - Cynthia had gone off alone in a taxi. When she got out of the taxi she left her handbag behind. As she told me,

'This was sheer forgetfulness on my part, Richard. I am becoming frightfully forgetful. But this was unforgiveable.'

'Perhaps it's not so serious? Did you have a lot of money with you? I hope you left your valuables and things in the safe?'

'Yes, I did, and that, I fear, is my concern. Yes, there is some money in the handbag but my passport and aeroplane ticket are locked in the hotel safe.'

'Well,' I was relieved - we had incidents in the past of lost passports and all the difficulties and delays that entailed, 'At least they are safe.'

'I fear not. They would be, if I had not taken the key to the hotel safe with me. It was in my handbag that I left in the taxi. The hotel tells me they have no duplicate key, so cannot open the safe, and I must report the matter to the police.'

We spoke again to the hotel manager. He was not very helpful: no, they had no key and only with police authority could a locksmith be called to change the lock. He warned that it would be expensive and would take some time. Cynthia was alarmed, and so was I: we were going home next day and needed the passport and ticket. The manager could call a taxi and ask the driver to take Cynthia to the police station.

'Oh dear,' I said, 'I think I had better come to the police with you…'

'Would you? I would be so grateful, but I really do not wish to take up your time…'

At the police station we had difficulties in making ourselves understood at first, and were told to wait. After about half an hour we were shown into the office of quite a senior officer, with immaculate uniform and really excellent English.

'I am sorry to have kept you waiting, my staff are not very perfect in English. How may I help you?' Cynthia began -

'I am frightfully sorry to trouble you, but I have foolishly *lorst* my handbag…' and went on with the story. He listened with a slight smile, perhaps amused by Cynthia's accent.

'Ah yes, I will certainly try to help you, but first we must see if we can recover your handbag. Did you by any good chance order your taxi from the hotel?'

'No, I am sorry to say I did not,' replied Cynthia. 'I was not at the hotel, but somewhere in the city. The taxi was in the street…'

'And I suppose you do not have the driver's card, or the car number?'

'I fear not.'

'No, then it will be difficult. As you know, there are hundreds of taxis in the city. Of course we will keep your enquiry and if the handbag is handed in we will contact you. But I must say, the chances are not very good, especially as there was some money in the bag. I must request you fill in some forms…'

'And the hotel says they need some kind of certificate from you to call a locksmith,' I said. We need to do this quickly as this lady needs the documents to fly home.'

'That is true, and we can do this, of course. I am just sorry I cannot be of more practical help. Such a shame… we have here several persons who could have helped as they are experts in working with locks.'

'Do you mean one of your staff could come and undo the hotel safe?' My hopes were rising - of course, policemen could pick locks - we could sort out the problem immediately and our worries would be over.

'Ah no, sadly not. You see, the experts are being held prisoner, here in our cells. I regret I cannot release them to help you, even under supervision. Such a pity.' He seemed genuinely regretful.

'But first I need to establish exactly where the lady took the taxi, and where did he take you? Was it near to your hotel?'

'Oh no,' said Cynthia. 'A number of us had been shopping and afterwards I wished to visit the National Museum. A passing taxi stopped to ask if I would like a ride.'

'Ah, I see, the National Museum. In that case, I must ask you to go to another police station - the station of the area where the bag was lost - as they must provide the certificate. Do not worry, I will provide you with a *chit* that will expedite the matter, and you can fill in the forms here. Pray use my office - this desk is free…'

He handed us several forms which Cynthia took.

'Oh dear, as well as my name it asks for the passport number, but…'

'Do not worry, just fill in such details as you have, a description of the missing items and so forth. Now if you will excuse me…' And he left the room.

Cynthia continued to write, but then turned to me.

'It asks for my father's name.'

'Well, we know that, I'm sure.'

'I do, but I am not sure what they require. You see he's *orften* just called Albemarle.'

'Well, can't you put that down?'

'*Orf* course I can, but that is a title. They may not understand. Should I put Earl of Albemarle do you think. Or just Albemarle? Or should I put in his name which is rather different? It is rather long.'

'If there's room, why don't you put both? It may cut some red tape…'

The policeman came back after a few moments and Cynthia handed him the forms. He glanced through them and the smile returned.

'Ah, I see you are from a noble family.'

'Well, er, yes. My father, you see…'

'I do, I do. But I must tell you, dear lady, that I am a democrat!'

The democratic policemen continued to be helpful. His desk sergeant called us another taxi and gave directions to the small sub-station that had to stamp the certificate. Whereas belonging to a noble family may not have cut any red tape, the *chit* provided by the democratic policemen clearly did, as the policemen in the small sub-station were very quick to respond. The certificate with several official-looking stamps was handed over (in exchange for the appropriate fee) and in due course the hotel called in their locksmith, clearly well-known - indeed, suspiciously well-known - to the hotel staff. A further hefty fee was paid, and the contents of Cynthia's safe were returned.

CYNTHIA'S SADHU

Although our guide tried to persuade us, we didn't want to see a cremation. Apparently this is a popular tourist diversion, but as someone in the group said, most of us were of an age when we would be going along to one before too long, and had no wish to hurry the process. But the view of the temple above the *ghats* on the Bagmati River, where cremations took place, was reputably one of the 'sights' of Nepal, so a number of us decided to visit the picturesque spot. It was there that we encountered Cynthia's *Sadhu*. The journey had been a little disconcerting, as, for reasons that were never made clear, we travelled the short distance by local bus and were really surprised to find that several of the Nepalese people, and especially the children, were holding animals on their laps. There were fluffy rabbits, some appealing kids, chickens and ducks… Where were they going? Some of the group asked if they were going to a special vet's clinic? Others wondered if there was a thanksgiving for animals at a temple? Naively, I considered both, and attempted to ask an elderly gentleman why all these animals were on the bus. He understood well enough, but didn't have much English to answer, instead pointing out of the window. There was quite a crowd walking along in the same direction, all quite smartly dressed, some of whom were also carrying rabbits, lambs, leading goats and a few sheep on leads. I glanced back to the gentleman, still puzzled, and his reply was a silent gesture - drawing the edge of his flattened hand across his throat.

'Oh my god!' said Betty, 'We're trying to avoid a cremation and we've blundered into a sacrifice! What else have you got up your sleeve for us?'

Fortunately we were able to take a different path to our destination after we got off the bus, and watched the procession of happy adults and children leading their animals down towards the river and the temple, while we climbed up through a wooded area. The first intimation of any disconcerting incident came, most unusually, from Cynthia. As you know, Cynthia enthused about all aspects of our tours - hotels, however decayed or run-down were always 'so atmospheric' or 'so very charming'; villages, however ramshackle were 'picturesque'; guides, however appalling, were 'interesting' or 'well-meaning'. So imagine our surprise when Cynthia, who had been walking quite far ahead with Lucy, turned and walked rather hurriedly back towards us, taking me on one side and whispering rather loudly.

'Oh Richard, may I suggest we take a different pathway?' Lucy, looking bemused, simply said,

'Yes, I do feel that another path would be more appropriate.'

'Oh dear, is there a problem?'

'I fear, Richard, that our fellow travellers may prefer… I fear they may not appreciate the attentions of a… well, one of his followers said he was a holy man. I fear he may not be what he claimed…'

Several of the others heard what Cynthia had said.

'What's the matter? Don't say we're going past the cremation? The whole idea…'

'No, no,' said Cynthia calmly, 'But I merely suggested there may be a different path that will lead us more directly to the viewpoint. This one seems to be, well, deviating…'

There were several criss-crossing paths through the woods, mostly leading uphill, and whether we took a different path or not we did not know, but we reached the viewing place without incident. The view was beautiful: we looked out over the Kathmandu Valley; in the distance were the foothills of the Himalayas, down below us the river wound its way between temples, houses and trees. Little plumes of smoke rose and there was the tinkling of bells and the sounds of temple music. But Cynthia's holy man was one step ahead of us: as we rounded a corner we saw a crowd had gathered at the view point for some kind of spectacle.

Now *sadhus*, who are just one kind of holy men of India, come in every imaginable form. No doubt the great majority are genuine devotees of whichever manifestation of god they worship. At the great *melas* - religious gatherings - along the Ganges or other holy places, they come together, some from remote fastnesses in the Himalayas where they live lives of great devotion and penance, to bathe in the holy waters at these especially auspicious times. Often long-haired, bearded, naked and smeared with ash, they take precedence at these vast gatherings, and are themselves venerated by the ordinary pilgrims who throng the bathing places. Just as medieval Christians sometimes walked long distances - to Canterbury, or Santiago - or penitents crawled on their knees, sometimes flaggelating themselves in holy processions, so some *sadhus* took vows to their deity, undergoing bodily privations - even mutilation and walking enormous distances as pilgrims to the temple of their god. Some have been known to roll on their sides - bleeding and bandaged - to the seven sacred cities of India, gathering devotees along the way; others live a life of quiet contemplation and meditation, living in caves or under a holy tree, offering occasional words of wisdom to those in need of spiritual advice.

There are some, however, for whom the temptations arising from the generosity of devotees proves too much. One totally naked *Baba* raked in enough in the way of offerings to buy himself a new *Harley Davidson* motorbike to ease the discomfort of walking to the holy places and roared off, still naked, to get to the sacred cities and more devotees rather quicker. As we know, several of the spiritual leaders of ashrams have accumulated great wealth - sometimes spending it on very creditable social causes. Some have claimed mystical, even magical powers; others have been exposed as mere charlatans. We never discovered which category Cynthia's *sadhu* best fitted.

The small crowd of twenty or so that had gathered at our viewing place were clearly captivated by more than the view. From the crowd we heard a plaintive angry shout,

'No photo! No photo!' in response to several of the crowd holding their cameras - some above their heads - in readiness. Now, 'no photo' is entirely appropriate. The famous naked *sadhus* are notoriously angry at photographers at the great *melas*. But now we could hear,

'No! First pay. Five dollar. Five dollar for photo!' In the crowd we could see a weedy looking little chap waving his arms rather angrily at the crowd. At our approach they stood aside so that we too could appreciate the spectacle. One young man, grinning broadly turned to us,

'See, very holy man. Very holy. You take picture?' His friend, clearly abashed by this cheeky effrontery to these elderly foreign tourists, pulled him by the arm, but thereby helped to clear the view of the main attraction.

Cynthia's *sadhu* was in a crouching position, his knees wide apart and deeply bent, a huge top-knot of matted hair falling forward over his brow. He was naked apart from smears of ash on his body and brightly coloured stripes painted on his forehead. As he slowly started to straighten his legs he began swaying slowly from side to side and backwards and forwards, which had the effect of swinging a rock, rather bigger than a house-brick, between his legs. This rock was tied by a harness of cord to another cord fastened to the gentleman's penis, which was stretched quite thinly by the effort and was almost undistinguishable from the cord.

The reactions of our group were very different,

'Oh, how frightful!'

'Oh, my god!' But a few were reaching for their cameras.

'No photo!' called our sadhu's assistant. 'Photo after. First you pay. Five dollars for small stone.' Indeed, at the sadhu's feet were two or three more rocks of different dimensions, each tied in a cradle of cord, ready to be tied to the penitent penis.

'Small stone only five dollars. Big stone, ten dollars.' There seemed to be no take-up on the offer from either the waiting crowd of mainly young men - maybe hoping for some payment from we wealthy foreigners - nor, I should say, from our group of mainly older ladies. The assistant was becoming a bit desperate:

'You want big stone? Big stone ten dollars. *Rishi* can do extra-big also.'

The group, anxious to back away, were also transfixed. One or two, I suspect wanted to see if *Rishi* could achieve extra-big without serious injury, but no ten dollars, or even five dollars were proffered, and the sage resignedly squatted down on his haunches, allowing 'small stone' to rest on the ground, awaiting the next, more appreciative tourist group.

'How perfectly frightful.'

'Richard, please make him go away.'

'Oh, do come away.' Cynthia was almost apologetic,

'I did try to warn you, Richard. Sadly the man took us unawares.'

'Not that he was demonstrating his prowess at the time,' added Lucy.

'No, dear, it is just that he appeared on the path before us naked.'

'True!' said Lucy, 'But he had a lascivious look in his eye. Of course we had no idea that it would turn into a most unedifying spectacle.'

'What is a *Rishi*, anyway?' asked someone. 'That awful slimy fellow was going on about *Rishi* can do this, and *Rishi* can do that. I've never heard of a *Rishi*.'

'Well,' I started to try to explain, 'As far as I know they are holy men who can achieve very advanced levels of yoga…'

'Well, I expect he was one, then,' said Betty. 'It looked pretty advanced to me. I've never seen that in my class in Winchester.'

HOTELS

A FEW WORDS ABOUT HOTELS

Planning tours means planning hotels and I don't mean just *any* old hotels; that would certainly not do. No, they must be the right kind of hotels, atmospheric, characterful, even charming (a word later bannd by my dear wife: 'How can you promise charm? *You* might think it charming…'), hotels where we would *not* feel we could be anywhere in the world. This is where we so often came unstuck. Having stayed in cheaper quite *reasonable* hotels when travelling around India on our own, Jill and I have often visited others that were so much better. Sometimes we went just to look, thinking that perhaps one day we may bring a group to stay; sometimes we treated ourselves to a meal in a smartish hotel restaurant. Occasionally, we went just to use the working western-style loos and washing facilities, sit for a while in an air-conditioned lobby, or have a swim. And, I must confess, in the case of Madras where we stayed so long in the university guest house, we also went to steal hotel toilet paper, as only the coarsest paper was supplied by the guest house and none was available in any shop. Why would it be? A nasty western practice. I might just mention that recently some of our Australian travellers bought a couple of those hose attachments, now often found in modern Indian loos, that have replaced the tap or bucket and cup: you know, the ones with a nozzle on the end for personal hygiene. They thought they would try one out at home, thinking they might even import them to Australia. One of the wives reported to me that the trial had not gone well.

'I don't think he got the pressure right, Richard. It went woo…oosh; an' I very nearly flushed me' clacker down the dunny.'

Despite having seen better hotels, for the first one - even the first two - of the group tours I still felt a puritanical need to keep the cost of our tours down to an absolute minimum. If we were to stay in a characterful 'grand hotel', then it would have to be a cheaper one - one that had probably seen better days, such as the faded Ritz in Hyderabad, or The Imperial in Delhi - more about these later. The mere names tell you what I mean, for in those early days they were neither Ritzy nor in any way Imperial. In fact nearly all the old grand hotels were faded in those days; the fashion was and is for new glitzy affairs. In the early days we couldn't really think of staying at the one positively not-faded very grand Taj Mahal Hotel in Bombay, which now, incidentally has attached the word 'Palace', called in designers for more make-overs and become even grander.

If we couldn't find old, crumbling and 'shabby-*grand*', we would search for smaller, still characterful places with some history about them. There are plenty of these in India: old guest houses in hill stations, palaces of maharajahs and lesser nobility in many places, and especially those parts which had remained under the nominal rule of the princes until Independence. After all, what were these former rulers and nobles to do with their palaces? Many had city palaces, country palaces, guest house palaces, winter palaces, monsoon palaces, garden pavilions, even palaces at important pilgrimage sites. Rajasthan and Gujerat have dozens, perhaps hundreds of them, and as tourism has grown, so more and more have been converted to hotels. Some of these erstwhile rulers have gone into the hotel business in a big way: one Maharajah (actually the only one with the even grander title of Maharana) has spread his net into neighbouring territories, taking over the palaces of his noble brethren, and named what has become his *chain* of hotels, rather ambiguously, '*HRH*'. Not, as you might think, those belonging to His Royal Highness, but an abbreviation of *Heritage Resort Hotels*. We have stayed in many of these, and very nice most of them are, too. But not all his efforts have been entirely successful: we looked at his newly acquired hotel in the desert city of Jaiselmer, but the building and the location were unappealing - ugly, badly built, no shade, too far from the delights of the town... I discussed the matter with our perceptive guide:

'No, no, you are right. I fear His Highness has bitten off a white elephant.'

We learned to be rather careful after one or two disastrous mistakes - mistakes, I should point out, that were entirely my own. Jaipur, capital of Rajasthan, not only has the grand palace-hotels of the Maharajah of Jaipur, but many of his courtiers have converted their town palaces or *havelis* into smaller mansion hotels, though sometimes hanging on to the word 'palace'.

It was our very first tour, and our arrival at the Bissau Palace was unfortunate. I had chosen this from the guide books, after our initial choice was disappointingly unavailable, for its 'authentic charm, with a pool in the garden', and should say straight away that the hotel has come on a long way since our first and only visit. We had been duped by an unscrupulous guide and driver into leaving our previous hotel at two am for the long and bumpy drive to Jaipur because, they claimed, we would be in danger from marauding loutish drunken youths as it was the Holi Festival. They would stop our vehicle, demand money, throw Holi colours over us, and worse... We must, they insisted, reach the safety of our hotel before eight in the morning. The warnings, uttered not to me but to the most nervous group members, hung in the air… In reality our guide and driver wanted to get back home to Jaipur for the Holi Festival and we were in little or no danger at all. Anyway, we were tired, some were ill and all were grumpy as we made our way through the Moslem meat-slaughtering and marketing quarter of Jaipur quite early in the morning. The goats' heads, feet and entrails perched on the walls as we entered the gates of the Bissau Palace did not lift the mood.

Nor was it improved on entering the hotel. We were due to stay for four nights in Jaipur, but very soon it was evident that the group - more or less compliant and agreeable up to now - were not going to like it. Some bedrooms, they pointed out, looked out over a rubbish tip. Some did not look out at all, with a high brick wall just two feet from the windows. Inside the rooms were dark, not very clean. The staff members, presumably also wanting to be elsewhere celebrating the Festival, were surly and unhelpful. The swimming pool was a stagnant green puddle in the lawn. I complained bitterly, and the young manager was mystified by my exasperation as he showed me from one bad room to another; what could be wrong with any of it? Finally he said,

'We have one more room - it is like an apartment, I can show you.'

'Please do,' and he led me upstairs. It was a bit more spacious, and I considered asking four of the women to share, but at a glance it was even dirtier than downstairs.

'Oh dear, oh dear, I am afraid this is even dirtier than some of the rooms downstairs. Look at that terrible filthy ring of dirt around the bath-tub…' He was very downcast.

'I can arrange to have it cleaned.' But as we were leaving the bathroom I noticed a pair of trousers hanging on a nail on the back of the door.

'And what about these?'

'Oh, yes, I am sorry. They are my trousers.' He turned out to be not only the manager showing us his own flat; the manager was in fact the noble owner, scion of the house of Bissau.

Soon, though, I came to realise that by paying a modest amount *more* money, the quality of comfort could be much improved. Not to the point of luxury, you understand, but greater charm and improved service. Choice is all important, but sometimes even when we seemed to have chosen well, things seem to go wrong. Why was it in those early days we would so often arrive in a hotel to find it *overbooked*, resulting in negotiations with the group members about who would share with whom? Would two single ladies share a room? Or would four people share a suite? Usually this only happened for a night or two, but it required people to agree at very short notice. The expectation of the hotels was either that we would not *all* turn up, or that we could simply adjust our room requirement to what was available. There was never a hint of apology or that any real inconvenience had been caused. On our very first tour we arrived in a biggish, rather splendid palace hotel in Udaipur, with a lovely view over the lake, to be told that there was a conference being held and we had three rooms fewer than booked. We sorted that out amicably enough, people agreed to share, but I had my son and his girl-friend with us, who we had brought at the last minute due to a cancellation. Thank goodness the room, yes *the room* had been allocated - purely by chance - *to them*. I was in the lobby and needed to speak to them a few hours after we arrived, so asked to be connected by phone. After an embarrassed pause and consultation with other staff the reply came,

'Sir that room has no telephone working. I will send boy with message.'

'Well, no, I need to speak to them in person. Where is the room? I'll go there myself.'

'Please, sir, there is no need, we will deliver message.'

'As I say, I do need to speak to them. Will someone show me the way?' With great reluctance someone did show me the way: I was led outside, up a long outside staircase; no-one replied to the knock at first, and then the door would not open. There was the sound of something scraping and my son pulled hard on the door to let us in. To do so he had dragged a bed, which was partly in front of the door, into the room. Two small iron bedsteads and a cupboard filled the small space, both beds were unmade, with bedding and towels strewn on the floor. There were, however two large swing doors that opened into the very large bathroom, which had a dining table and six chairs between the grubby old iron bath and the even grubbier lavatory. The table had not been cleared of dirty plates. Now my son was very untidy at home, but it was six in the evening of the day we arrived, so I said, quite gently,

'My goodness, your room's just like you keep it at home. Doesn't this girl mind?' I didn't like to ask how, during a period alone, they had managed to throw so much bedding from both beds on to the floor.

'No, it's all right. It was like this when we arrived. It's OK.'

My guide was still standing there so I enquired,

'Was the room ready for hotel guests?' He was silent.

'And, tell me, why is there a table and so many chairs in the bathroom? Who has been eating here' He remained silent. At the reception desk I asked the duty manager the same. He looked sheepish.

'So, may I ask,' I enquired, 'is this room, the one with no telephone, no beds made with clean sheets, no clean towels, not cleaned or prepared in any way, but with six chairs and a table in the bathroom a regular hotel room?'

'Oh yes sir! Certainly.'

I am ashamed to say we made a bit of a fuss and they told us that as the conference was ending next day they would give us some more rooms for those sharing, and even though my son was not at all concerned, they offered to change his room as well. The next day we were offered the President Suite, The Viceroy Suite and several other grand-sounding suites to replace the shortcomings. They were enormous, each with anti-rooms, dressing rooms, additional rooms, several huge four-poster beds, balconies… it was also interesting to notice that they had clearly not been in use for some months.

All this sounds like a litany of complaint, but by and large hotels have been reasonable, often delightful and only occasionally disappointing. Even when they were disappointing they often provided rich if inadvertent humour. If they were disappointing it was no doubt because our expectations were unreasonable, and over time my choices, my reluctant acceptance that we should pay a bit more, and my expectations were all modified. And over the same period many Indian hotels improved, and if they didn't, they sank ingloriously, at least below my horizon. Towards the end of what I thought a quite successful tour in Rajasthan, where we had stayed in some very nice small palace hotels, we arrived in Agra. Nearly all tourists to India go to Agra to see the Taj Mahal, and there are a lot of hotels there, but none of the sort I like to offer our travellers. Instead of atmosphere, a modern, reasonably efficient 'tourist machine' is the best we can do.

One grumpy disaffected member of our group, a German lady, wife of an unfortunate university colleague of mine, the only one, I may say, of the many hundreds who travelled with us, and who positively disliked everything Indian from the outset, complained at one hotel that,

'It is very dirty. I hav spent ze evening cleaning ze surfaces in ze basroom. Tomorrow I must clean ze surfaces in ze bedroom.'

'Good heavens,' said someone, 'Did you bring cleaning materials?'

'Of course! Always my cleaning items I am taking.'

When she saw our hotel in Agra she perked up,

'Zank goodness, zis is ze first place which is acceptable. Vy haf we to go to all zose old palaces and zinks like zat? Zey are terrible. Vy could you not choose proper hotels?'

BRIEF ENCOUNTER

I suppose this incident belongs at first with those concerned with trains, as it began with a brief encounter - all too brief an encounter - on a railway platform. No, it didn't involve a smut in the eye, and quite unlike *that* Brief Encounter, moved rapidly on to a hotel room. Not for a romantic interlude, I hasten to say; quite the reverse, for this hotel very nearly caused a divorce. It was probably the worst hotel we saw in India, although we have come across some nearly as bad, sometimes in the most unlikely places - Turkey, Italy, even in Bath.

I should have known better on this occasion, but Jill and I had successfully used *Indian Railway Retiring Rooms* once or twice in our earliest travels. These are very inexpensive and convenient, if rather basic rooms at railway stations that could be rented by *bona fide* passengers. My mistake was that on this journey, arriving late in the night, I thought it would be very sensible to rent one of these *on arrival*. We had been told by the agent in England who sold them, that our precious *Indrail (1st Class)* passes would ensure not only priority reservations on trains, but also in Retiring Rooms, and we'd had no difficulty in using them before. Our train arrived in Aurangabad station very late at nearly three am. Despite presenting the *Indrail* passes we were told (a) by the ticket inspector who had descended from our train that the retiring rooms were locked and the key was with station master who was out of station, (b) by the deputy-assistant engineer, summoned when we demanded to see someone in charge, that the rooms were under renovation, (c) by a sub-inspector that they were fully occupied, and (d) by a deputy-assistant station master that the rooms, which we were standing outside throughout the discussions, clearly labelled '*Retiring Rooms*', were 'discontinued'. I later learned that station master, far from being out of station, was most certainly in station, in fact in residence *in* the retiring rooms - yes rooms *plural* - together with his extended family. During the lengthy, sometimes heated and ultimately futile discussions, we had been approached by a very disreputable-looking character with dirty clothes and an old towel wrapped around his head - probably, I only realised later, in league with the station staff. He handed me a grubby, dog-eared business card which read.

EXOTICA HOTEL
Near to Station
Clean and Sanitory
Running Water in all Rooms.

'Look,' I said to Jill, 'We're obviously getting nowhere with this bloody station, but this' - showing her the card - 'this looks just the thing.'

'Are you mad? Have you seen the state of him? Have you seen the state of the card? Did I not say we should book a hotel? But oh no, you wanted to save a few pence, you would…' But it was too late, the man had somehow swung both our bags on top of his head and was trotting, almost running down the platform and out of the exit. It was all we could do to keep up with him, with me shouting,

'Hang on! Stop! Wait a moment. Where…' And him calling back.

'Very good hotel, five minute only…' without slackening his pace. We tried to keep up, at least fifty yards behind. The road became narrower, the street lights petered out; the road became a track. We were puffing and shouting,

'Where the hell are you taking…'

'Very good hotel, five minute only.

It seemed more like twenty minute only, but we were hot, exhausted and Jill very angry, mainly with me. We saw our man stop, put down our bags and carry them through a doorway into a dimly lit entrance passage. A man who had clearly just woken up, tousled and grumpy, said,

'Room? You want room? Sixty rupees. You want breakfast also? Sixty rupees. Breakfast extra.' I may say that sixty rupees in those days was about four pounds - a bit more than we usually paid elsewhere for quite good rooms.

'Er, can I see a room?' But again it was too late; our station platform man was carrying our bags up a staircase. There was very little light, but we could see that it was a rough concrete staircase with no hand-rail on the *outside* of some building. We followed, feeling our way, out on to an external corridor, with unglazed windows on one side, and spaces for windows but instead of window-frames and glass, there were alternately and very crudely laid bricks, making a lattice pattern window. There were dim lights inside some of these rooms, and we could see several beds with sleeping occupants. Jill's patience was clearly at an end. She said nothing, but the atmosphere was heavy. Further down the corridor our host opened a door where there was no light inside and started to *feel* the beds to discover if there were occupants. There were!

'Have you a room with no-one sleeping in it?' Jill's voice was menacing.

But after another couple of attempts he eventually found a room which had both a light and no-one sleeping in it. It was dreadful; the 'hotel' was a newly built but incomplete something, we never knew what. Our room had a concrete floor, concrete walls, brick lattice 'window' liberally spattered with cement, a naked light-bulb. In the corner was a wash-basin (*Running*

Water in all Rooms), and there were five iron framed beds. The bed sheets were grimy and Jill, tight-lipped, asked for clean ones. Sheets were brought, our host contemptuously stripped off the dirty sheets and then proceeded to put *the same sheets* back on again. Jill's tight lips had now become an open mouth, until she recovered herself, tightened her lips again and said slowly and clearly,

'You have just put those same filthy sheets back on my bed.' Speeding up, she added, 'Here give them to me. Oh my god! The one's he's brought are no better.'

Our host departed. Jill made up her bed only saying,

'If you think I'm lying on those sheets you can think again. Why the hell I agreed to come…' and proceeded to unpack most of her clothing, first lying a raincoat on the bed, then various towels and other items, finally lying down herself, fully clothed. I thought I would at least undress and wash; there *was* water in the tap. But as I started to wash I felt water splashing on my legs and feet, and found that the waste was not connected to anything: the water simply poured from the waste hole onto the floor. I got *into* my bed, between the sheets, still undressed, and felt clammy and incapable of sleep. Jill was already fast asleep. I did not sleep, thinking of impending divorce and how to get back to England (we had just started this three month visit to India). At six o'clock I woke Jill to pack. We paid the sixty rupees (no breakfast) and carried our bags back to the station, to ask a taxi-driver to take us to 'the best hotel.' This is a foolish and dangerous thing to do: best often means 'best commission'.

However, by our standards it was the best hotel. It was the government-run Aurangabad Ashok Hotel, with reasonably clean bed, wash-basin-connected-waste, even a swimming pool. We stayed here over the next few days to explore the rock-cut cave temples of Ellora and Ajanta, some of the greatest of India's wonders, and decided to stay here again for our group tour a year or two later. But that was because we did not know what can happen in a year or two.

RETURN TO AURANGABAD

We went back to Aurangabad two years later with our *very* first group to India. At the time we imagined it would be our only group to India, but in the event it was the first of very many, and even the first of several to Aurangabad. We had at least learned a few things from our previous visit: the monuments at Ajanta and Ellora were too important to miss out - real wonders of the world that would give the most dramatic introduction to Indian art and religions; to get there we should not attempt to go by train; we should not think of staying in the Railway Retiring Rooms at the station and should always book our hotels in advance. Elementary, you may say? You are right.

When I suggested to the agents that we stay at the Aurangabad Ashok Hotel for this first *group* tour they had not demurred. Mind you, these were the same agents who told me I could certainly bring a group of thirty five to *fill* a thirty five seater coach (imagine!), who gave us some really terrible guides, and put us in some of the worst hotels. Later, when planning another trip, our *new agents* had been quite shocked to learn we had stayed at the Ashok.

'It is not at all recommendable,' they had faxed an urgent message, 'Service is not up to the mark. We definitely suggest you do not take group.' They were quite right. Hotels are often rather like the moon; they wax and wane, though unlike the moon, sometimes, having waned they don't wax again. It took our return visit, accompanied by twenty-five others, to learn that the Ashok was in a permanently waning phase.

The journey to the hotel went remarkably well. Our flight was on time, we arrived in the tiny Aurangabad airport in lovely soft morning sunshine, our coach and guide were there to meet us and we set off through a beautiful pastoral scene. Bullock carts laden with the grain harvest ambled along the road in caravans of ten or twenty at a time; flocks of sheep and goats grazed at the roadside. Our excited group, most of whom had not been to India before, demanded we stop the coach for photographs. The cart drivers - men in white 'Ghandi' caps, shirts and *dhotis*, women in colourful long skirts, blouses and head-scarves - smiled at us and we smiled back. We continued to smile until we drove into the Ashok forecourt.

It had been two years since we saw it. That time, after a disastrous journey and appalling night, it had appeared so welcoming. Yes, it was modern, cement, big, a bit bleak, not charming, but it was a refuge. There were just the two of us and our priorities were to shower, sleep, and reconsider whether the recriminations and our likely divorce were imminent. When we surfaced from the long sleep we found the hotel had a garden, a swimming pool, a restaurant and, as I say, the things there are to see in and around Aurangabad are so wonderful as to make the hotel seem relatively unimportant. There are not only the rock-cut cave temples; there is an enormous fortress, a Mughal tomb, interesting crafts - fine weaving and *bidri* ware, a special kind of inlaid metalwork - to be explored in the bazaar.

Arriving with the group, the hotel looked a good deal less cared for than when we last saw it. The white painted exterior was streaked with dark monsoon mildew, the lawn parched and bare and edged with a few marigold plants in un-watered beds, the tarmac drive-way had potholes and ruts, and litter was strewn about - plastic bags, newspaper, old soft-drink cans. Inside it was a bit better: there was a welcome drink of Coca Cola, and after arranging a rendezvous for departure to the caves, people dispersed to their rooms. As I say, this was our first group, and most of the people in it had not been to India before. This was their first hotel and expectations were not so high. But soon it became clear that whereas I may have felt that the hotels were of secondary importance to the wonders of India, many of the group soon felt differently. They were on *holiday*. That was the essential difference. I was still thinking of it arrogantly as an Indian *tour* and even felt a slight and misplaced sense of pride when, after their return, people would say,

'Christ! I needed a holiday after that! Experience it may have been, holiday it was not!' Some, I should say fell in love with the experience of India immediately, and the more Indian the experiences the happier they became. Dear Rosie, on her return home, dismayed her family by painting the house in Indian colours and motifs and burning incense, bored her friends with hundreds of photos, and would bury her head in her travel bag to recapture the smells of India. She and a small minority didn't like the Ashok because it was too western, but others didn't like the Ashok because it wasn't western enough.

The complaints were quite minor: a few damp beds, lumpy pillows, missing towels, missing shower curtains, broken light bulbs. All these, the reception staff promised, would be rectified by the time we returned from our first sight-seeing visit to the caves at Ellora. And some were. What could not be rectified were the mysterious large pieces of plywood nailed on to the walls in some of the rooms. When some of our travellers attempted to turn on the air-conditioning, they discovered what these plywood panels were. They were covering the voids where the air-conditioning units had been removed. The manager explained the problem.

'I am sorry to inform that my predecessor is in the District Court and has been charge-sheeted with the removal of hotel A/C units and purloining proceeds. He was saying that ITDC (India Tourism Development Corporation) has not paid due salary, and he had taken A/C units in lieu. That is also why he is my predecessor. I regret inconvenience.'

We returned to the hotel after our sight-seeing at the Ellora caves, hot and exhausted, some duly impressed with the carvings and sheer magnitude of the task that the temple builders had set themselves. But by the afternoon the temperatures are high, the sun has soaked into the rocks and radiates the heat back at you, and to tell you the truth our guide was pretty useless. His English was impenetrable, his knowledge slight and his enthusiasm non-existent. What he wanted was to take us shopping for silk and other items to earn his commission, so tried to rush us through the caves.

'First caves are not-at-all highlights, so we will go immediately to Number 14, then Number 16…' The idea of going anywhere *immediately* in that heat was off-putting; it is quite a long walk to the caves and from one to another, with much climbing up and down steps. And he was missing the point about which caves were Buddhist, which Hindu, which Jain. He rattled off a few incomprehensible stories of some of the gods and goddesses, not allowing us to take in any of the lovely carving. I tried to interject what I thought was some necessary information, but could see people were flagging and I felt dispirited, especially when a few only brightened up at the prospect of shopping! At my insistence we did spend a bit of time at the wonderful Kailasha Temple, the one that isn't a cave but a vast temple carved from the solid rock, and people were impressed - impressed but exhausted.

It was starting to get dark by the time we returned to the hotel. Although tired, some of us decided to have a swim. There were quite a few broken tiles on the steps, and it was Tom who pointed out that the pool lighting looked odd - rather beautiful, but certainly odd. Quite a few of us were already in the water which was refreshing and looked quite clean, lit from below by the pool lighting. In fact it was lit from unusually low. Normally pool lights are not far below the surface, but these were on the bottom, only because they had been detached from the sockets near the surface and hung down on their cables, resting on the bottom of the pool. The pool had been filled before the electricians had finished their task. We could see the wires very clearly. How the whole system had not shorted out, and how we survived electrocution, we never knew. After raising the matter back at reception, next day the pool was

'Closed due to renovation'. It remained closed for the remaining two days of our stay. It also remained full of water, the electricians could not fix the lights, and the water turned a deep billiard-table green. On our last evening we could still see a dim glow from the lights through the soupy mixture.

The cave temples of Ellora and Ajanta remain wonders of the world, and we have returned to Aurangabad, the nearest jumping-off point, quite often. There are hotels available which are perfectly adequate, if not to my personal taste, but the poor Ashok, from what I can discover, has not so much waned as had a total eclipse. Nor have I found any trace of the Exotica Hotel, close to Railway Station.

ALL ROOMS ARE SAME

I had chosen the Ritz Hotel from the guide books for our first hotel of the tour. They didn't actually say 'redolent of old world charm' - after all it wasn't the Cotswolds - but one did say: '*For a touch of the days of the Nizams of Hyderabad, head for the Ritz Hotel... This former palace is rated as a four-star hotel, however it's getting shabby and the musty rooms are overpriced... Restaurant...pool, tennis court and spacious lawns affording beautiful views...*' Apart from the bits about 'getting shabby' and 'overpriced' this would be perfect. Not for us the sanitized anonymity of a modern five star luxury hotel, where we could be 'anywhere in the world.' No chain hotel, unless it could offer charm, ambience and location. No, here we would have the atmosphere I was looking for - especially as I read somewhere: '*Hill Fort Palace was where the younger son of the last Nizam, Prince Moazzam Jah, stayed. It is later known after Ritz Hotel. Built originally by Sir Nizamat Jung, the architectural style was based on the Trinity College in Cambridge where he had studied, and the castles described in the novels of Sir Walter Scott. The building was completed in 1915 and named as 'Hill Fort Palace'*. I was excited at the prospect of atmospheric charm as our coach drew up at the hotel entrance.

The Hotel Ritz, even, perhaps, when it was Hill Fort Palace, may never have been in its prime. It certainly did not appear to be at this moment. The rather curious architectural mixture of Indianised Tudor College and Scottish Baronial had produced a stone 'castle', with crenellations and Gothic windows. More recently, perhaps when being converted to a hotel, someone had decided to paint the grey stone white with a bright blue edge to every surface. Each window was edged with blue: each facet of each battlement, the edges of the plentiful verandah roofs, and the even more plentiful balustrades. Blue is a colour that fades in strong sunlight, but it had not faded uniformly or beautifully. Both the white and the blue now appeared to have some scabrous disease; rough, flaking, peeling paint and stucco were everywhere, streaked with dark mildew. The once perhaps sumptuous lawns, planted in the European style, but always impossible to maintain with uncertain water supply and summer temperatures, were now mainly dust. The clipped low hedges and topiary were ragged and missing rather vital parts. However, there were some colourful flower beds of Canna lilies and some trees - a lovely frangipani in full flower with its waxy white blossoms stood in front of the entrance, and two dark green trees offered shade.

'Here we are, ladies and gentlemen - our first hotel - The Ritz!' I cried cheerfully. 'I know just how tired we all are - so let's get our rooms and some rest.'

From the brightness outside, the deep gloom of the lobby did not look very welcoming. Dark wooden panelling, huge hunting trophies of heads of deer, buffalo, and a leopard lined the walls. On the floor was a threadbare,but once beautiful carpet. Some dusty upholstered sofas (some inexpertly patched, others in need of patching where the stuffing was escaping) stood around. Behind a reception counter at the far side of the large room were three members of staff, all men in dark suits and ties. They did not look up as we approached.

'Here is Travel Club,' said Sadam, our guide, cheerily. 'Where is welcome drink? We are here for check-in.'

'Good,' I said, 'I hope you are expecting us. I hope our rooms are ready?'

'Give me passport list,' was the only reply. One man looked up; the others did not.

'Well, I do have a passport list, but it's with my luggage. But surely you have one? Mr Sadam, they should have one?'

'Certainly you should have one. One has been sent.' There was no response.

'Well, anyway' I broke the silence, 'Please let us have the keys to our rooms. I'll give you a list when I get my baggage, but the people are very tired after a long journey, and we need our rooms. As you know, we need 12 double and 3 single rooms. Oh, and we need 9 rooms with large beds and 3 rooms with twin beds.'

'All rooms are same, sir.'

'Do you have no large beds?'

'All rooms are same sir, all have two beds only.'

'This seems a charming place' I heard the unmistakable sound of Cynthia's voice, 'How clever of you to find it; so atmospheric.'

'Christ! What have you brought us to?' Jill hissed in my ear. 'Have you seen the waiter? Have you looked in the loo? You better look at the rooms before you dish out the keys. If the loos are anything to go by…'

'Can we look at the rooms?' I asked.

'All rooms are same, but for you we have reserved suite-room - state room on 3rd floor. Mohammed will show you.'

'No, we want to see all the rooms,' said Jill firmly. 'Send someone with me and half the keys, and someone with my husband and all the other keys.' I was alarmed at her initiative.

'Can we have our rooms please?' The group, very tired after the long journey, was getting impatient

'Yes, yes, I'll be back in a minute,' I said, the familiar feeling of mild panic was returning.

'We're just going to check which rooms they've given us.' So Jill with one porter, I with another, armed with many keys, set off up the wide staircase to make a very hurried inspection. Jill disappeared from sight and I was shown the first room. Already apprehensive, I started to look and with each room the gloom deepened. For the most part the rooms were very large and had very high ceilings - all good - but all had frayed carpets, peeling walls, stained bed spreads, fly-blown photographs of grandly dressed Indians, old motor cars and dead tigers. I turned back the bedspreads - the sheets looked reasonable; there were grey stiff-feeling towels; the vast bathrooms had white tiles but no shower curtains. Strangely, considering what I had been told downstairs, some rooms had enormous double beds, some twin beds, some three beds, some four, one had five. Nearly all the beds were very high from the floor, many with elaborate frames for mosquito nets, but there were no mosquito nets. I lost count of the rooms - perhaps six or eight, but couldn't remember which was which and returned to the lobby confused and dispirited. Jill was there with the list which she had carried off.

'Well? I've seen four'

'Well, they're all much of a… not much to choose between them. They're all pretty awful'

'Do we get rooms or don't we? We've been hanging around…' The group was closing in.

'What were they like?'

'Well, it's hardly the Ritz,' I joked weakly. A mistake.

'I'll dish out the keys now.' I turned to the clerk, 'You told me all rooms are the same, they are all different - there are double beds, twin beds, triple beds, how could you…'

'All are same. Same tariff for group.'

'Look' I said to the group 'to save time I'll dish out the keys. Have a look at the room you get, if you find it unsuitable, please swap with one another. They don't seem to know which rooms have twin beds, or which have double.'

'But you've just been to look. Fond as I am of Cynthia, I don't want to share a bed with her,' Betty, at least, was laughing.

'Yes, have a look at the room - check the beds, the bed linen, the towels, the hot water, anything, and come back to see these men if there's anything wrong.' The three men behind reception were now looking alert, even wide-eyed. So far two had done nothing and merely looked aloof. Now they all looked anxious. The vocal one spoke,

'Now, sir, I am on off-duty. My duty is completed. Here is my colleague who is on on-duty. He will be duty reception.' The colleague glanced up from his newspaper. 'I may now depart?' asked the now off-duty clerk.

'No, you may not. Please wait. You are the receptionist who has allocated the rooms and given me the keys. Please wait.'

'What for, sir? My duties are completed…'

'Kindly wait.' We waited. Within two minutes Jackie was back at reception. 'Ah, Jackie, is the room OK?' I asked.

'It's much as I expected, but there are three Indian men living in my room.' I had vaguely noticed that there seemed to be some clothing strewn around in one of the rooms. The clerk was in conversation with the about to be on-duty man.

'Excuse me, there appear to be three Indian gentlemen living in this lady's room.'

'What?' he looked very anxious and immediately smacked the top of the brass bell on his desk and shouted in Telegu. The other two were taking notice. They seemed somewhat sheepish. Just then Ron appeared at my elbow. He looked puzzled.

'Ah Ron, is everything alright?'

'Well no. There's no bed in the room. Otherwise…'

'No bed? Excuse me, there is no bed in this gentleman's room.' I had not seen a room with no bed. Surely Jill would have…

'What?' exclaimed the receptionist and smacked the bell again. 'You see' I said politely, 'Your duties are not complete.' And that was not the end:

'We asked for a double bed, but there are three that look like camp beds,'

'We need twin beds but there is an enormous four-poster,'

The lobby was once again filling with people: group members, unknown Indians, a bed was being carried through and then a mattress. More staff were beginning to collect luggage.

'Shall we try to have a room' said Jill to me. 'There's not much you can add to this.' I had a large key with a brass tag attached to it in my pocket.

'Where is this room?' I hissed at the three scared staff, thrusting the key at them. One hit the bell again, but Jill cut in, 'Just tell us which floor - which direction.' We made our way up the stairs to the 'State Room' followed by a new servant wearing a tea-towel as a turban, who had been told to help. He took two of the hand bags Jill was carrying and the key from me and after a long climb and a long walk, let us in. It was certainly big. It was four rooms, all leading from one to the next. Each room was darker and mustier than the one before. Sofas, sideboards, tables, chairs, cupboards, wardrobes littered the rooms. In the last room was a huge bed some three feet from the floor.

'Is this OK?' I asked. Jill was examining the sheets,

'Oh let's have it, for goodness sake. I want to sleep.' She turned to the turbaned man. 'Please *on* the geyser and bring the luggage for HUNT to this room.' He smiled but did not understand. 'Baggage' she said louder. 'Baggage for HUNT.'

'I'll get it' I said. 'It will be quicker.' But I needed the lavatory, I needed sleep. Very reluctantly I put my shoes back on and trudged down to the lobby. Only a few people remained. The bed that was being carried through was now lying on its side, a very unsavoury-looking mattress draped across it. The pile of baggage was a good deal smaller, and our two bags were among it.

'Hasn't the bed gone to that gentleman's room?'

The now on-duty man was surly. 'Guest says bed is hard and dirty. But we are giving clean bed-sheet. Now we have given another room. We have given Viceroy suite.'

'Is he happy now?'

'Yes, yes, now he is happy. But room is different tariff.'

'You told me all rooms are same.'

A SWIMMING POOL AT THE RITZ

A sign in the lobby said *TOILET & WAY TO GARDEN*. One of the guide books had said of the Hotel Ritz, 'Swimming pool in attractive garden' and this had been a factor in my choice, admittedly a very limited choice, of hotel. We had a day 'at leisure' in our itinerary. What would be nicer for the group to relax beside the pool, read, snooze and cool off? I had pictured the group lying on teak sun-loungers, with white covered mattresses, under parasols, waiters bringing iced drinks… I was beginning to have doubts. I needed a pee, but thought I might take a look at the pool. I asked at the reception,

'The sign says 'Way to Garden'. Is the swimming pool that way also?'

'Yes, sir.'

'Can I have a swim now?'

'Yes, sir.'

The gent's toilet did not reassure me; it was rather smelly and not very clean, but I thought I might have a look at the pool before going back to our room. I walked further along the corridor, past the sounds and smells of a kitchen, some discarded plates and the remnants of meals on the floor, through a door labelled *WAY TO GARDEN* and out into the bright sunlight. I was indeed in a garden, with more greenery than at the entrance of the hotel, with pots of geraniums and marigolds and a large stone fountain that had no water in it. Further off was a another very decayed sign that read *SWIM-ING POO-Reserved for Resident only* and beyond it a tall concrete structure supporting what was clearly a high, large diving board. As I drew nearer I could see the pool. It was enormous, white tiles shining in the sun. It was also very deep at the deep end, but very nearly empty. At the bottom of the deep end was just a small pool of dark green stagnant water with some scum and one old orange-coloured life belt just visible submerged below the green slime, and an upturned metal chair, with rusting legs sticking above. Various tide marks stained the walls and many of the tiles were missing, or broken. The paving around the pool was also broken, uneven and weeds grew in the cracks and gaps. I returned to the reception. Only the newly on-duty clerk was there.

'The swimming pool is empty.'

'I will check up, sir and let you know.'

'No, I am telling you, the pool is empty.'

'I will check.'

'There's no need to check. I have checked. It is empty. A few minutes ago I asked you if I could swim and you said 'yes.'' Silence.

'Pool is under renovation, sir'

'Is it? I checked with our agents that this hotel has a pool, which usually indicates we would like to use it. When will it be ready?'

'I will check up, sir and get back to you.'

'Who will you check up with? Can I speak to the General Manager?'

'He is in a meeting, sir.'

'When will he finish his meeting?'

A pause. 'In three or four days, sir,'

'Three or four days! - for a meeting?'

'The meeting is in Delhi, sir. The GM is taking care of his business.'

'Isn't the hotel his business?'

'Yes, sir, he is the GM.'

'So what business is he taking care of?'

'The GM is having many businesses, sir.'

'So who is in charge while he is away? Are you in charge?'

'No sir, I am only the F & B in-charge, sir.'

'The F-ing B? What is the F-ing B?' I was tempted to expand the abbreviation.

'It is Food and Beverage in-charge, sir.'

'Food and beverage? But you are in reception.'

'Reception in-charge is out of station, sir. Night duty reception in-charge is off-duty and day duty reception in-charge is out of station. I am only…'

'I know what you are. Is the day-duty reception in-charge also in Delhi?'

'No, sir, he is in family function.'

'So who is in charge of the swimming pool? Is he in Delhi or a family function?'

'The GM only sir.'

'Is see. So how long has the pool been under renovation? Will it be ready before we leave here in four days?'

'I do not know sir, I am only working here, sir, for past four months.'

'Do you mean it's been under renovation for longer than that?'

'I don't know, sir.'

'Have you seen the pool?'

'Yes, sir'

'You said, when I asked you, that I could have a swim in it.'

'Yes, sir.'

'But you have seen the pool. Do you think I can I have a swim in it?'

'Pool is under renovation, sir.'

At that moment an elderly waiter walked by with a tray of dirty plates and cups.

'Please ask this gentleman if he has worked here longer than you. Perhaps he knows about the pool?'

The waiter turned pleasantly and smiled. He put down the tray on the reception counter and joined in the conversation.

'Yes, yes, sir. I am waiter here this long time.'

'Good. Can you kindly tell me how long the swimming pool has been not working?'

'Is not working?' It sounded like a question.

'Yes, I mean no. It is not working. How long has it not been working? This man here says it is under renovation.'

They conversed for a few moments. The waiter resumed his account.

'Yes, sir, it is definitely under renovation. But renovation has stopped for some time.'

'How much time?'

'Oh maybe - five (a pause) maybe six (another pause) years?'

'Years?'

'Maybe seven years.'

'Seven years? So it's not under renovation? It is abandoned!'

'Oh no sir, there is some dispute. It is in renovation…'

I climbed the stairs slowly, wondering how we might make use of our day at leisure.

A POST SCRIPT: It is some thirty years since this, our only visit to the Ritz Hotel in Hyderabad back in the 1980's. I thought it would be interesting to see, with the magic of Google, how the hotel has been getting on. A *Times of India* report of 2006 stated: HYDERABAD: *The private promoter of erstwhile Ritz Hotel has dragged the A(ndhra) P(radish) Tourism Development Corporation (APTDC) to court after the latter slapped a notice of termination of the 33-year lease executed by the two in 2000.* Perhaps the swimming pool was at the centre of the dispute at the time of our visit? Or perhaps just a victim?

DINING AT THE RITZ

It all started with a visit to the bazaar. It was the first day of the tour; we had checked in to the hotel, had some rest if not sleep, and were off on our first adventure into old Hyderabad. Mind you, we had left quite a few of the group behind, catching up on sleep, or just too exhausted after the long, long journey to go into town. It was deep in the bazaar when Tom, riding in one of the front cycle rickshaws of our cavalcade, called out,

'Can we have some of these? Some of us went without lunch.' I couldn't see what he could see, but the smell drifting out was certainly delicious and I could see smoke and steam billowing out from a grimy stall.

'You want to try?' asked our guide, calling back to the rest of us.

Try what? I couldn't see, but the group members were dismounting. A smiling man in a grimy vest and *lungi* stood beside the stall, banging a lump of dough on a wooden block, then twirling the flattened dough into a large flying saucer on one finger, and spinning it very expertly onto a large upturned and blackened metal dish, which he had greased with something held in his other hand. Beneath the metal a hot red fire was burning.

'You want to try?' asked Sadam again.

'What is it?' said some;

'Certainly' from Betty.

'I do,' said Tom, 'I'm hungry.'

'It will not sicken your stomachs?' asked Sadam again.

'Nonsense,' from Betty 'They're fresh and hot, what harm…'

'You must be mad,' said Betty 2. She and her husband were not eaters of local food; they claimed to have brought most of their food for a three week tour with them from England. Several of us gathered round watching the cooking. Another man squatted beside a vast basin of what may have been ground or pounded meat, adding finely chopped onion and garlic, an assortment of spices - grey, green, red - from battered aluminium pots and mixing it all with his fingers.

'And what's this?'

'This one is *paratha* - special Hyderabadi *paratha.*' said Sadam, indicating the smiling twirling man. 'And this one is *kebab* or pattie - also very special in Hyderabad. Inside is restaurant.'

We entered under the very low roof to the interior, where there were a number of battered and rather grimy chairs, stools and tables. It was rather dark and there were only a few customers who looked very surprised and a little uncomfortable as we squeezed in. Growing accustomed to the light I became a little anxious - the tables were decidedly dirty, the place was very hot - hardly surprising as another great fire was belching flames and smoke from under a black upturned metal dish the size of a large dustbin lid. Sticking to this were small flat patties, sizzling in the high heat, while a man deftly turned them and flicked them off onto a stack of metal plates. A small boy squatted dangerously near the fire, poking in sticks.

Some of us ordered plates of patties and *parathas*; others looked on in horror. Within a couple of minutes the plates loaded with food arrived and we fell on them.

'Only a liquid lunch, you see,' explained Betty, 'in our room back in the hotel.'

'Absolutely delicious,' exclaimed Cynthia.

'Oh yes, these are terrific,' said Tom. And they were: the *parathas* were light, flaky, hot and very slightly oily; the patties the size of small flattened cup-cakes, crisp and brown on the outside, melt-in-the-mouth soft inside, flavoured with garlic and cumin and coriander and chilli.

'What meat do they use?' asked Cynthia?

'Best not to know,' said Betty, tucking in. Several re-orders later we left.

'Shan't want much dinner' said Tom. 'Good job, too, considering the state of the restaurant back at the hotel - what was it?'

'The Ritz. What a joke! If only their grill room was a patch on this place…'

'Which Ritz?'

'Well, the London one, if it comes to that.'

'Ah, there you have the advantage of me…'

We all smelt of wood-smoke and spices as we left the smoke-blackened 'hotel' where we had just dined.

'I don't know how you could' said Ian, husband of Betty 2. They had remained outside. 'I'll bet you're all down with…'

'Well, you don't know what you've missed,' several shouted.

'It certainly was so delicious, I can't remember…'

'I asked Tom to film it, you know,' said Ian, indicating the video camera. 'And I shall be showing it to my health inspector friend when we get back. We had a good talking to from him when we told him where we were going and this will just show him how right he was.'

'And we'll know who to blame,' added Betty 2 knowingly, 'When you all go down with something horrible.'

'Oh, I don't expect we shall,' said Cynthia. 'It may not have been fine dining in the strictest sense, but was certainly one of the most tasty and interesting meals of my experience... I do hope we come here again.'

At dinner at the Ritz later that evening the group slowly gathered. A long table had been set down the centre of the room, with overlapping tablecloths in varying states of cleanliness. The green ones looked worse than the blue, with large stained patches. The only other guests were a middle aged couple sitting finishing a meal at a distant table on one side, and three suited business men equally far away on the other. From the walls, some rather flea-bitten, dusty hunting trophies looked down dolefully. The antlers of one large stag had some old Christmas decorations still attached. It was only March, but the decorations may have dated from several Christmases before.

'I'm not sitting here - look at the state of...'

'Excuse me, waiter, this table cloth is very dirty,' from Jacky.

'Where Madam?'

'Here, and here, and here, look. Here...' A jabbing finger.

'But here, Madam, is not dirt.'

'Of course it is. Can't you see? Look at this great stain: small ones, here and here...'

'But that is not dirt, Madam, that is sauce...'

The rest was drowned in a huge explosion of laughter. My side plate had a trickle of oil on it from a previous customer. The large grey napkin, warm and newly ironed, was resting partly in the oil. Waiters were going around taking orders for drinks. Beer bottles were appearing and being opened. Jill ordered mineral water and pointing to my plate added,

'Please change this plate and knapkin. They are oily.'

'Certainly Madam.' He took the offending articles away.

Slowly the food orders were taken. News of the bazaar *kebabs* and *parathas* had spread among those who had stayed in the hotel.

'Have you some of those meat patties the others had in the town?' someone asked. I tried to explain to the puzzled waiters what we had eaten. He pointed to the grubby and rather worn menu "*Tong-tikkling shish-kebab Hyderabad steel*.' I read this out to the group. 'I guess this is what they mean.' Some dishes were ordered. The waiter looked doubtful. 'Will take too much of time,' he muttered.

With much chat and excited information passing from the city visitors to the sleepers, beer was drunk and some food started to arrive.

'Well!… I ordered mine long before…'

'What is this? This is not what I ordered…'

'Over here, that's mine…'

'What about the rice? I want to eat this with the rice, while it is still luke warm…'

'Coming sir, coming Madam. Food is getting ready. One more beer. No sir, this is *Hyderabadi Biriyani*, this one is curd. You do not wish for curd? Who wish for curd?'

'This dish is cold. Please take it back…'

Our own meal came - a simple meal of *nan* bread, *dhal* (lentils) and *aloo jheera* (potato with cumin). The nan bread could be placed on a side plate, but mine had gone.

'I asked for a clean side-plate and napkin for my husband' said Jill.

'Certainly Madam.' He picked up a plate and napkin from an empty table nearby and brought them over. He was a portly man with a very filthy uniform, especially filthy over his paunch which was wrapped in a grimy cummerbund. The plate looked perfectly clean, but Jill made a point of picking it up to examine it, twisting it to the light.

'Is clean, Madam?'

'Yes, thank you. It seems clean.'

'Make clean, Madam,' upon which he picked up the plate again, clasped its eating side to his paunch with both hands, and rotated it a few times. Then he attempted to remove the newly acquired grey grease stains with an equally filthy tea towel he wore over his shoulder.

'Here, Madam,' he beamed proudly as he replaced the plate.

'*Shish Kebab, Shish Kebab*, special order.' A waiter carried two large platters to the table.

'Here, here' were responses from different parts of the table. The platters were placed with great style. They contained almost black, shrivelled items bearing no resemblance to the delights of our bazaar experience. Hands reached out. The platters were passed up and down.

'You said they were delicious.'

'Mm… they're terrible. You said…'

'I can't get my teeth into…'

'Nearly broke mine…'

'Here (to me) you try one. We only asked for them because you said…'

I bit into one. The hard dry unyielding exterior did, with effort give way to an only slightly less dry unyielding, but rubbery interior. 'Yes, they do seem a bit overdone…'

'Overdone! They're cremated.'

Patties with one bite taken were pushed back onto the serving platters. Genteel ladies surreptitiously put napkins to their mouths to remove the offending remnants. The downcast waiters looked on and saw their tips withering away.

THE LALITHA MAHAL: A PROPER COURIER

I was once described in my absence as *not* behaving like a 'proper courier'. Admittedly this was in the context of a tour where I wasn't actually the 'tour leader', but had organised and accompanied a tour led by a friend. My offence, although both had committed the same offence, was grievous: 'D'you know, he sat down and ate with us at meals!' It was a relief, then, to come across a couple of 'proper couriers' and by chance they were both at the same hotel.

The Lalitha Mahal Palace is the flagship of the Indian *government*-run hotel chain. It was and is a very grand place indeed. Modelled, some say, on the White House in Washington, some on St Paul's in London, it was built in the 1920's for the Maharajah of Mysore to put up the Viceroy of India and his entourage, and subsequently his other foreign guests. Its location, a few kilometres out of Mysore, was partly to give it a certain privacy in its own gardens, but also to keep the Maharajah's carnivorous guests a suitable distance from the purity of his own vegetarian kitchens in his own very much grander palace in the city. A devout follower of Shiva, he was, rather unusually for his caste and status, a strict vegetarian. The guest house really is a magnificent, over-the-top building - a huge white stucco and marble Classical affair, with a great pillared portico, surmounted by a domed turret, long shady verandas behind more pillars and arches. The grandeur continues inside - the magnificent double marble staircase ascends from the entrance hall (if one chooses to use the stairs rather than the antique electric lift). The dining room, the ball room, the billiards room and the magnificent guest suites all continue the opulence. Until, that is, one tries to stay there.

We had seen the building some years before; at that time the Lalitha Mahal Palace was just being converted to a hotel and we were shown round the main rooms on the half-pretext that I plannd to bring a group to stay. I certainly did not think it would ever happen. Some of the vast bedrooms, with four-posters, silk hangings, ante-rooms, dressing rooms and enormous bathrooms, could have accommodated the whole group. I remember 'sneaking' a very refreshing swim in the large oval pool in the gardens "Strictly for Residents Only" while Jill kept watch for security guards. We loved Mysore and in the planning of the tour I had in mind that a combination of the delights of the city with the nostalgic grandeur of the palace would make a real highlight. To my surprise, the price didn't seem too unreasonable.

When we all eventually arrived at the hotel I was ignored. I felt a little miffed - the welcome was no better than our hotel in Hyderabad.

'Excuse me,' I said. A clerk looked up. 'I am checking in with the British group. Have you our rooms ready?'

'What is the group?' No effusive welcome, a rather abrupt retort.

'Well, we are the British Group - The Travellers' Club group. We need our 15 rooms.'

'We are having many Britishers. Not your group only. The hotel is totally sold out. We have allocated 11 rooms and 2 suites for your group.'

'What? How can… We booked 15 rooms and you say…?'

'Suite rooms are very commodious. You can accommodate. We are putting cots into suite rooms.'

'Cots? Do you mean cots? Can you see my group? Do they look as if they need cots?'

'Cots are folding bed. Very comfortable…'

'But it's only three in the afternoon. You can't have given our rooms to others already?'

'Hotel is totally full. We are giving two suite: there four persons can easily accommodate… Also suite room is much more costly, and we are giving at no extra charge…'

The group was marvellous: with no complaint, offers came forward to share, led by Cynthia and Betty. Without looking at any of the rooms, and with remarkable harmony, the women decided among themselves how eight of them could squeeze into two suites. At that moment a new, loud and very strident English woman's voice was heard:

'Where are our welcome drinks? I trust you have our rooms ready? I am Lady Blank-Blank and this is the Lady Blank-Blank tour.'

In the discussion with the clerk about our rooms I had not noticed the arrival of the Lady Blank-Blank tour. But now I turned round and saw a dozen or so pale and refined British ladies and gentlemen, Panama or Tilly hatted, demure voices, accompanied by a very large quantity of smart and smartly labelled luggage.

'I hope *this* group has fewer rooms than booked, and not only my group?' I murmured to the reception clerk.

'Oh yes sir. They too have two rooms too few.'

Lady B-B was talking to another reception clerk:

'What? This is outrageous! Do you know who I am?'

I am not sure whether he knew who she was or not, but by pure chance, I did know. She was the wife of a former British High Commissioner to India. At the end of our very first group tour to India we had been accidental guests of her and her husband. One of our group members, who also had 'Lady' in front of her name, was in the process of divorcing a husband who had been briefly a member of Mrs Thatcher's cabinet. Somehow the Foreign Office had relayed notice of her visit to Delhi to the British High Commission, but neither the FO, nor the High Commission knew of the impending divorce - I'm not sure the husband knew, either. As happens in these matters, our Lady was duly invited to take drinks with His Excellency at his Residence, but she had said that she wanted to bring her tour leader and his wife along. The visit did not turn out to be a great success. Immediately before our departure for the drinks, our group had held its own 'final evening' party in the old - at that time quite scruffy and run down - Imperial Hotel, at which quite a lot of drink had been taken. Jill and I had been garlanded with extravagant flower garlands, and while we remained reasonably sober, our Lady was less so. She insisted we did not remove our flower garlands when we left the hotel, and rather cavalierly dismissed the taxi when we arrived at the Residence.

We were met by a smartly white-uniformed servant and ushered into the presence of His Excellency and his lady. The evening began with us being offered a mild rebuke for turning up at the door wearing the garlands. Indian custom, we learned from Lady B-B, required the immediate removal of a garland, as only Gods may continue to wear them. Mere mortals should show humility and remove them immediately after they were hung around the neck. Ann's eye looked steely as she told the B-B's that they were a gift from a very appreciative group who regarded us as their Gods and would certainly not wish them to be removed. The smartly dressed servant, with tall turban and now with white gloves, plied us with more and yet more drinks.

'Gin and Tonic, sir, madam.' He said more than once, bowing low with his tray. Unfortunately he did not offer anything to eat, or even to nibble. The G & T's were making me a little unguarded and I recognised that Lady B-B's irritation seemed to increase when, after they mentioned that their son was at New College Oxford, I blurted out 'What a coincidence, so's mine.' It happened to be true, but somehow the coincidence did not strike a happy chord.

We learned quite a lot about not only Indian customs, but what was customary for visitors (meaning us) to India. The conversation was reasonably amiable for a while, if a little one-sided and aloof, with Lady B-B doing most of the talking. Quite soon it was made very clear that the B-Bs were going out to dinner that evening. Ann was oblivious and took up the conversation quite happily. So, rather too late, I suggested we leave.

'You have your car?' enquired his Excellency, largely as a matter of form.

'Er, no, I'm afraid not,' I mumbled. 'We rather imagined we could get one from here, so we paid him off.' My voice and mannr were perhaps not sufficiently apologetic, perhaps altogether too casual.

'Well, that's not frightfully convenient,' replied Lady B-B. 'The custom here is to tell one's driver to wait.'

'Oh dear, I'm sorry about that... perhaps we could 'phone?'

H.E. beckoned to the G & T bearer, who stooped to hear the muttered instructions. I heard '...telephone...car...Lady... and her guests...' but not much more. A little more stilted and awkward conversation continued until, after a remarkably short period, the servant returned.

'Car is waiting, sir' he said.

We stood up, bade our thanks and, accompanied only by the servant, exited from the front door. There, under the portico, was a white Rolls Royce, with smartly uniformed chauffeur holding open a passenger door, the British coat of arms on the pennant flying from a little mast on the wing. Ann merely said 'Oh jolly good,' and stepped in, calling loudly 'Imperial Hotel.' Jill and I followed her in on the other side and the rather startled driver set off. The Rolls, we learned from the driver, was to convey H.E and Lady B-B to dinner. Whether the servant had understood his instructions, or our taxi was ever ordered, or whether the B-Bs used our taxi or waited for the return of their car, we never learned. It took over half an hour to reach The Imperial Hotel, where the large, uniformed commissionaire very rapidly came to open the door with an elaborate salute. The look of disappointment was evident when he saw who was inside. Sadly, none of our group were there to see our arrival.

A Postscript:

Now, several years later, to my great surprise, here was Lady B-B leading a tour in India. I came across her in the swimming pool next day, and took the opportunity of thanking her for her hospitality. She said she did not recall our visit,

'There was a constant stream of visitors,' she explained, 'and I was seldom responsible for the invitations.'

When visiting the Mysore city palace later, a small group of tourists was depositing cameras at the time that some of us were retrieving ours: it was the Lady B-B group. They were so obviously British that several of our members said 'Good morning,' but received rather muted replies, and Lady B-B's stance, seen at some distance, appeared to give off an air of studied indifference. Clearly she wasn't going to recognize me either here or at the hotel. She was gathering her group firmly around her. However, I saw one of them talking to Betty, who pointed to me and they both came over.

'This is Richard,' She said, by way of introduction. 'I was telling this gentleman about you, as he was asking about our group.'

He was a genial-looking man perhaps in his sixties and he extended his hand.

'Hello, yes, I was just asking this lady about your group.' He had a warm Scottish accent and smiled. 'We saw you in the hotel, and I was wondering who you are?'

'Well, we're just a group from England…'

'Yes, I know y'are. So are we, but *you* seem to be having a *good time*!'

'Oh dear! I hope you are having a good time, too?'

'Well, yes, I suppose we are. The wife seems to think we are. We're off to some wild-life place tomorrow.'

'Oh, that sounds a good idea. By coincidence, I have met your tour leader.' I volunteered. 'I believe she is very knowledgeable about India.'

'Yes. Have you? Yes. I suppose she is. But I think I know more about Indians and Indian customs than I wished to know…'

'Oh dear. I'm sure…'

'And it's a bit like travelling round with a rather cross head-mistress… I'd better go,' he said turning round, 'I'm getting a look!'

ANOTHER PROPER COURIER

After the confusion of securing our own rooms, and the minor satisfaction of overhearing the outrage of Lady Blank-Blank, who was shouting that her people *could not* and *would not* share rooms, I started to walk away from the foyer when I was tapped on the shoulder. A man, who I had noticed reading a newspaper in the foyer, had approached.

'Wot ees your groupe?' he asked confidentially in a heavy French accent.

'I beg your pardon?'

'Zees groupe. I ask again, wot ees zis groupe?'

'Well, it's just a group. We are from England… Oh, I'm not with that group' - I indicated the Lady B-B people who were all now squabbling in the foyer.

'Yes, yes, I know, I know. They also are from Eengland. I know you also are from Eengland, but wot kind of groupe eez your groupe?'

'Well, I think you saw… they are quite a mixed lot. Some rather elderly…'

'But I see zees group. I see when you arrive and zees hotel does not av enough room. It ees ze same with me. For me also zay say zat we av not enough room. But your group - when you ask zem to share a room, zay *agree wiz you*. When you say you will share a room, zay *agree*! *Incroyable*!'

'Well, yes…'

'My group, zay nevere agree. Zay will not agree and I, oo av been ere many time, I am given the room of a chauffeur.'

'Oh, I'm sorry but my wife and I are also in…'

'Bah!'

The same evening as we entered the dining room I noticed my French counterpart. He was sitting at a small table in a corner near the door, alone, once again reading his paper. A bottle of red wine was almost empty at his elbow. Our group was sitting at four large round tables of six or seven people, and further up the room was another long rectangular table of noisy French people. Jill and I went over to our people to see their reaction to the surroundings; there was much mirth at the grandeur of the dining room: it was rather like being inside a huge china Wedgwood box turned inside out. Blue and white classical pilasters, arches, rich silk turquoise hangings, an arcaded upper floor gallery, all lit with grand chandeliers. Above this was a stained glass ceiling. Seated on a stage at the far end, a *tabla* and violin duo played Indian classical music, and in the centre of the room a large buffet dinner was laid out on elaborate white and turquoise satin table cloths. The waiters wore

Western evening dress and the whole effect was magnificent and overblown. Several people wanted to tell us about their rooms, their four poster beds, their wonderful huge marble bathrooms. In one case there was a graphic description of a seven feet tall urinal, in another an elaborate shower that sprayed water from many angles, mainly over the floor but none over the bather. In many cases the plumbing did not work at all, nor the air conditioning, but everyone seemed to have the correct luggage, some had swum in the pool, some had found the shops and there was a general air of contentment and bemusement.

We spoke to all our tables before sitting down to join Jean, Molly, Jacky and David, where spaces had been left for us. As we settled down everyone looked up to see Lady Blank-Blank leading in her group. She strode ahead of them wearing a long, rather florid dress; most of the men wore jackets and ties and the ladies were in smart dresses suitable for evening wear. They quietly went to their allocated table, very close to the French group. The mannr of the Lady B-B group was politely reserved, but not so the French, who appeared very animated, but apparently by anger rather than *bonhomie*. There were some aggressive demands addressed to waiters and explosions of irritation. Wine bottles were poured into glasses, but these were sniffed and passed round to cries of disgust and pulled faces.

'Well done, Jean! I'm glad you have come in for dinner.' I sat next to her. Jean did not respond well to food.

'I don't suppose I'll eat much, but Molly said I should come to look at the room.'

'It is rather impressive, isn't it? Do you like the Indian music?'

'I can't hear it. Those people are making a lot of noise.' This was true. The French group, who were closest to the musicians, were not displaying appreciation, and from the Lady B-B group the dominant voice was that of Lady B-B. Among the snatches of conversation I could overhear came a loud, confident and familiar 'No, I think you will find that the custom here is…'

'Well, let's go and have a look at the buffet,' I said to Jill, anxious to avoid any eye-contact with Lady B-B. I had mentioned she was staying here and Jill was not keen to resume our connection. Most people had already started and David was on a second helping of soup: a brown and not altogether recognizable soup.

'I had better fill up on this,' he said. 'They say it's French onion soup, but I can't find any onions in it. They do have some fish but it appears to be curried. The fried chicken may be all right, but there are no chips! Nearly all the food is *Indian*!'

Like most hotel buffet dinners, the presentation was a good deal more impressive than the content, but we found some dishes that were quite acceptable and enjoyed an agreeable meal. Among the bright pink and green 'European' desserts was what a waiter explained to me was 'Chocolate Mouse,' but there was also a very nice Indian sweet - carrot *Halwa* - sweet and syrupy. I felt quite contented. While we were eating, several members of the group came across to ask about the next day's programme, so I circulated from one table to another, just mentioning that we would meet at nine to visit the temple and the great Nandi Bull, and then the Maharajah's palace. When we were leaving the room, the French tour leader beckoned to me with his newspaper and I walked across to him.

'I am watching. You allow zees people to speak to you *during ze dinner*?' He asked incredulously.

'Well, yes, I ...'

'I watch you and I see. Moi? Nevere, I nevere allow eet. 'Ow can you allow eet? Boef!'

'How was your dinner?'

'Ze dinner? Eet ees terrible. Only ze wine ees good.'

'Really? I've never found... And your group did not seem to like the wine...'

'Of course not. Ze wine zey 'ave zere ees terrible. But zees is my wine. *Naturellement* I bring ze wine from France... *Naturellement* I sit 'ere, I do not sit zere wiz zem.' He became more confidential.

'Non. You see, I am a *professional*.'

[illegible]

OUR ROOM AT THE LALITHA MAHAL

While I was still trying to deal with the room sharing resulting from the over-booking at the hotel, listening in to Lady Blank-Blank dealing with the same problem, and receiving my new French friend's advice on how to conduct a group, Jill went off with our key and a man with our luggage. Before I had finished, she was back.

'Have you seen the room they have given us?' she was clearly not pleased.

'No, he just gave me the numbers. He knows I am the leader, so I was hoping…'

'Yes, well, he's given us a cupboard under the stairs.'

'A what? What do you mean?'

'You'd better come and look. There's hardly room for the bed…'

It was true. Half way up a narrow servant's staircase was a low door. It opened into a very small room, with a small double bed squashed against two walls, and a minute shower. There was no window. The only space for the lavatory was directly beneath the shower.

'Oh Christ. I thought when he said it was for the leader, he was giving me one of the best rooms.'

'Well he didn't. This is awful. It has no window - it's just awful.'

Back at reception the implacable clerk remained implacable.

'Hotel is not only totally full, it is over-full. You can change with another of your group.'

'Over-full? You mean over-booked! No-one else will want that room! It is not even a guest room.'

'It is a room for tour leader. Maybe tomorrow you can change.'

It was time to clutch at straws. 'Yes, yes, definitely we will change. My wife is very unhappy…'

So before we set off for our next day's sightseeing, I had an important task: to secure a change of our room. We had not spent a very comfortable night: it was hot, there was no space for our modest luggage, and neither of us had yet used the shower poised over the lavatory. Jill reminded me of this before I went for my swim and again at breakfast. I approached the reception desk in the lobby.

'You promised me a change of room *today*. Which room will you give me?'

'Hotel is totally full, Sir. Tomorrow you can have different room.'

'Ah, no. I was promised another room today, your colleague…'

'Yes, yes, he is out of station. When he returns…'

'When will he return?'

'He is the morning duty. He will be duty reception at ten yay yem.'

'Well, we leave here at nine a.m. and my wife insists we have another room before we go. Why can't you give me another room now?'

'Hotel is full, Sir. Until guests have checked out I cannot give a room.'

'Look, we have packed our bags, which are in room 138. We will be going out at 9 o'clock. We will be back by one p.m. At that time guests will have checked out, and you will have moved our bags to our new room. Is that OK?'

'I will inform reception duty.'

'Have you got us another room?' asked Jill when she appeared in the lobby. She was carrying my hat, books, folder, water bottle and her own handbag, ready for our departure.

'Er, um, I think so. But we won't know which room it is till we get back…'

We spent a rather exhausting morning and now it was back to the hotel. 'Find out which room they've given us,' said Jill as we got off the coach. While the others made their way to their rooms to prepare for lunch, I returned to the lobby. There was the reception clerk who had made the promise.

'Ah, good. I spoke to your colleague this morning. You have changed our room?' I asked.

'Why?' was the abrupt reply.

'Why? What do you mean why? Because yesterday you gave us a terrible room with no window and you promised to change it today. Can I see the manager?'

'Ah yes. Kindly wait. I will check up.' I did wait and after some delays another man appeared from the office behind the reception.

'I am sorry to keep you waiting. You are Mr Hunt, I believe, can I help you? I am Chaudhary, the duty manager.' He presented his smartly printed business card.

'Yes I am, and you can. I have been waiting for a change of room since yesterday. They gave me…'

'I see. Are you staying at this hotel?'

'Am I staying..? Yes I am. I am the tour leader with a group of 27 British tourists; we arrived yesterday and my wife and I were given a terrible small room with no window…'

'I see, but Mr Hunt, the hotel is very full, in fact overfull.'

'Well it shouldn't be overfull. You mean you have overbooked. Already my group has had to be squeezed into too few rooms…'

'Yes, I am very sorry. Let me see what I can do. Please give me some time. Why not take your lunch and we will do our level best.'

Back in the room Jill was not placated. Our bags were still there, packed and ready to go. She had washed and changed and was sitting on the edge of the bed. She had to move so that I could get past her to the bathroom. As I peed the shower dripped on my head.

'Well?'

'I've told you. He'll fix it while we have lunch.'

A buffet lunch was available, to the accompaniment of more, rather good Indian classical music - this time played on flute and *tabla*. Or we could order sandwiches or snacks beside the pool. There would be some leisure time available - a snooze or a swim - before an afternoon expedition that I had suggested to the flower and vegetable market in the city. Rather to my surprise, another room had been found and the duty manager arranged for the luggage to be moved there. Our own leisure time was taken up by the move to another room. We walked along behind the porter to another floor in a distant part of the hotel, with bits of clothing over our arms and assorted items of hand luggage. Arrival at the room was not too promising. It was in the 'new' wing - more modern rooms, each with a small balcony overlooking the garden - but when the porter opened the door we were immediately confronted with a battered, paint covered metal step-ladder. Above it, a panel in the ceiling had been removed and hanging down was an ominous assortment of electric cables and hosepipes.

'What is this?' I asked the porter, indicating the hole above our heads.

'It is maintenance; maybe it is Yay C' he replied.

'Do you mean the A/C is not working?' I could foresee either a return to the unacceptable room, or accepting non-functioning air-conditioning.

'Engineer is working.'

'Where? Not here, he isn't. Is he up there?' I pointed up the ladder. 'No, he's not up there, and the A/C, how long has it not been working?' The question hung in the air. I called up to the void above the ladder, but there was no reply. We spent the next three nights of our stay with the step-ladder, occasional ill-timed visits from maintenance and no A/C, but a fan working and the door quite pleasantly open on to the balcony.

THE HEAD WAITER

It was quite late when Jill and I made it into the dining room. The French group had gone, the Lady B-B group had gone, and apart from our group, the room was largely empty. Most of our own group were there, no longer sitting at the familiar round tables. They seemed disgruntled and I asked if anything was wrong.

'Yes,' said Betty, 'we've been ordered to sit at this table. He was quite rude.'

'Who was rude?' The dining room staff had been perfectly pleasant and helpful up to now. Instead of the rather nice circular tables that we had dined at before, our group was sitting at one long table, previously occupied by the French group, uncomfortably close to the live music on the stage. Our old circular tables beyond the buffet were still there, quite empty.

'He says he is the head waiter, and we are to sit where he tells us! Bloody cheek!' Mary was clearly put out.

'Who? Which one?' I was puzzled. At that moment a waiter we had not seen before walked through the restaurant. He was perhaps in his fifties and walked in a rather awkward mannr, almost on his toes and leaning forward.

'That's him!' came a chorus, and we watched his jerky movement as he gave peremptory orders to some of the waiters. Clearly I was expected to do something about this, so I walked over to him.

'Excuse me. I believe you are the head waiter?'

'Sir, I am the head waiter. You wish for something? One of my staff will assist.' He turned to move away.

'Well, I would like to speak to you.'

'To me? What do you have to say to me?' It seemed to me that he was making a poor attempt at a French accent. I plucked up courage, knowing my group was watching.

'My group tells me that you told them to sit at that table. For the past two evenings we have been sitting perfectly happily at those round tables over there. Why have you moved them?'

'They must sit together. They are a group.'

'We have been sitting at those four tables up to now. Why should we move? This table is too close to the music and too close to the buffet. And they told me you spoke rudely.'

'I am not rude. I am not rude. But one said she does not wish to sit on your table and I insist. Group will sit at group table.'

I was feeling quite nervous, but could see the group had stopped talking and were watching and listening. I had to be brave. 'Well, *I* insist that they sit where they wish. And I will be reporting your rudeness to the manager.' There was applause from my group, some of whom were already moving back to the round tables. The others followed suit. I was shaking, but there were cries of 'Well done', 'Quite right' and 'What a bloody cheek!'

The head waiter walked away rather quickly, his forward lean and tip-toe stance even more pronounced.

At dinner Owen offered a curious explanation for the head waiter's behaviour. Owen was an elderly, long-retired psychiatrist, who had amused us with tales from his clinical past. Another single man, Philip, travelling in our group had been firmly but kindly rebuffed by Owen when seeking advice about his own mental condition - 'Sadly I am firmly retired, and I fear my fees were exorbitant…'

For better or worse the would-be patient did receive some forthright advice from his room companion, who had listened, as had many of us, to a good deal of Philip's complex history of relationships. On a long coach journey he burst out, rather loudly and impatiently,

'Look, Philip. We're almost the same bloody age. I calculate we have about 2000 days to live at best. I suggest you start living yours now!'

Owen had told us with a very serious voice but knowing smile that he found India fascinating, and was thinking of working on a Freudian analysis of Hinduism, and in particular the mythological origins of *Ganesh*, the elephant headed son of *Shiva*.

'Yes,' he had told us musingly, 'There's a lot of material there. I'm rather surprised it's not been done… I might do a paper on it…*Oedipus and Hindu Mythology* perhaps, or maybe just *Ganesh in the Psychiatrist's Chair*? I see a lot of scope…'

He had been unusually silent during the dining room complaints, but now said,

'Poor man, I think he is unwell.'

'Unwell! I think he is unhinged!' cried Betty.

'Ah yes, I think the illness can, indeed, manifest itself in that way,' Owen said, musingly. 'Particularly in the most serious third stage. Poor man.'

'What illness? Manifest in what way?' asked someone. We were all puzzled by his sympathetic concern.

'And I think the walk confirmed it. I remember a colleague of mine - he was a venereal consultant at the University - he told us all about it…'

'What do you mean the walk? What's his walk got to do with him ordering us about?'

'That odd gait,' explained Owen in rather hushed tones. People were leaning forward and straining to hear. 'Did you notice? Walking along on his toes and leaning forward. It is an indicator, I believe. And it is associated with bad temper… almost paranoia… I believe it may be an advanced stage.'

'Odd gait? Well yes, he certainly walks curiously. What's that got to do with bad temper?'

'Well it's only what I was told, it's not strictly speaking my field, but I think the poor man has *syphilis*.' Owen's voice was down to a whisper.

'Syphilis!' The word was shouted out by at least six or eight people and echoed round the room. The other diners put down their cutlery and looked in astonishment at our group.

A WELCOME AT THE FERNHILL PALACE

The Fernhill Palace is a strange and fascinating place. Let us say at once that the location is wonderful. It is perched high on the edge of the very scattered hill station of Ooty, with long views over blue receding Nilgiri hills. But the palace itself, at the time of this and some subsequent visits, was less than wonderful: atmospheric? certainly; interesting? undeniable; comfortable? sadly not! As palaces go it was less palatial than the Mysore Lalitha Mahal we had just come from - indeed, in the world of palaces it is in a minor league, though that is a bit picky, as the word 'palace' has come to be used all over India to describe the least likely of places. One can find 'Snack Palace' (over a tiny wooden shack at a bus station offering tea), 'Handloom Palace' (over a small shop selling plastic buckets and T shirts) and 'English Wine Palace' (selling hard liquor). And of course we have stayed at many palace hotels that were not. So to be fair, the Fernhill Palace was certainly intended to be a palace: it was built for the self-same Maharajah of Mysore whose grandiose city palace we had just seen, and in whose former guest-house we had just stayed. This one was his hot-weather retreat at the by-then well-established and very fashionable hill station of Ooty. Mysore is within an easy day's drive of Ooty - after all we had just made the journey by coach - but not so easy before motor cars. More Maharajahs were to build up in these southern hills very much more distant from their homelands than Mysore: Jodhpur in Rajasthan, and Baroda in Gujerat are very far off in the north, and the Nizam of Hyderabad had a long journey from the east, but they all built palaces up here. The name 'Fernhill' fitted in with the British residences, Rose Cottage, Dove Cottage, Summerhill and the like, and the Maharajah of Jodhpur chose 'Arranmore' for a Scotch flavour, but, like Mysore, couldn't resist adding 'Palace', as befitted the residence of a Maharajah. Arranmore eventually became a government guest house, but Fernhill (with 'palace' still attached) became our hotel. It was certainly big enough for a Maharajah's retinue and guests, and was built to accommodate all the essentials for a season in the hills: a ballroom, billiards, garages, stables and kennels for the hounds (HH was MFH from time to time, except that here they hunted jackals, rather than foxes - so perhaps he was MJH). There were enough drawing rooms and dining rooms and bedrooms and bathrooms for the house-parties, all equipped with tiled fireplaces imported from Britain in case one chose to be up here in the cold weather, or felt cold at this altitude in the hot weather.

It was that glorious time of the early evening, shortly before dusk, when we arrived. Everything looked reasonably promising from the outside and the group looked agreeably surprised. Vaguely Gothic in style, the mainly single-storied buildings were spread out over a considerable area along a ridge. The colour was a peeling pinkish terra-cotta, with the Gothic windows and crenulations picked out in discoloured white, but at first glance considerably smarter than our dear Ritz in Hyderabad. The gardens were quite well maintained with bricks, in saw-tooth arrangements edging the lawns, alternately painted in the same pink and white. Inside we felt rather more dismal: the lobby was a very large panelled room, with very high ceiling, but cold and dark, and with an ugly modern reception desk. The response of the staff, while quite polite and welcoming, was not at all reassuring as once again they appeared to have no knowledge of our booking. But with some prompting, the desk clerk made some phone calls and sent an assistant with messages into an interior room; after some time one of the staff emerged with keys which we handed to the group. I made the usual announcement about:

'If you are not happy with the room please do come back and take it up with these gentlemen…' And they did. Before all the keys were distributed Alwyn and Hugo returned to the desk.

'I think you should come and have a look at our room, it's just along here.'

'Is it no good?' I asked.

'We think you should take a look. It's just nearby. Come and see.' Alwyn and Hugo were not given to complain. Indeed they had stoically accepted some of the least acceptable of rooms and had been quite vocal in their disdain for those who complained. But I could see why they may not be satisfied when I entered their room to find a very large, high-ceilinged room, with a polished wooden floor, panelled walls and fireplace but with no furniture. Their luggage had been delivered and stood, alone, inside the door.

'Is this it?' I enquired, mystified. Surely this must be an ante-room and the bedroom must be beyond?

'Look for yourself,' they replied, so I opened another door to find a huge bathroom, the floor tiled in black and white marble and equipped with vintage bath, basin and loo. It was ready for use with towels and shampoo and toilet paper. A piece of paper across the lavatory seat said 'Sanitised for your convenience.'

'But where is the bedroom?' I asked again.

'We were hoping you would tell us'. There was no other door and with no bed, wardrobe or any other stick of furniture, we agreed that the room, although a perfectly good room, was unsuitable. Hugo and I returned together to the lobby. Jacky had arrived just ahead of us and was talking to the reception man.

She turned to us.

'I'm just telling this man about our room. I think you should see it. I don't think we can stay there'.

'Oh dear, I'll come in a moment. Just let me ask about Hugo's room'. I spoke to the lobby man.

'Excuse me. This gentleman's room has no furniture.'

'Yes, sir. Furniture is all Maharajah furniture from antique time.'

'I dare say it is, but in this room is *no* furniture. No bed, no furniture. Please go with this gentleman and look, and then provide a bedroom with *bed*.'

I went with Jacky to look at her room. It was another large room, but this time generously furnished with two large four-poster beds, high off the floor, with wooden steps on each side to enable people to climb up into bed. There were wardrobes, chests of drawers, a sofa, some upholstered chairs, bedside and other occasional tables, table lamps. On the floor was an old, worn, but possibly once-fine carpet, and in the huge window were rather glorious curtains, hanging from ceiling to floor but which curiously extended along one wall.

'I think you should see this', said Jacky, and pulled back part of the curtain to reveal a wall that was covered in grey-green and white mildew and was actually wet to the touch.

'Oh dear, that's not too good'. There was a pause.

'What was the matter with Hugo's room? Was that running with water too?'

'Well, it didn't seem to be. No, it had wooden panelling. No, it's just that it didn't have any furniture.'

'No furniture? Do you mean *no* furniture?'

'None! No bed, nothing. But the bathroom was ready, and they had their luggage delivered there…'

It was nearly six o'clock, almost dark and I still hadn't been to my room. When I arrived I found the door open and inside Jill was sitting on the high bed with a book. It was a rather grand room with another very high ceiling, elaborate draped curtains and a large, high, four-poster bed. There were tall, rather beautiful, very old glazed doors opening on to what might have been a terrace that looked out to the last glow of the setting sun and a lovely view beyond. The room smelt rather musty, but seemed so much better than those I had seen.

'Oh, this is rather good,' I said. 'One of the rooms didn't have any furn…'

'Don't sit on that chair… or that sofa.' But I already had, and clouds of dust came out of the cushions.

'I told you. I did that and couldn't breathe for a bit. That's why the door is open.'

'Oh dear, did you open these doors to the garden?' I indicated the huge pair of glazed doors.

'I tried, but they seem stuck, and rather flimsy.'

I had a go as she said this and, indeed they did seem stuck at the bottom. As I pushed, the doors were certainly rather flexible and there was some movement near the top but none at the bottom. But at a further push they did burst open but as they did so two of the panes of glass fell out and crashed on to the concrete outside. I stood for a moment and then as I tried to close the doors, three more panes fell out.

'Now what will you do?' asked Jill. 'It's cold enough in this room without holes in the door.'

'Oh dear. Er, I suppose I can ask for another room… or maybe…' I reached as high as possible to see if I could pull the curtain across. I could, but as I did so I could see that the lining was hanging in shreds and clouds more dust were shaken into the room.

'Oh dear. Well, I wonder what I'd better…'

'And, speaking of cold, the water is cold. I started to wash my hair, and it's completely cold.'

Cold water! And in cold weather. Oh dear. I knew from long experience that this was serious. To have rooms with no furniture, or rooms with damp walls, to have missing window panes - these were minor problems. To have cold water when washing hair… I returned to the lobby.

DINNER AT THE PALACE

The dining hall of the Fernhill Palace was another cavernous wood-panelled space, with a very high ceiling and a number of heads of deer and bison and jackals staring down at us from high up in the panelling. Elaborate chandeliers with just some of the bulbs alight lit the room, and two dimly-glowing one bar electric fires on the floor heated the room from each end. A long table had evidently been set for our group, some of whom were sitting there, swathed in the dark yellow hotel blankets. Nearer to the door was a smaller table with an Indian family; the portly father in a smart shiny suit and tie, a wife and a mother or mother-in-law each wearing several heavy shawls, and three small children in balaclava helmets topped with woolly hats.

'Jolly cold, isn't it?' said the gentleman, smiling as we walked past. 'Just like in your country. We enjoy very much.' The wife and grandmother did not appear to be enjoying very much. 'The rates in off-season are very much lower,' he went on, confidentially. 'That is why we are coming here. But it is too damned cold!'

'It is, and we have come to your country to avoid the cold climate at home,' I offered. 'We've just come up from Mysore which was quite warm. It is very cold in our country at this time of year…'

'We are from Bangalore', he offered. 'There the weather is very pleasant. But we have brought my mother-in-law for a jolly outing.' Mother-in-law did not look at all jolly, scowling at us, the room and the table.

'Ask uncle, "*whatisyourcountry*?" He abruptly snapped at his children. In unison they shouted back, using that familiar piercing, high pitched shriek.

'They are learning English,' explained the father. 'They are in English Medium school. Ask uncle again.'

'*Whatisyourcountry*?' shouted the children, louder than before.

'My country is England,' I dutifully replied.

'Very good. Very good country. Ask uncle "*whatisyourname*?"' demanded the father.

'*Whatisyourname*?' shouted the children.

I was obliged to play the game for a few moments, but Jill had already walked away to our table, where others of the group were arriving. Winter fleeces, scarves, even one pair of gloves, presumably worn to Heathrow and then packed away until our return, had now reappeared. Some of the group appeared to be pleasantly jolly and a bit flushed, but this did not prevent quite an outburst:

'You said we may need a cardigan, but nothing like this!'

'Why didn't you tell us? It's bloody freezing!'

There followed a 'set' dinner. Waiters brought bowls of a pale, thin soup with no really discernible flavour but which reminded me of post-war austerity soup served in Kardomah Cafés. Could it be potato? Or cabbage water? This was followed by communal bowls of rather grey-looking rice and several other dishes of brownish-looking curry which all tasted and looked very similar. The one distinguishing feature was that some of them had large and sometimes splintered bones in the sauce.

'What is this?' I asked the waiter. He wore evening dress with black bow tie, but also a green woolly hat.

'Non-veg,' he replied.

'What kind of non-veg?'

'This is the mutton curry, sir.'

'And this one? What is this one?'

'Veg,' was his terse answer.

'What kind of veg?'

'Mix veg,' he replied.

There was also a very thin *dhal* (lentils), which was certainly the best thing on offer, and the meal was rounded off with a dessert of what may have been blancmange, but was proudly announced by the waiter as 'Souffle', pronounced as 'Soofal'. It was one of the worst meals eaten in India, and we were staying here for two days. But the evening was relieved to some extent by copies of the hotel brochure that Catherine handed around. She had discovered them while asking for information at reception, and as she handed them round, she and Val and some others were almost crying with laughter. Obviously the leaflet had been printed some time ago, perhaps when the Fernhill Palace had first opened as a hotel, aiming with great foresight, though perhaps over-ambitiously, at what was to become the very lucrative markets of corporate entertainment and Indian honeymoon clients. The copies were rather dog-eared, the colour printing not very accurate and the text and pictures had an unintentional 'shadow' or double image, giving it a lurid and blurred appearance. Nonetheless, the cover had a picture of the hotel exterior, looking quite spruce. Inside, there was a conference room, labelled '*State of Art Conference Facility for Live-Wire Business men*'. Another picture showed a narrow passage with a sloping glass ceiling. Most of us had walked along this dingy corridor, noticing the cracked glass, the green mildew and the creeping outdoor plants that were making their way inside. The brochure labelled it as

'*Lover's Lane for the Honeymoon Conscious*'. The lane was certainly only wide enough for lovers in very close embrace; dark and dingy enough for a certain seclusion, but nowadays the lovers would be in danger of falling glass.

Fortunately the brochure distracted us from the reality of the '*Tongue-tickling Treats*' among the '*Grandest fare of them all*' on offer with '*Sunlit graced service*' in the '*Romantic candle-lit Grand Royal Banquet Hall.*'

DINNER AT THE CLUB

Hugo approached me after breakfast. 'Dear boy,' he said, 'D'you mind if we take an evening *orf* this evening?'

'No, no, of course…'

'Thought we'd go along to the club. Years since we were there. Used to come up here from time to time when we were in Bombay.'

'Oh! Were you a member? When were you in Bombay?' I had heard about the Ooty Club. Strictly members only. I was wondering how Hugo, even if he'd been a member, could get in now.

'Well yes. Left in '47. In Bombay I was in the Yacht Club and I've kept up the membership'. I remembered that Hugo was from Lymington and from the sailing fraternity. No doubt he had membership there too. 'There's a reciprocal arrangement up here, you see,' he went on. 'Thought we might go along for dinner, see how the old place has changed. Matter of fact Alwyn and I were wondering if you might like to come along with us - we can take a couple of guests. Why don't you and Jill join us? Dinner at the club? How about it?'

It was tempting: dinner at the club! After all, dinner in the hotel had been really dreadful. But should we leave the group to solve the inevitable problems that would arise? Log Fires? Wet Beds? Awful Meals? Was Jean still trying to go back to Mysore? What if...? But dinner at the club? It was certainly tempting. I was reminded of the only other time we had been invited to dinner at a club in India. It was in Madras in the early days of our first arrival, when Peter, a friendly and very helpful official at The British Council had learned of our 'plight' staying at the University Guest House and invited us to dinner at the club.

'Can I invite you and your wife to dinner at the Madras Club?' he had asked on the 'phone. 'If we dine on the terrace, there's no need to wear a jacket and tie. Just a shirt and slacks will be OK. Pick you up around seven for a drink? Oh by the way will duck be OK? It's Tuesday, so it's duck on the menu…'

We had only been in Madras for about two weeks, feeling my way at work and experiencing the Guest House food - the same fish curry every lunch and every evening for two weeks, and with the prospect of only the same for the next *three months*. 'It's duck on the menu' was certainly an added attraction. So started what turned out to be a very welcome and rather bizarre evening. Peter collected us in his small car and drove - rather bravely, we thought - through the Madras traffic and out into the suburbs, through the gates of the

Club, along the sweeping drive set in lawns, past the grand 1830's portico. We went into the building to the library, with battered leather club chairs, newspaper reading stands (empty), standard lamps but with no members. Apparently we were not supposed to enter without jackets, but Peter said the servants would not mind us looking around as there was no-one there. There were several servants who stood around, white uniformed, looking a little anxious, evidently waiting for us to leave.

'Lucky you're a member,' I offered. 'We're very grateful to be here. Have you dined at the University Guest House?

'No I haven't had that pleasure, but I have heard about it. Are you really staying there for three months? No-one has ever stayed there beyond a couple of days so far as I know. Oh, by the way, I'm only an associate member here. The Council gets us associate membership when we're posted. Here everyone's an associate member because there's only supposed to be 100 members, but most of them retired or left India and there are quite a lot still living in Cheltenham or Bath who keep up their membership. Of course, there are quite a number of Indian members nowadays, but they don't come often.'

We went out onto the terrace where a few tables were laid for dinner under more standard lamps. We were the only diners. Peter mentioned again that duck would be the menu.

'Duck!' said Jill 'Yes, Richard told me. Duck! How lovely. We've had nothing but the same fish curry every day since we arrived!' So, on the terrace, lit by standard lamps, served by waiters with white gloves and white uniforms, we ate a kind of stewed duck with brown gravy and potatoes in a temperature of around 80 degrees.

'Well?' said Hugo, bringing me back to Ooty with a start, 'How about it? 'Fraid we chaps will have to dress up a bit. Frocks for the ladies, jacket and tie for the chaps…'

'Er, well, I'm just wondering if I ought to stay with the group and make sure everything's all right,' I said, knowing I would make no difference. I was also wondering about my wardrobe in the light of Hugo's comments - no jacket and no tie - but the thoughts of irritations over temple music, leaking water bottles, and anxiety over Jean in a taxi, all hung in the air. Perhaps I should stay?

'Wouldn't you like to ask any of the others?' I asked. Hugo and Alwyn had often sat with Jacky and David at meals and they had sometimes had drinks together, so I suggested 'Wouldn't Jacky and David like to go with you?'

'Well, I dare say they may, but we thought we'd ask you. But if you feel you'd better stay with the others, we can ask them.'

That evening, while some of us were having a drink in the garden of the Fernhill Palace, Alwyn appeared, ready for the expedition to The Ooty Club. Alwyn was a tall, statuesque woman and she wore a voluminous kind of floor-length kaftan - something she had bought earlier in the trip back in Mahabalipuram. It was a vivid blue, but decorated with quite large white and orange flowers and other motifs. She wore several necklaces and rings and carried off the whole ensemble with a very confident air.

'Well, we're *orf*, dear boy. Sorry not to be taking you, but Jacky jumped at it. Ah here's Hugo.'

Hugo's appearance was very different. He was quite a small man and now looked rather like an elderly 'Just William' of Richmond Crompton fame. He certainly had a jacket - in a dark blue - but it looked very crumpled, ill-fitting and rather dusty. He also had a tie - also in a dark blue, perhaps with some kind of club motif - but it was also crumpled and awry, with vestiges of soup or porridge on it. It was tied round an equally crumpled shirt collar. Light coloured trousers and old shoes completed the dress, but Hugo was as confident as ever.

'*Orf* to the club!' he called to our small group of drinkers cheerily. 'You're not missing much: food was pretty awful in the old days, but then it wasn't much to cheer about here! We'll compare notes when we get back.'

In contrast to Hugo and Alwyn, David and Jacky made a very smart appearance. David wore a crisp blue and white striped shirt with a yacht club tie, smartly creased navy blue trousers and polished black shoes. Over his arm he carried a navy cardigan. Jacky looked the picture of 'going to the club': skirt and jacket, handbag and shoes to match. Their car was waiting for them and with smiles and waves they set off in high glee for their evening-at-the-club.

We continued to drink; some had not yet showered and changed and dinner was fairly late. Our hotel meal was a slight improvement on the previous evening - an improvement that almost certainly had nothing to do with our complaints. It was not approaching good - but at least not awful - and it did take a long time to serve, so the party was breaking up and some had already left when the dinner-at-the-club foursome came into the dining room. Jacky was laughing, David looked a little crest-fallen and the other two showed their usual *sang-froid*, with distant enigmatic smiles on their faces.

'I must tell you', said Jacky, addressing the company, 'We've had a hilarious evening: David was refused entry to the club because he was improperly dressed!' She could hardly get the words out with laughing.

'David was?' said several.

'He's the smartest of anyone.'

'Not properly dressed? - David?'

David looked mildly embarrassed. He was now wearing the navy cardigan and looked every inch the English gentleman. Hugo looked on, crumpled as ever, with an innocent smile.

'No,' said Jacky, 'Look at them: Hugo's got a jacket, and David's cardigan just would not do!'

'Well,' said Hugo, 'I did wonder when we set *orf.* After all, dear boy, rules is rules. You see,' addressing the rest of us, 'The chap was simply not wearing a jacket.'

Jacky butted in, 'Anyhow, at first they weren't going to let him in at all, but Hugo had a word and they looked him up in the register. Finally they said we could go in, but couldn't eat in the dining room. *They said we could eat in the nursery*!'

There were howls of laughter from the rest of us, but I remembered our Madras Club experience and felt sympathy for David. Nursery? We had at least dined on the terrace.

'Was the food good?' someone asked, 'Ours wasn't so bad this evening, but it did take an age to come.'

'Oh, the food was frightful,' said Alwyn, 'Some totally unrecognizable soup, then a brown stew of bones, uncooked boiled potatoes and overcooked cabbage. I think the pudding was the same pink blancmange left over from here last night…'

'Yes, it was pretty disgusting,' Jacky was dying to tell the story, 'but it suited David pretty well - just like school, he said - but I asked for Indian food. They didn't seem to know what I meant. "Indian food? Indian food?" they kept asking. I said "Yes, Indian food… you know, curry". "Curry Madam?" they said, "we do not serve curry in this establishment!"'

'Sounds like nursery food in the nursery,' laughed Betty, 'Didn't the people in the dining room have Indian food? Presumably most of the members must be Indian? Can't you eat curry if you have a jacket?'

'We'll never know,' said Jacky, 'There was no-one there.'

'What?' People were incredulous.

'I tell you there was no-one there.'

'Nobody?' a chorus from the rest of us.

'Nobody! Only the servants. We were the only ones there the whole evening!'

HOT WATER AT THE FERNHILL PALACE

'The water in my room is cold.' The receptionist looked up, calm and not surprised.

'What is room number, sir?'

'Number 37. And some glass is broken in the window…'

'Yes, yes, we will on the geyser at 6 p.m.'

'It is now six-fifteen.'

'Yes, hot water is just coming…'

I had little faith in the water coming now. Geysers usually take a long time to heat up, and the antiquated equipment and general maintenance of the Fernhill Palace hadn't done much for my confidence.

'Perhaps it is, but my wife wants hot water now. She has been trying to wash her hair, so please send a bucket of hot water now.' Buckets of hot water had quite often been the saving of our marriage when it came to washing - especially hair-washing - in several Indian hotels on our travels, and to be fair, the hotels had usually obliged. I remembered a previous visit Jill and I had made to Ooty, when we had spent a couple of very cold nights in a cheap guest house in the town, so I now said, 'And do you have hot water bottles for all the guests?' remembering that it was hot water bottles, rather than buckets, that had saved our marriage on that occasion.

'No sir, we are having water bags only.'

'Bags? I mean for the beds; to put into the bed to make it warm.'

'Yes, sir, bags for the bed. We will supply after the dinner.' This was very good news, and rather unexpected. We were a big group, and I had seen other guests in the hotel. Could they have enough bags?

'You have enough bags?'

'Oh yes, sir, we have enough.'

Later that evening, after the long drive up from the plains and the minor problems of settling in, and a deeply disappointing dinner, I for one was ready for bed. At the end of the meal we were very pleased to see two hotel servants distributing the hot water bags.They were conventional rubber hot water bottles, some even with fleecy covers. This was very cheering to the members of the group who gathered round to receive them.

'Well, this is better…'

'Just what we need…'

'Who would have thought…' and the hot bags were pushed under the blankets people had wrapped around themselves and carried off to their rooms. Like the others, I took the two bags offered to us and put them in the bed when we reached the room. The buckets of hot water were now quite cool, so while Jill fiddled around doing some repacking, I sorted out a few papers ready for tomorrow, undressed and started to get into bed. Pulling back the top sheet revealed that it was only a partial sheet, covering only about one third of the bed and it more or less came away from the bed as I pulled it back. I pulled the now exposed blankets back to find the next section of sheet, but sadly this revealed a large patch of damp, warm, bedding where the water had soaked into my side of the bed. I pulled out the hot water bottle to find that the neck of the bottle was badly perished and partly detached. When carried upright it was OK, but when laid down in the bed the water very quickly found its way into the sheets and mattress.

Back at reception, three more of the group had placed their leaking hot water bags on the counter. Jackie, wrapped in a dark yellow blanket was laughing.

'It could only happen here! You can't help laughing! I spent half-an-hour before dinner in their linen cupboard punching pillows to try and find one that was not like bricks. One was a bit better than the others, but would you believe? When I got back to the room with the water bottle I put the pillow into the bed with the water bottle on it to get warm, and now the only remotely usable pillow is soaked!'

'Well, never mind the bloody pillow, it's my bloody mattress that's soaked, which is not so funny!' said Ian.

A house keeping man was approaching with his arms filled with sheets, and the next hour was spent supervising the turning over of mattresses, remaking of beds, with, in most cases, several sheets required to cover the area of that would usually require one. Certainly the beds were large, but the sheets were not. What was to have been an early night became rather a late one. Ian, unlike several of the others, was not amused by the turn of events.

'It's bloody cold, the place is a disgrace, the food was terrible - it's a good job we brought those rolls from breakfast in the last place and we'd still got some of our sardines from home! And now we're up half the night changing bloody mattresses and bed sheets! Christ almighty! I can't imagine what you are all giggling about! I just want a decent night's sleep.'

LOG WALLAH

In the lobby Catherine, Val and some others were at the desk, wrapped in hotel blankets, demanding extra bedding and that the fires were lit in the rooms. The mellow sunset was fading and the temperature was certainly falling.

'Yes, yes, extra blanket and fireman will light fire at six p.m.'

'But we're cold now!' they cried in unison, 'We want blankets and a fire. It's nearly six o'clock and we want a fire now!'

At well past seven o'clock it was seriously cold. Jill and I were getting ready to go for dinner when there was a knock at our bedroom door. A voice called loudly,

'Housekeeping, fire, fire.'

'My god!' cried Jill, fearing the worst. She had not overheard the earlier conversation in the lobby. I opened the door. It wasn't an announcement that the hotel was on fire, but that a fire was to be lit. There, in the corridor stood a man with a handful of twigs and a plastic bottle; behind him was a small wooden cart on wheels, rather like a baby's pram, with more twigs. He repeated,

'Fire, fire. I am housekeeping log man.' Despite the very large size of the room, our fireplace was a very small, narrow, tiled affair - the kind that could be seen in late Victorian or Edwardian bedrooms in England and in the hills stations of the British Raj. The iron grate held a few long thin twigs, each the thickness of a finger, which had been pushed up the chimney, so that the fireplace was filled with thin vertical sticks about two feet long, disappearing from view. Our fireman approached the hearth with his plastic bottle filled with what I learned was petrol, which he poured on the sticks and then set them alight, leaping back as he did so. They twigs flared into life and roared up the chimney, giving a glorious, if rather alarming blaze. I asked,

'Do you have any logs? These won't last long.'

He had put the few sticks he carried into the room in a fire bucket in the hearth. He pointed to these and said,

'Here is log for more fire.'

'No, I mean *logs* - thicker logs, you know - *firewood*, logs to make the fire last…' But he had gone; he had left the room and we could hear him knocking on another room, calling 'Fire, fire…' After a few minutes all the sticks collapsed into the hearth and continued to burn for a few more minutes before going out. The handful of twigs in the 'log' container in the hearth were too long to lie across the dying embers, and too flexible to break into shorter pieces, so it was very difficult to get them to light. I went to the door and by good luck the fire-man was returning along the corridor.

'The fire is out,' I said.

'More log. I bring more log,' he replied. I called at the room opposite, where I knew Cynthia and Betty were. They were sitting close to the last vestiges of their fire.

'The fire-man tells me he will bring more log,' I told them.

'Oh, don't worry, we are warmed from within,' said Cynthia. 'Would you care for a Scotch whisky?'

'How kind,' I said.

'Do bring Jill, I am sure she would take a whisky?' Cynthia poured out large measures.

'I'm sure she will.' As I opened the door the fire-man was pushing his small handcart along the corridor. It was loaded with more twigs.

'Good,' I said to him. 'Please bring to this room, and also that room there,' pointing to our room opposite. Jill did not join us - her hair was still wet and she was sorting out layers of the warmest clothes in our luggage. I took her a glass of Cynthia's whisky and returned to Cynthia and Betty's room where we watched the new blaze while sipping whisky. When I returned to our room the second fire had gone out again, some sticks had fallen forward and were smoking into the room. Luckily Jill was still in the bathroom. For the rest of the evening before dinner the poor log man was racing up and down our corridor with his log cart, occasionally replenishing his supplies, while people came to their doors calling,

'Log wallah!'

'Fire, fire!,'

'More wood, more fire.'

At dinner Cynthia said,

'That poor log-man, he worked so hard, running up and down replenishing our fire. We were very grateful, and I am afraid we may have rewarded him rather over-generously.'

'Even if the fire only lasted for five minutes,' added Betty.

'Fire? What fire? We didn't have a fire!' chimed in several of the others.

'Oh, we did. He came to us with more wood. Mind you, they only lasted…'

There was a general hubbub of protests from those who had no fire, those who only had one fire, counteracted by others who boasted three and even four fires. Someone asked if there had been any hot water. I remained silent.

OFF THE ELECTRICITY

During the late night disturbances caused by bed-wetting I needed to walk up and down several corridors and enter several rooms. From some of them I could hear the far distant but insistent sound of temple music - both instrumental and vocal - the vocal bits sung in that high-pitched, penetrating, rather nasal female voice that is a feature of some Indian music. The verses were interspersed with short bursts of orchestral interludes that were also very strident. Clearly all this was coming from a loudspeaker, but we couldn't tell where it was coming from. Back in our room, with the missing window panes and drawn curtains, it was a little louder, but Jill was already asleep and I found the music quite soothing and soon fell asleep myself. Waking occasionally, the music was still playing, but I had a good night.

Next morning the music was still audible and on our way to breakfast I encountered a rather grumpy Ian.

'Christ Almighty! There you are. What the hell is all that noise? I haven't had a wink of sleep; it's been going on all night.'

'Oh dear, I'm sorry about that. I think it's…'

'I couldn't stand it. Got up in the night to find out what's going on and tripped over some bloody bundles in the corridor. Turned out that they were hotel servants sleeping in the bloody corridor for Christ's sake! What kind of a place do you think you've…'

'Oh dear.'

'One of them got up, so I tried to ask him what was going on. Couldn't understand what he was saying, but something about a goddess? I ask you…'

We were near the rear door to the hotel, from where the music was louder. The glazed doorway opened out on to a terrace and the lovely view across the hills. It was a beautiful crisp morning, the sun shining. Ian was working himself into a rage.

'Ask him', snapped Ian. 'Ask this fellow.' He was pointing to an elaborately uniformed security guard standing outside on the terrace.

'I'll try to find out…' I offered lamely.

The music was louder as we went out of the door and seemed to be coming from the direction of the view - still loud and high pitched and piercing, but a long way off.

'Excuse me', I addressed the guard. 'Do you know what is that music and where is it coming from?'

'Music is from temple, sir. It is new temple they are inaugurating.'

'I knew it!' snapped Ian, 'Some bloody temple. It's been going on all night.'

'Yes, sir', said the guard, 'Night and day also they will sing.'

'What? All day as well?' Ian was becoming even more enraged.

'Yes, sir, for seven nights maybe they will chant the name of god. It is Hindu temple; this is what they do.'

'*Seven nights*? *SEVEN NIGHTS*? What do you mean seven nights? You mean they will do that tonight? As well? I can't have that!'

'Yes, sir. It is what they do. They chant the name of god.'

'For seven nights? Christ almighty! How can they chant a name for seven nights?'

'No sir, It is not Christ they are chanting. It is Hindu temple. They are chanting Hindu gods only. There are so many names. But Christ also is having many names. He is Jesus also, he is Messiah also, he is Good Shep…'

'I know what he is for Christ's sake! You don't have to tell me about Christ, for Christ's sake! But they can't go about…'

'And Hindu gods are having so many of names, sir. Shiva, he is having so many - maybe 1008 names, and Durga also she is having 88 names, and Lakshmi, she also is having…'

'Look!' Ian was now shouting, red in the face. 'I don't care how many bloody names they are having, I can't have that bloody racket going on all night.'

He turned to me. 'We can't have that! Our room's just there. Betty's furious. We can't have that!'

'You do not like?' asked the security man. He sounded calm, almost dead-pan.

'No, I do not like.' Ian was very red in the face. 'Where the hell is this bloody temple? Surely to god…'

'It is there only; in the valley.' The man pointed vaguely over the escarpment in the direction of the blue receding hills. 'You don't like?'

'In the valley? It's bloody miles! How the hell do they make that much noise?' We were now receiving a piercing instrumental interlude on a wailing, reeded instrument.

'They have electric loudspeakers, sir. The electric is coming from here only…'

'How do you mean "from here"?

'Yes, sir, from here only. There is no electric in that valley. Only from here. The Hindu priests asked for electric cable for the inauguration.' Our guard pointed overhead to what was evidently a temporary thin electric cable disappearing on poles in the direction of the music.'

'You mean you are - the hotel is - supplying the electricity to *allow* that dreadful noise?'

'Yes, sir. It is from here only.'

'But this is supposed to be a bloody hotel, for Christ' sake. People are supposed to bloody *sleep* here…'

'Sir, if you do not like, I can *off* the electricity.'

'You can?' Ian and I spoke together in astonished unity.

'Oh, yes, sir. From here I can make it off.'

'You can?' we repeated. But I was concerned - I knew a bit about the sanctity of temple worship, the auspicious nature of an inauguration. A mere hotel could have no say in opposition to the celebrations of a temple.

'But won't you mind? If it is for the Goddess… Won't the people be upset? Won't you be upset?'

'I won't mind, sir! I can definitely *off* the electricity.'

'Really?

'No, sir. I don't mind. You see, I am Roman Catholic.'

AN IMPERIAL BREAKFAST

Today the Imperial Hotel is very grand indeed. Following a long drawn out, no-expenses-spared renovation it is the essence of a luxury hotel - supremely comfortable, with wonderful service and elegant and tasteful décor. It even retains much of the charm of the colonial days of its beginnings - with its public rooms and even bedrooms hung with a fabulous collection of prints and drawings of the 19th and early 20th centuries the envy of many museums. It is certainly the place where anyone wanting great comfort and a wonderful location in New Delhi, and with nostalgia for a by-gone age, would want to stay. So it is a bit unreasonable to suggest that the dear old Imperial has gone a little too far in the direction of grand-luxe by following the fashion for the make-over at the hands of the interior designer. Now the sumptuous, no-doubt old fashioned, beautiful flower arrangements in huge vases have been replaced with sculptural shapes of flowers brutalised into contorted modernism by a floral artist regularly flown in from France; the elegant old white painted cane furniture on the terrace has been replaced with new that is stark, black and functional. The crockery is fashionably square, replacing the familiar round plates with the Imperial crest, and the drinking glasses are - would you believe - coloured and not upright! A *Chanel* shop dominates and distorts the symmetry of the wonderful lobby... But why am I making such a fuss? It is a lovely place to stay - if you can afford to.

The Imperial was not always like this. On our first visit in 1979 it was threadbare. On our last night in India, after a three month stay in a very spartan university guest house, we treated ourselves to dinner there. Sadly we found a band attempting The Beatles and other 70s music not very well in the dining room; the food was non-descript; the service shoddy. But the place had great atmosphere and later, when planning our first group tour to India, I thought it would be rather wonderful to stay there. We needed somewhere with history, that reminded us we were in India, not in a high rise anonymous place. In some ways even the first group visit was wonderful, and even not so expensive, and we have taken groups there through thick and thin - even through the 'Great Renovations' over the past 30 years.

To give you an idea of what it was like early on, let me tell you about Jacky's breakfast. The trouble is that all these little anecdotes sound as if we are constantly *complaining* about poor service or inadequate facilities. That is not really the case, because in reality the incidents are what we so much enjoyed - certainly what we remember. The truly kindly and well-meaning staff are so endearing in their efforts to please and their inability to understand our intolerance, or our failure to understand our cultural differences, that our heart goes out to them. We are after all, visitors to *their* country.

Anyway, Jacky had decided she did not want to go sightseeing with us that morning, and related her story to us afterwards. No, she would have a morning of real leisure, reading in the garden in peace and quiet after a solitary breakfast on the terrace. So she came down towards the end of the allotted breakfast time after we had all gone. Alone at her table, in the sunshine, with her newspaper (delivered to the bedroom - even in those days) she was approached by a waiter.

'He came up to me and said,

"Good morning Madam. Do you wish for breakfast?" Imagine! That's what he said! Why else was I sitting at a breakfast table? So I said to him,

"Of course, yes I would like breakfast."

"Group has finished breakfast, Madam."

"Group may have finished but I haven't started mine,"

"But Madam, for group breakfast we have served already and…"

"Look! I was not with the group. I am with the group - that is I am a member of the group, but this morning I am not and I have not had my breakfast…" I can tell you even I was getting confused, but the poor man… Anyway I told him,

"Yes, I would like some breakfast please. I would like porridge and some scrambled eggs, Some tea, some toast…" He hummed and haahed for a moment and then he came out with,

"I am very sorry Madam, but in the Imperial breakfast there is the porridge *or* the yegs," and he produced this very dog-eared and grubby menu.

"There is Imperial breakfast, Madam, or Continental breakfast, or North Indian breakfast, or South Indian…"

Well, of course, I wasn't having any of that.

"Nonesense! I would like the porridge and the scrambled eggs, please. And some tea and toast. Oh, and some fruit."

"But Madam, fruit is with Continental only, and Imperial is allowing porridge or yeg only!"

"Look! I've been travelling with this group for the past three weeks and every day we have porridge AND eggs."

(I must interrupt: this was not quite true, occasionally we had porridge and eggs, but porridge was only rarely available. Jacky resumed:)

"So please bring me the porridge and the scrambled eggs. I like the eggs only lightly scrambled. Not cooked too much. Do you understand?" He nodded and said "Just one moment please" and disappeared for a few moments. When he came back he said

"Yes, Madam, but the porridge will take too much of time." I told him,

"I don't mind about the time. I am taking the morning off, so I have plenty of time, Please bring my order!"

"But also, Madam, kitchen is saying porridge is not of best quality in the market, and will take so much of time!"

"It's perfectly clear that you don't want to bring my order. Can I see the manager please?"

"No, no, Madam. Kitchen in-charge is in charge. He is saying..."

"Well please tell kitchen in-charge that I always have porridge in India, I don't believe this story about not best quality, and would he please prepare some porridge. I would like it before my eggs. I don't mind if it takes a little time to prepare it, I can read my paper. How long will it take?"

"In-charge says it will take at least ten minutes, Madam."

"Ten minutes is perfectly acceptable. Please bring me some fresh fruit, and I will sit here and read my newspaper."

The poor fellow went away very downcast, no doubt to face the wrath of the kitchen that thought it had finished with breakfast, let alone having to make porridge. But within five minutes or so he was back with a plate of porridge. He put it down on the table, looking ever so sad.

"Here is porridge, Madam."

"There you are," I told him. "Thank you. That's very good! Here's the porridge, and it's only taken five minutes. You said it would take ten minutes. It's only taken half the time." He was very slow to respond, sounding sadder than ever.

"But the porridge is only half-cooked, Madam."

RUNNING REPAIRS AT THE IMPERIAL

I suppose if I were running a hotel I would want it to be in good repair and at the same time try to maximise the profits. But would I wish to offer rooms unsuitable to clients - damaged or unfinished rooms, for example? Ah, but wait! that is unfair; in a big hotel I suppose it is quite possible that only some people may know about which parts are undergoing repairs, and haven't told others who allocate the rooms? I hasten to say that we can find hotels with unfinished building work going on all over the world. I have a builder friend who used to go on cheap holidays in Spain *in order to watch* other builders working in his hotel.

'I could just stand in the pool, doing nothing, with a beer, watching someone else doing all the work. Lovely.' He was deeply disappointed if there wasn't a building project. I suspect he was unusual - his wife didn't enjoy it - and on our group tours running repairs usually meant trouble.

I mentioned that our dear old Imperial underwent a very long and very major refurbishment. It was really necessary as the old air-conditioning system smelled very badly and the place had become very frayed around the edges. But all the way through the refurbishment the hotel kept going. This didn't usually impinge too much on our comfort, but the day before we were leaving India to go home, two or three ladies came to me to ask if I had seen Gerry's room. I had not.

'Well, you should. It's not fair!'

'It's positively unsafe. His breathing's not good anyway.' Gerry, I should say, at 89 was one of our oldest members, not only of this group, but of all our groups. He was only overtaken by Melanie, 91, and Sandy, 92, later on. I also knew that Gerry was not coming home with us next day. He had plans to stay on in India to meet some friends, but he hadn't told me the full details.

'Oh dear, what's wrong with his room?' I asked. 'I 'specially got him a room on the ground floor.' Many of our rooms were looking very spruce, newly decorated, very nicely furnished… The Imperial was really coming along.

'The damp! It's terrible. You'd better go and see. We don't think he's at all well.'

Gerry was in the room, and he didn't sound so good - wheezy and a bit frail. Half of the room had been newly re-wallpapered in a pretty, traditional paper. The other two walls had been stripped in readiness, but obviously abandoned because of the severe damp. From floor to ceiling there was grey and green mildew, with black irregular stains. There was a strong smell of damp. The slightest touch on the walls produced green, moist stains. Some of the new wallpaper was blistering and peeling away. Yet the rest of the room was properly equipped - polished wooden floor, oriental carpet, well furnished, comfy bed. Gerry was bemused by the whole thing and couldn't see what all the fuss was about.

'Don't like to complain,' he said, 'I assumed all the rooms were like this. It is a bit musty and I find it gets on my chest…' His friends had come along with me for the inspection.

'You can't stay here, Gerry!' said one.

'You ought to get some compensation,' said another.

'Well, I don't know about that. Actually, the thing is I have to stay an extra night in Delhi after you've gone home, so I have to move to another hotel tomorrow anyway. I don't suppose another night here will kill me!'

I felt it better to avoid this possibilty; we had been at the hotel for three nights and tonight was our last. I asked to see the manager. (I should interject that this particular manager was not there for long. The Imperial refurbishment went through several stages, and included refurbishing management.)

'You wish to see me? How can I help you?'

'I hope you can. Have you seen Room 105?'

'No, not recently. Is there a problem?'

'Yes, there is. One of my clients is in it. He's 89 years old, and the walls are running with damp.'

'I'm sure that cannot be the case. I will check and let you know.' By now, if you haven't experienced this response yourself, you will know that it is was one I have met very often. It is presumably taught in schools of hotel management.

'There's no need to check and let me know. I do know. I have just come from that room. Do you have a moment to come and look for yourself?'

'Actually that is the duty of my floor manager, I'll just find out if he is free.'

'Well you are the General Manager, and I am talking to you. If you don't mind giving me a moment more of your time, the room is quite nearby. I think you will find it interesting to see it yourself.'

He did come. He walked angrily with me along the two corridors until we were back at Gerry's room. Gerry and the three ladies were still there. He looked at the walls in silence.

'Damp, I think you will agree?' I said.

'Well, there does seem to have been some kind of slip up. Yes, the room is unfinished.'

'I agree, and it should not have been allocated to my group, or anyone else for that matter.' The poor GM was not pleased to be chastised. Presumably that was his floor manager's role.

'I will see if we can change this room,' he said, grimly. 'If you will please give me some time.'

'Certainly,' I said, 'but there is the question of compensation. You have been paid for three nights for a room that should not have been sold, and this gentleman has put up with these conditions. The damp has affected his breathing. What do you propose?'

'We will move him to a very nice room. I am sure he will be more comfortable.'

'I'm sure he will, but that will be for only one night, so you will have been paid for three nights for a room that should not have been occupied.'

'I will look into it and let you know.'

Gerry was moved within an hour or so to another perfectly acceptable room with no damp walls. We discussed the matter of how we may ask for compensation, but Gerry was more concerned about the extra night he wanted to stay on in Delhi.

'Of course, I couldn't afford to stay on *here* after you'd gone, so I was going to look for a cheaper hotel. But I wonder if they'd let me stay here for another night?' I wondered too, and we went on to discuss a possible strategy.

After several hours I had still not heard from the manager, so I asked to see him again, and took Gerry along.

'Can I help you?'

'Yes, thank you. You said you would look into the matter of this gentleman who was in room 105 and get back to me.'

'Yes, I requested he was moved to another room. Is it OK?'

'The room is OK, but we were discussing some compensation for his inconvenience.'

'I regret it is not hotel policy to provide compensation.'

'Well that seems a pity, as the hotel has made an unfair profit from the situation.'

'But we have given the gentleman an *upgraded* room.' Gerry now spoke up.

'It was certainly upgraded from the unfinished room, but didn't look any different to me, except it isn't running with damp. In any case, I didn't want an '*upgrade*'.

'No,' I butted in, 'He wants compensation. However, I have a suggestion. This gentleman needs to stay one extra night after our group departs tomorrow; why don't you allow him to stay in the room for that night?'

'I am afraid that will not be possible. If the gentleman pays the tariff, then we will see what we can do.'

'I wasn't thinking of paying,' said Gerry very firmly. 'You've put me in a room you shouldn't have given for three nights and now you're asking me to *pay* for the extra night? *Pay*? You should be paying me.'

'I am sorry, sir, but you cannot stay free of charge. It is hotel policy…'

'Is it?' Gerry was now warming to the task. '*Is it*? Well let me tell you this, if I can't stay in my room for the night, I will sleep on the sofa in reception. See how you like that! I'll shift all my stuff and unpack in your lobby.'

'No, sir, that is not possible, we cannot allow…'

'What are you going to do about it? I'm going to be 90 in a month's time. Are you going to get your staff to carry me outside and put me on the pavement?'

Gerry came to see us off next morning. He was smiling broadly. The duty manager was also in the lobby. He was not smiling broadly.

'Goodbye, you lot,' said Gerry. 'I bet you're all feeling jealous. An extra night at The Imperial! How about that!'

A FAREWELL DINNER AT THE IMPERIAL

Many of our tours in North India started and ended in Delhi, where we were lucky enough to stay at The Imperial. And on our last evenings there we always tried to arrange a farewell dinner *outdoors* - relishing a dinner under the stars on a warm evening, contrasting this with what we could expect back in England in February or March. Nowadays the hotel is so grand that we don't have quite the freedom we had in the old days. We do still arrange dinner on the terrace, but in the old days we could have a table set up for us down on the lawns, in privacy, beyond the terrace. Gathering for a drinks party beforehand in one of our rooms, finishing off the last of the duty free, or the more recently acquired drink, we always went into the garden to eat, tempering our high spirits with a certain sadness that our Indian trip was coming to an end.

The sadness was a little more than usual on this occasion, as quite late the previous evening, after we had retired to our rooms, our phone had rung.

'Hello?'

'Oh, Richard. This is Elsie, I'm sorry to ring you so late, but I'm afraid Noreen's had an accident. I thought I'd better tell you.'

'Yes, of course. Oh dear, what's happened?' Elsie and Noreen were sharing a room.

'Well, it was very foolish of us. I feel I'm to blame. Poor Noreen. We went out for a stroll after dinner - just to let the dinner go down, you know - so we thought we would just walk up a little way towards Connaught Place. And poor Noreen fell down a hole in the pavement!'

'Oh dear! Was there much damage?' The pavement outside the Imperial had a lot of holes in those days - quite big holes, and it wasn't well lit.

'I'm afraid there was. We've been to the hospital and they've put her leg in plaster. We don't really know if she's broken her ankle, or torn something, but the poor thing is in a lot of pain.'

'Oh heavens! What a shame! Does she need any pain-killers, or anything?'

'No, no. She's got everything. The hospital arranged lots of things from the pharmacy.'

'I'd better come along to your room to see her…'

'No, there's no need, and we've got her into bed. The hospital was very good, and the hotel people were very kind. But she won't be coming out with us tomorrow. That's why I phoned you really - to let you know. And I may stay with her, too.'

At about eight next morning the phone rang again.

'Hello, Richard, it's Elsie. I'm sorry to ring you so early.'

'Ah, yes, I was about to ring you. How is she? Did she manage to sleep?'

'I'm afraid there's some more bad news. She wanted to go to the loo this morning, and was *hopping* across the room, but she fell forward, *and now she's broken her wrist*! The hotel has just arranged to get her back to the hospital. We're leaving in a few minutes.'

'Oh, crikey! The poor thing!

We didn't see Noreen until lunch time, when we were back after a morning's sightseeing and she and Elsie back from the hospital. She was back in her room, sitting propped up with pillows on her bed, her leg in plaster raised on more pillows *and an arm*, also in plaster, held up in a sling. She was putting a very brave face on it.

'Entirely my own fault, I should look where I'm going.'

'But it was very dark, dear,' said Elsie.

'Well, we shouldn't have gone out. But it's going to be a bit difficult getting on the plane tomorrow. They tell me to keep my arm up in this sling and also to put my leg up all the time.'

'Don't worry about that,' I was trying to be reassuring, 'We can arrange a wheelchair at the airport, and the airline will get one at the other end. And I'll get the agents to tell the airline you will need a seat where you can have your leg up.' I was being optimistic; I had no idea if this would be possible. Noreen went on,

'I'm just so sorry to miss the sightseeing this morning. I told Elsie to go, but she insisted on coming with me to the hospital. Now she's not seen the *Qutub Minar* you told us would be so good. I was looking forward to that.'

'Don't worry about it, dear. I have an excellent post-card of it...'

The hotel staff was excellent. They brought one of the pool loungers into the garden so that she could have her leg up during the afternoon, pushed Noreen along corridors, in and out of the lift, and helped her off and on the wheel-chair. They helped her back to her room to change before dinner, wheeled her to the drinks party and eventually lifted her wheelchair down the steps onto the lawn for our farewell dinner. It was quite a jolly affair, and Noreen entered into the spirit of the thing - raising her glass as everyone toasted her recovery. It took a long time to order the meal, and another long time for it to even start to arrive, but we were in no hurry. As it was already dark, no one really noticed the gathering clouds blotting out our star-lit evening. But just as the main courses were being brought to the table by the procession of waiters - all in their splendid red and gold jackets and turbans - there was a great clap of thunder, and very soon after, the first few large drops of rain. People looked up anxiously, and then there was a flash of lightening, followed a few seconds later by more thunder. It seemed very close - almost overhead. Then the rain started in earnest - a sudden, lashing deluge. The waiters came running to carry off the food, the group started to their feet and began running for the terrace, and the shelter beyond.

Poor Noreen was stuck in her wheelchair, Elsie trying to hold a starched linen knapkin over her head. I shouted to the waiters to bring umbrellas. Jill and Elsie and I were trying to protect Noreen from the rain which was bucketing down, and all of us getting soaked in the process.

'Umbrellas! Bring umbrellas,' I kept shouting to the waiters. But there were no umbrellas. Instead they were running, carrying tablecloths.

'No umbrella, sir. We are bringing cloth.' And with that they threw a large green-checked tablecloth over Noreen and her wheelchair and four of them tried first to push, and then to lift, the wheelchair and carry it to the terrace and the inner dining room. Jill and Elsie had another table-cloth over them, and I am sorry to say that as other waiters opened the glass doors for us to get into the dining space, there was a great cheer and applause from not only our own group standing there, but the entire dining clientele of the hotel who had gathered to witness the spectacle. Soon Noreen was deposited among the others, with her four drenched waiter-attendants, still in red and gold and with dripping turbans. She was still in the wheel-chair, draped in the table-cloth, now soaking wet, looking not unlike those prints we had seen of Indian ladies in *purdah* palanquins.

As I lifted the cloth off, she looked up, her hair bedraggled, the sling and plasters wet.

'I don't know what my husband is going to make of this. He didn't want to come to India, but I told him I was going with Elsie if he wouldn't. I'm not sure he'll let me come again.'

[illegible]

[illegible]

[illegible]

[illegible]

PAKISTAN

Why not Pakistan, someone suggested. After all, it had been part of India; it had many of the great monuments of ancient and even quite modern India, it had quite marvellous scenery and famous places; Kipling's Kim was there… We had taken groups to many parts of India, so why not Pakistan? Why not indeed. The time we are talking about was after the wars between Pakistan and India and before we'd even heard of Al Qaeda or Taliban incursions from Afghanistan. Of course there were plenty of tensions - assassinations, political strife, Sunni and Shia, the Indo-Pak squabbles, trouble on the North West Frontier - but there were no reasons to think that we would be especially unsafe: the Foreign Office, though advising caution, didn't say actually say no. Even today it doesn't say a firm *no*, except to those places one would most like to visit: Peshawar and the border with Afghanistan, the Karakoram Highway up to Gilgit…

Apart from all this, my mother, daughter of an Indian Army family, had gone to boarding school up in the Murray Hills, near 'Pindi, which gave me a personal interest in trying to get to Pakistan. Maybe the Loretto Convent was still there? She had told such alarming stories about it. The nuns were very strict and screamed their displeasure when, on her first day at the school at the age of seven she had taken off her clothes to have a bath. No! *Holy Mary Mother of God!* She must undress under a *shift* and lower herself into the bath wearing the shift. A few days later she had been bullied by older girls into undertaking a dangerous mission. All the girls had to eat up everything on their plates, but they all hated *suji* pudding - a very glutinous kind of semolina - and they had adopted the secret practice of sticking the pudding to the underside of the table and selecting a victim to creep into the dining room after the meal to remove the sticky mess and dispose of it. So my mother - the youngest and newest girl - was the scapegoat. She did as they made her - stealthily entered the dining hall, crawled under the tables and tried to scrape the *suji* pudding off with her finger nails. Some fell on the floor, but where could she put it? She resorted to pushing it into her voluminous new school knickers; but she was unlucky - she was caught by a nun as she left the room. The kind nun was lenient: she had to stand and recite only twenty '*Hail Marys*'. I didn't learn what happened to the pudding.

I began the protracted planning and negotiations for our tour. We had plenty of people keen to travel with us, nearly all of whom had already made several Indian journeys. All we needed was an itinerary, a plan! Before too long it began to emerge that it was not going to be all plain-sailing. A clue came when the agents responded to my request that we make certain journeys by rail. I still had an out-moded and unreasonable nostalgic wish to travel by rail, and besides, trains had been so prominent in tales of the North West Frontier, and even in the horrific accounts of the massacres following partition in 1947. The correspondence was by fax machine.

'For your journeys we do not recommend by train. The train is not having A/C and will not be comfortable…'

'We do not mind about the A/C. We have travelled on many trains in India where there are only fans. Fans will be acceptable.'

'Fans may be there, but to have them working will be a bit of a fancy. Also trains are not running…'

We did not use trains.

The flight out was not too good, either. We flew by PIA - Pakistan International Airways. Well, if I tell you that some months afterwards I got into trouble with my agents for apparently insulting the President of PIA, you will see what I mean. It was at a huge travel market in Earls Court. Earlier in the day I had been entertained to some wine and very little food at the Cyprus, then Malta, then Canary Island stalls, but now I was with my friends - the agents for Pakistan. With great show and pomp, along came the PIA people, including the President, all garlanded and important, bestowing grace and favour on the various Pakistan agents at the show. Unfortunately I was introduced as a client.

'Ah,' I said, 'You're just the person I want to see. We've just flown on PIA and we're not very pleased with you.'

'What? What? What is the problem? You have a complaint?'

'I most certainly do.'

'Here, (he turned to a flunkey) take down this gentleman's complaint. What is your complaint?'

'It's not one complaint, it's lots of complaints: the 'plane was filthy, the lavatories were bunged up within half an hour, the food was uneatable, it was late, we were stuck on the tarmac in some remote part of the airport…'

'We will take immediate action. Which flight was this?'

'It wasn't one flight, it was all the flights… Let me tell you, we can't possibly travel with PIA again. I am going to have to use Uzbek Airways…'

My agent colleagues had been looking horrified at this exchange. The President of PIA had attended to be lauded, not harangued. He and his party moved on, stern-faced, displeased; but a little blond-haired lady who had been listening, came up to me.

'Excuse me, but I strongly recommend if you take groups to Pakistan, you should use PIA.'

'Really? They were appalling. I'm planning to use Uzbek next time; we may even include Uzbekistan…'

'Yes, but even so, you will find PIA is very much better. I know very well. You see, I am Uzbek.'

What we did not reckon on was the weather. In Rawalpindi it was dull and threatening before it started to rain, and then the rains began in earnest. Very heavy continuous *unseasonal* rain. We had a very good, rather elderly guide, Mr Hafiz, conducting us around Rawalpindi for those first few days; very informative, very smart with dark suit and rolled umbrella. But as we were about to fly to Gilgit, we would lose Mr Hafiz at Islamabad airport and another guide would meet us at Gilgit. But we didn't fly to Gilgit; our flight was cancelled due to the continuous rain, and we were informed that our only option was to go by road. Mr Hafiz was detailed to accompany us, and then return from Gilgit. Mr Hafiz, I may say was a Lahore city guide. The only reason he was in Rawalpindi was that a tourist had left a passport behind in Lahore and Mr Hafiz was asked to courier it back to the owner. Well, we never got to Gilgit at all. The rains were so bad that they caused very severe flooding: the road in front of us was washed away, but we had driven up the road a good distance and then the road behind us was washed away. We turned round and got back as far as Abbotabad, a town that we had passed though earlier. This town, curiously named after a British Mr Abbot, was where Osama bin Laden met his end many years later. Here we were lucky enough to get some rooms in a hotel, and where we were stuck for a few days. We had to make do with what we had: Jill and I shared a big room with Val and George and there was a certain amount of other room sharing to squeeze us in. There was an American group also staying at the hotel, but they had plannd to be there, whereas we were refugees. I was concerned that we might have taken some of the American rooms, but the clerk said,

'No, it is not a problem. We have put you in the upper rooms, but the Americans are much too old to reach the upper rooms.' We, I should explain were not too young, but when I tell you that the American group called their seventy-five year old tour leader 'Baby', you will understand what he meant. The Americans had also had trouble with the floods and had to get off their coach that day as it crossed the causeway to reach the hotel. One intrepid ninety-two year old told me,

'I was not worried one bit; I was wearing *galoshes*!'

The rains stopped after two or three days, but with roads and railways washed away we had to re-jig the tour on a daily basis, and Mr Hafiz, who had only brought his pyjamas and his umbrella with him, expecting to be away from home for only one night, remained with us throughout. We never went to Gilgit, but spent time in the Swat Valley (where the Taliban now roam), Peshawar and up the Khyber, and finally returned Mr Hafiz to his home in Lahore. Jacky told me later,

'It wasn't what we signed up for, but then it seldom is.' And Mr Hafiz told us that he had never enjoyed a tour so much in his life. He was certainly a godsend to us and, after the first discomforts of hotels, even saved me from myself and me from the group when my errors of judgment became too evident.

FLASHMAN'S, DEAN'S & FALETTI'S: OUR ATMOSPHERIC HOTELS

Whereas the agents dissuaded me from using trains in Pakistan, I was more obstinate when it came to choosing hotels. For the big cities the agents strongly recommended a modern chain of business hotels all called Pearl Continental. But my mother had spoken of train journeys to school and had mentioned the romantic-sounding names of some old hotels in pre-war days. In Rawalpindi, where her father had been stationed for a while, there was *Flashman's Hotel*; another, *Faletti's*, was in Lahore; *Dean's* in Peshawar. These were the old colonial hotels, what could be better to evoke a sense of history? Before you begin to judge me too harshly, by the way, my decision was made in a pre-Trip-Adviser era.

So when we drove up to Flashman's, our first stop after arriving at the airport from London, it was a bit of a shock to see that it had been turned, at first glance, into a modern business hotel - not a high rise affair, true, but with tell-tale 'modernist' touches of perhaps the 1960s. The main addition was a curious stucco facade, but sadly one whole section of stucco was missing, another had stucco partly detached, leaving one section intact and other patches with bits of the old Flashman's showing through, and an ugly jagged scar, a crack in the stucco repaired with cement, highlighting the join.

'Christ!' called David as we drew up, 'Where have you brought us? The front's fallen off the building!' I was not the only one to notice the unsuccessful modernisation.

'What's this 'Flash' mean?' said Betty, 'Not much flash about this.' She was right: even the '*...man's*' part of the name *'Flash...man's'* had fallen off, leaving our hotel rather inappropriately called *'Flash...'*.

Nor was our reception and room allocation especially welcoming. We dispersed to our rooms which were certainly not modern or business-like. Ours led off a swimming pool courtyard, and was certainly spacious, with an ante-room, which led in turn into a dark bedroom. The rooms smelled musty and there were very evident damp, peeling patches on the walls and part of the ceiling. However, we were off sightseeing shortly and there was little time to check on the condition of other rooms. Before we left there was a cluster of our people around the reception desk reporting non-flushing lavatories, missing light-bulbs, absent shower curtains, hard pillows and other not uncommon features of a badly run hotel.

Yes, yes, they would check-up and get back to us. No problem. So after an indifferent dinner we spent a not-very comfortable night, disturbed by loud thunder, flashes of lightening and heavy rain. The dining room was a little distance from the courtyards. Had we known about it, some could have reached the dining room via covered walk-ways, but many of us did not know, and as the umbrellas that should have been in our rooms were mostly missing, several reached the dining room very wet from the steady downpour. There was a distinct atmosphere of gloom as the group stared at their breakfast.

'These eggs taste quite horrible,' said Jacky. 'They taste as if they have been cooked in some kind of disinfectant - Jay's Fluid I would think.'

'Yes, they are inedible,' agreed someone. 'How can a hard-boiled egg taste of TCP?' They were quite right; there was a pervading smell of disinfectant hanging in the dining hall and the eggs seemed to be the cause. As breakfast comprised two hard-boiled eggs brought to each diner by the waiter, with some rather stale, sweet-tasting bread, butter and a dollop of very red jam, this seemed to be rather unsatisfactory. I turned to the waiter.

'I would like my eggs fried, please.'

'Egg cook is out of station,' he replied, 'Boiled yeg only.'

'But these eggs taste very bad.'

'Bad yeg? Not bad yeg.'

'All right, not bad, just very horrible.'

'Horrible yeg? I do not understand.'

As there were also a number of complaints about the shortcomings of the rooms over the breakfast, I decided to go in search of the manager. But I had to join a queue. It wasn't a queue of complaining hotel guests, but apparently a number of business men, mostly in dark suits, who told me they had urgent business with the manager. On enquiry some assured me that, no, they were not there on hotel business; one was a road contractor who told me the hotel manager supplied road-building materials. My thoughts went to the missing façade of the hotel. Eventually I was ushered into a very busy office. The manager sat at the central desk, talking on the telephone and intermittently bringing his fist down on a brass bell on his desk, calling instructions to assistants who rushed about with files and sheets of paper. After five minutes or so it was my turn.

'Good morning. How can I help you? Kindly forgive the delay, there are so many pressing matters.'

'Good morning. I am a guest in your hotel.'

'Really? Ah, yes. Good. I hope you are enjoying your stay with us?'

'Well, I have to tell you that there are several complaints.'

'Complaints? I am sorry to hear that. What is your complaint?'

'As I say, there are several, concerning the rooms and also the food. I have just come from the breakfast.'

'The breakfast?'

'Yes, breakfast. They brought us eggs that are inedible…'

'They brought you breakfast?'

'Well, yes, but it was very poor and the eggs…'

'But they brought you breakfast?' He seemed astonished. It was quite difficult to continue the complaints session.

I recall another member of another group, on listening to some complaints by others, telling me that he had learned not to complain when in the army. Roger was a very aware, but rather doleful story teller, who related the incident as a lesson to others.

'Yes,' he said slowly and deliberately. 'I learned to watch my step when I was doing my National Service. We were in the canteen having our dinner, an' this little jumped up officer in the Catering Corps - a little lieutenant, I think he was - he came in.'

"Right-ho, you men. How is the meal? Are you enjoying the meal?" Very sharp and clipped he was, you know the kind. But I thought the food was 'orrible, so I said,

"Well not very much, sir. I don't think it's very good."

"What? What? That man there, was that a complaint?"

"Well, sir, not really, sir. You asked if the food was OK. I just said…"

"Is that a complaint? That man there is making a complaint! Call the Cook Sergeant, call the Cook Sergeant!"

Well, blow me if they doubled in the Cook Sergeant. One, two, one two, one two…

"Cook Sergeant! Cook Sergeant! There's a man here making a complaint about the food! Deal with it! Find out his complaint and deal with it!"

"Wo's wrong wiv the food?" The Cook Sergeant was shouting at me. "You, wo's wrong wiv it?"

"Well, Sarge, it's the chips. They're horrible…'

"Sergeant!" shouts the little officer, "Taste the chips, tell me what's wrong with them."

"Well, sir," I said, "They're 'orrible.."

"I didn't ask you, I asked the Cook Sergeant! Did I ask you? You speak when you're spoken to. Well Sergeant?" Well, the Sarge, he was picking up the chips and tasting them. After a minute he gave me a look, an' he said,

"They're not fucking chips! They're fucking parsnips!"

I can tell you, I never complained again.'

The rain continued intermittently all day, making our sight-seeing equally intermittent, and punctuated with the news that our flight the following day may be cancelled if the weather did not improve. There was much discussion of the alternatives open to us: to stay in Rawalpindi, residing at Flashman's until the weather improved; or to make the journey to Gilgit by road. We were a pretty adventurous bunch of people and setting off by road was the unanimous decision. This required the agents to sort out a vehicle and Mr Hafiz to accompany us, and revise our accommodation. We would start early in the morning. But it was in the early morning that one of our group had a small adventure.

Anthony had joined our group as a single traveller. He was a tall, almost elderly, rather grand gentleman, frightfully well-spoken in a slow languorous way, slightly aloof. I learned much later that he had never admitted to his friends and associates that he had joined a *group* tour, which he condescendingly would call a 'package', but instead claimed that his journey to Pakistan was a 'private tour'. He did have a sense of humour, or at least I took it that he was displaying a sense of humour, that same evening, when I feared we would be stranded on the washed-away road and admitted to the group that we may have to spend the night in our coach, he said,

'Well I shall not mind too much, as I booked a *single room*. But where will you all sleep?'

But in the early morning, before we set off for the attempted drive to Gilgit, Anthony decided to swim in the pool. Several of us had swum in the warm rain the previous day, but, as I say, now it was very early. It was still raining, and not yet light, and Anthony decided to have another swim, this time naked - as he said, he didn't want to be carrying a wet swimming costume around with him. His room opened directly to the pool courtyard and it would be quite easy to slip into the water alone and unseen. Unfortunately, he did not reckon on the wind, which had slammed his door shut behind him and which he found locked on his return - keys, towel and all means of modesty locked inside. Some precious minutes were spent trying to get into the room while the sky lightened. Several more of us were up early, putting luggage outside the rooms and were mildly surprised to see Anthony striding off to the reception desk, decorously holding up the wet doormat taken from outside his room, to ask to be let in.

Much later in the tour, after many ad hoc arrangements resulting from the floods, we reached the 'frontier' city of Peshawar and checked into Dean's Hotel. The old images of Dean's had shown that it was 'by appointment' to the Crown and also, with the three feathers, specifically to the Prince of Wales. It had been part of the associated Hotels of India, which included those memorable institutions - Flashman's of course, but The Imperial in Delhi, The Grand in Calcutta, Cecil's in Shimla and many others which we knew and loved. Sadly, today, Dean's is no more. Not just closed, but demolished, and I suspect that on our visit it was on its way to this ignominious end. Indeed, our arrival at Dean's was deeply disappointing, and even I was beginning to see that the advice of our agents to choose other hotels - indeed *avoid* the old colonial hotels - while ignoring sentiments of nostalgia and history, had a certain practicality.

Dean's shortcomings were brought home to me quite sharply almost immediately. A small timid lady member of our group, who never complained, soon returned to the reception desk holding disdainfully, at arms-length, the damp, dirty and very smelly bath-mat from her bathroom. The patient and watchful Mr Hafiz was standing beside me and I voiced my exasperation to him.

'I had no idea that it would be this bad', I said to him. 'We're here for four nights!'

'Let us see what we can do,' he said to me. 'Let us go together in the coach to another hotel and I will try to facilitate. I think they will not like this place.' I also thought they would not like this place. Our room was disgracefully dirty; in comparison, Flashman's seemed luxurious. So Mr Hafiz and I slipped away, our driver taking us to the Peshawar Pearl Continental Hotel. Here Mr Hafiz displayed his true abilities as a resourceful, perceptive and devious guide and tour manager. First, he asked me to remain out of sight. I was wearing a pair of shorts, a short-sleeved shirt and pair of quite scruffy sandals. He was in his dark suit, white shirt, tie, carrying his rolled umbrella. I did as I was asked and hid behind a pillar, within ear-shot of Mr Hafiz's conversation with the reception clerk.

'Good evening, I am the tour manager of the British Travellers' Club Group. We are checking in shortly. You have our rooms?'

'Er, What is the name of your group? I do not appear to have a note…'

'What? You do not have a note? How can you not have a note? This is a VVIP group, they have booking for 14 rooms! Is there some slip-up?'

'I am very sorry, I cannot find any note… How many nights are they staying here?'

'How many nights? How can you be asking "How many nights?" We have confirmed reservation of 4 nights at this hotel.'

'I am very sorry, there seems to have been a mistake, and tonight there is no room at the hotel. Tomorrow there will be rooms, we have a business conference leaving tomorrow early, but tonight…'

'This is disgraceful and my company will be taking the matter up. I will report the matter to my company and they will certainly be taking the matter up. And the Britishers will be very angry. How can they be treated in this way? They are all VVIP's, British army people are there, judges are there. Anyway, please ensure that our rooms are ready first thing in the morning. They will require early check-in. 14 rooms, do you understand, and by way of compensation you will of course ensure they all have up-graded rooms…'

Mr Hafiz had already indicated to me to keep out of sight, and now marched purposefully out of the hotel entrance. I crept out, trying to remain hidden from the reception staff, and met him at our coach.

'Will that really work?' I asked in astonishment and wonder.

'I hope - maybe - it will. It is most reprehensible of the agents to have booked you into that Dean's. It is certainly to be dis-recommended. I will telephone them to ensure they have now made a reservation, so we can inform group members to move in the morning.'

It did really work. How it worked or why it worked we never knew. But we informed the group they were all shifting next morning and there was a kind of jubilation at our one and only evening at Dean's Hotel. Even the evening meal seemed not so bad, and it is amazing what one can put up with, knowing that the experience is coming to an end. We arrived at the Pearl Continental hotel next morning and at first were a little disconcerted to read a permanent notice in the lobby that I had not noticed when hiding the evening before. It was painted in white elegant lettering on a large varnished wooden board:

PEARL CONTINENTAL HOTEL
It is the policy of the hotel that all
Arms and Ammunition must be deposited
at the Reception.
Hired gun-men are not admitted to the hotel
and must remain outside the building at all times.

Despite this, we found clean rooms, comfortable beds, good food. A number of questions hung in the air: we had presumably paid for our rooms at Dean's, but not at the Pearl Continental; there must be a considerable price difference between the two; we had no actual reservation - were we taking rooms reserved for others? We stayed in considerable comfort for the remaining three nights, making visits to the bazaars, the Khyber Pass (with armed escorts), to the gun-making village of Darra, where we had to persuade Mary, a gentle spinster school teacher, to return the hand-gun she bought as a gift for her little nephew. At no time either during our visit, or ever since, were we questioned about how we came to leave Dean's and stay at another hotel.

Mr Hafiz did, however, suggest that before we reach Lahore towards the end of our tour, that I should change the booking I had for Faletti's and book instead at the Pearl Continental Hotel. He suggested that we would not find Faletti's to be too different from Dean's. Lahore was Mr Hafiz's home town and he knew the conditions of its hotels. We took his advice. Recent information suggests that Faletti's may reopen, but it has been closed since 1990 - clearly our visit in the 1980's would have been during the later stages of its decline. I am slightly ashamed to say that, having insisted on making a reservation there in the initial planning of our Pakistan tour, we did not even make a visit.

TRAINS

SHOULD WE TRAVEL BY TRAIN?

Don't you think that an Indian train journey should be part of an Indian tour? Isn't it said to be a part of experiencing India - that elusive 'real' India which *travellers*, rather than mere tourists, claim to be searching for? We have all seen Indian train travel on television: old films like *Bowhani Junction* or *A Passage to India* perhaps, or documentaries on Indian Railways. Or we have read about it in novels, or come across Paul Theroux's *The Great Indian Railway Bazaar*. There are several train journeys in Paul Scott's *Raj Quartet*. People - mostly people who have not been to India - have often said to me: 'Oh, yes, I would love to travel on an Indian train.'

In truth I had included travel by train in my plans for our *group* tours partly to save money - after all, an overnight train journey would save the cost of a hotel room - and partly to ease the long journeys by coach over particularly bad roads. But partly it was to ensure that the group should 'enjoy' a very 'Indian experience' of stations and trains. And there was my own sense of nostalgia - hoping to recapture a fragment of my own past. As a small child I had travelled with my mother on Indian trains, sometimes with her bearer (man-servant) and my Aya (woman-to-look-after-me-servant), and had often heard my parents reminisce about other train journeys made with their friends: talk of servants; baggage; bed-rolls; blocks of ice in tin baths to cool the carriage; picnics; breakfasts with porridge and eggs in stations; meals ordered at one station and delivered at another. Novels and memoirs often spoke *with affection* about railway travel in the days of the Raj.

Armed with all this, I had persuaded Jill when planning our earlier visits to India that travelling quite extensively by train would be the thing to do. We had bought *Indrail* cards - giving unlimited rail travel for each of our three-month visits - which were so inexpensive that we allowed ourselves the luxury of buying *first class* rail passes. Now, for the price of a first class *Indrail* card we could travel either in 1st Class (Non Air-Conditioned) or 2nd Class (Air Conditioned) if the particular train we were travelling on had such carriages. I had been assured by the agents - a rather seedy outfit I came across operating with an address '*Inside Earl's Court Station*' - who were selling the *Indrail* Cards, that these cards would *ensure* a reservation. Indian trains often travel full and prior reservation was always necessary, whereas the holder of an *Indrail* Card, they told me, would always have priority. 1st Class (Air Conditioned) was also available on a very few trains in those days, and if it was available it was at a much higher price - the equivalent of flying. The only people we ever encountered travelling 1st Class A/C were Indian politicians ostensibly on their way to political gatherings. There were and are many other classes of rail travel, including the 3rd Class (3 tier) sleeper and, lowest of all, General Class. Jill wisely persuaded me to discard consideration of any of these. Of course 1st Class (Non A/C) on Indian Railways in the 70s and 80s was not, we supposed, equivalent to first class on our own dear British Rail, then in the process of being broken up into the confusing array of private companies operating bits of the system over Railtrack (not that we ever travelled 1st Class at home). Indeed we were proved right, and although we were younger then, even in 1st Class, at no time over the many rail journeys we made the length and breadth of India could we say that it was comfortable. The fault was ours: our expectations were unrealistic and, most importantly, we never learned that essential of overnight train travel - the ability to sleep on any surface. Many Indians have this enviable capacity. Quite apart from coping on trains where beds of some sort are often provided, we have seen the most amazing sleepers: families asleep on railway platforms and on pavements of course; but a museum attendant fast asleep with his bottom on the floor and feet and head raised on wooden stools; a man on the parapet of a bridge no wider than his hip while he lay on his side; another on a low wall, with his legs and arms actually entwined among the railings to prevent his rolling off.

The Indian trains were usually very full and, sadly, seldom very clean. Often we could only see a blur of the passing countryside due to the state of the windows. The beds were very hard. The bedding provided was still called 'bed-rolls'… (how I had enjoyed playing with my father's real bed-roll when I was a child, a great khaki-coloured canvas bag containing a mattress, blankets, sheets and a pillow, all rolled up and fastened with leather straps, always carried by his army servant like a huge kit-bag across his shoulder, which he had shipped home to England (both the bed-roll and the servant) when we all left India. I played with the bedroll with my eight year old gang of friends - pretending we were on a great adventure as we laid it out on a building site (a frontier battleground) in austerity England, the smell of the canvas bringing back memories of India). But returning to India in the late 1970's, I found that bedrolls were no longer a roll at all, but a rather awful armful of sheets, blankets, pillow, pillow cover, sometimes a towel. These were all newly washed perhaps, but somehow rather grubby and often torn from being stuffed into grimy metal lockers. Mind you, the ragged tears were sometimes repaired with darning and patches. I recall one hole, about the size of a saucer, in the middle of a sheet, which had not been patched but neatly edged to prevent it getting bigger.

In those days, most trains in India provided the slowest means of getting to one's destination. Coaches, even on bad roads, were much faster - the terrifying night coaches, with music blaring or, worse, videos flickering in garish colours and blasting soundtracks - carried and still carry the brave, or unaware, or urgent passengers. Aeroplanes carried the wealthy. Today there are a few prestigious and moderately expensive express trains, with smart seating carrying expressive names: Shatabdi Express trains have 'Executive Chair Cars', but for most Indians, trains still provide a cheap and very slow way to travel enormous distances. And while Indians are tremendous travellers - working or returning from work in far-distant states, visiting relatives, on pilgrimage - they are seldom in a hurry. The trains stop - often not at stations - for long, unexplained periods. Or, sometimes the stops are at stations, but for equally long, unexplained periods. On one occasion, travelling from Udaipur to Jodhpur in Rajasthan, a journey that would take perhaps six hours by road, the schedule indicated departure from Udaipur at 2 pm and arrival at Jodhpur at 6 am next morning. It was picturesque travelling through the Aravali hills and at about 6 pm we reached Marwar Junction, where we remained for a long time as the light began to fade. Someone came to take an order for dinner 'Meals, meals? Veg, non veg?' but the train did not move. After over an hour, I wandered along the platform. Passengers were drinking tea, smoking, chatting, buying oranges or peanuts, eating snacks. No other trains came or left. I asked an official when the train may move.

'Ah yes, after some time. You see here at Marwar Junction is *very busy*. Bogeys are coming from here and from there, so we always allow 3 hours flexibility at Marwar Junction. Have you taken your dinner?'

As I say, when we had bought our *Indrail* tickets I had been assured that we would have priority on bookings and there would be no difficulty in making our journeys. This, sadly, proved not to be the case.

THE BOOKING HALL

Soon after our arriving in India for my job at Madras University, I had been invited to attend a conference in Delhi. We naturally intended to travel by train, using our precious *Indrail* passes. Other delegates from Madras were to fly (perhaps three hours), but our express train would leave in the early morning and arrive before mid-day on the following day. This would be our first train journey and I discovered that obtaining tickets was not the simple operation that the *Indrail* Card salesman had indicated. I went to Madras station about three weeks before the plannd journey. Naively I entered the 'First Class Booking Hall' and queued up at one of the long lines waiting for the counters for each of the bewildering number of trains that departed from Madras. My queue was for the *Tamil Nadu Express* to New Delhi. I chatted to fellow queue members and slowly realised that very few of my companions intended to travel. Most people in the line were professional queuers, paid to stand there and obtain tickets on behalf of middle-men. Several kindly offered me the cards of their agencies (*First Class Travel Agency; PayGo Agency; Prontoticket*) and their services to stand in line if I would hand over the ticket money and a little more. Although sorely tempted, I had already been in the line an hour or so and decided to wait. After another half an hour of quite pleasant and interesting conversation, I reached the small ticket window. I explained that I wanted two first class return tickets to Delhi and held out the *Indrail* Cards.

'Where is your application form?' A brusque demand from behind the grill.

'Application form? I just want…'

'You must have application form. You don't have?'

'Er, well, can you give me one?'

'No. You must apply for application at Application Form Counter.'

'What? Where…'

'There, look, see. On the other side of booking hall. Next.'

'But I have these *Indrail* Cards, here, you see…'

'Application form is a must. Next.'

I turned to my neighbours in the queue.

'Yes, yes, Application form is a must. You see we are professional men. We already have application form for client.'

'You don't happen to have a spare one?'

'No, it is not permitted. You must apply in person.'

'But you are queuing for someone else.'

'Yes, yes, but we are professional persons and will be making application for authorised persons. For you, too, we can make application.'

'I see, can you do that here, as you are now at the front of the queue?'

'No, no, that is not possible. We also must apply at Application Form Counter for Application Form. See it is there…'

I looked there. On another side of the booking hall was indeed another long queue lined up in front of a prominent over-head sign: *Application Form Counter*. Reluctantly I gave up my treasured place at the front of the *Tamil Nadu Express* queue and joined the back of the *Application Form Counter* queue. The line moved rather faster, and after only another half-an-hour I was at the counter. Now I was learning fast: we intended making other journeys quite soon, so to save time I asked,

'May I have four application forms please?'

'What for?'

'Because I want to make four train journeys.'

'Only one form at one time,' a patient, deliberate response.

'But there are two people and I want…'

'Two people can be on one form, but one form can only be for one journey. For more forms you must be in line.'

'Am I not in line?'

'Yes, you are in line, but for more forms you must be in line again'

'What about the return journey? Do I…'

'Returning is requiring another form.'

The impassive young lady was only inches away holding a book of yellow application forms from which she had been tearing one form (in triplicate with carbon paper) at one time for each applicant; there was no grill at this counter and the window much larger.

'May I look at the forms?' She handed the book to me.

'May I tear out four forms?'

'Certainly. Why not? Next.'

I joined the back of the queue for the *Tamil Nadu Express* counter once again. Ahead of me there were all the other counters, each displaying a prominent overhead sign, each with a long queue. Several were for more journeys that I hoped to make: the *Nilgiri Express*, would take us on a journey I plannd to the Nilgiri Hills *en route* to Mysore. The *Hyderabad Mail* would take us to visit friends working in Hyderabad. These and others were among ones I hoped for. Must I queue for each? Already I had been in the station for well over two hours. So I abandoned the queue (asking my new neighbour if he would save my place should I fail and return; he smiled, indicating that a gratuity would be in order) And wondered away to the front of the queue and into the front corner of the booking hall, near the row of small grilled windows. There was a side-door, which was slightly ajar. I peeped around it and stared into a large busy room. In front of me I could see the side view of about 20 booking clerks, all facing the queues on the other side of the grilles. Behind them was a sea of desks piled high with papers, ledgers, files and many more clerks shuffling papers, writing, some on the 'phone, some moving about carrying piles of files. Fans whirled overhead. A khaki uniformed lady behind a big desk looked up.

'Yes, what do you want?'

'Er, I was hoping to book some train journeys…' I waved my clutch of yellow forms.

'Yes, there is booking hall. What train do you want?'

'To Delhi. I must go to Delhi…'

'We are having numerous trains to Delhi. There is booking hall. You must select. You have timetable?'

'Well, I have to go to a conference in Delhi. I am at the university, you see…'

'Are you VIP?'

'Well, I suppose…'

'If you are not VIP kindly go in line in booking hall.'

'Well, maybe…'

'Are you VIP?'

'Er, well, in a way… yes.'

'OK, then kindly be seated. Most welcome. How can I help you? Which train? Would you care for a cup of tea?'

Only an hour later, I emerged in triumph, slightly ashamed that a white skin and white lies had cut so much red tape. I had been given a cup of tea, a spicy pastry, a biscuit and I held my tickets for Delhi, Ooty, Bangalore, Hyderabad, and the returns. And for the first time, perhaps the last, I had been VIP.

A TRAIN ESCAPE

We did travel on the *Tamil Nadu Express* to Delhi, in the luxury of a first class private couchette on a special VIP quota. We were able to use our *Indrail Card* to pay for the booking, but it hadn't been the card that got us the reservation; it had been the helpful lady who recognized me as VIP. Ours was a narrow two-berth compartment (one up, one down), with a solid grey metal sliding door to the corridor, austere grey plastic seats and very thin mattresses for seating and sleeping. The small low window opposite the door was barred. It was reminiscent of scenes from prison escape movies - the kind where prisoners are being taken on trains to prison, but make their escape from the train. Come to think of it, that is what happened.

Although January and only seven in the morning, it was hot in Madras railway station: the train was not air conditioned and, along with the rest of the 1st Class carriage, our couchette was cooled with ceiling fans that whirred noisily above us. To try and keep a bit cooler, and to be able to see out of windows on both sides, we kept the door to the corridor open. Very unusually, I was wearing my new, unused 'conference suit,' a light, creamy coloured summer suit that I thought would be very appropriate for a Commonwealth Conference on Development. The jacket hung on a hook in our compartment. The choice of clothing proved to be a mistake. Soon after the train set off, a sweeper moved along the corridor on his haunches sweeping the dust and debris along in front of him with a small sparse hand broom but with no receptacle to receive the rubbish. The dust rose and was circulated rapidly by the ceiling fans. Over the next 30 hours, the sweeper appeared frequently, the dust rose, was distributed and settled again, mostly on us and my suit. We went to bed that night sweating and hot - it must have been about 30 degrees - but were surprised to see that the evening shift of train guards (guarding against '*dacoitry*' I was told when I enquired - in this case bandits who would board the train to rob passengers) were wearing long greatcoats and woollen balaclava helmets and carrying very long old rifles. We awoke shivering at about one in the morning, with the temperature down to about 5 degrees.

We got a bit warmer after the sun came up, but we were still feeling the cold when the train, which had been travelling very slowly, and stopping very frequently, finally seemed to stop at around 12 noon - about an hour after our scheduled time of arrival in Delhi. We were not in a station, but on a high embankment some distance from the city. The train did not move for half an hour or more and I wandered along the corridor to enquire what was happening. Other passengers were happy to tell me that this was a frequent occurrence and it may take another half an hour or perhaps an hour before we arrived at our destination of Old Delhi railway station. Now Old Delhi is north-east of New Delhi, but I could see from road signs and from a fairly detailed map of the city that we were in the south and not so far from our hotel in the *Lodhi* Gardens. I checked with fellow travellers that we were indeed looking down into the *Lodhi* Gardens and as we were to stay at the *Lodhi* Hotel, we were much nearer now than we would be if we went on to the station. Couldn't we get down here rather than carry on? Couldn't we just climb down the bank, take a taxi and find our way? We would not be alone: we had seen several people - mostly men, but even some families - clambering down the bank, some laden with luggage.

'No, no, to get down would be most unwise,' urged some passengers, 'The bank is so steep and you will not find a taxi to take you to your hotel.'

'But we are so near,' I said. 'We are already late and it will take us a long time to travel back here. Besides, all those other people have got down…'

'But those are ticketless passengers! They are escaping the ticket collector at the station.'

Against the advice of other travellers, and certainly against the advice of my dear wife, we did get down. Collecting our modest luggage together, I clambered down from the train, finding that the drop without the benefit of a platform was much greater than I expected; Jill handed the bags down to me and I helped her down. We stood looking down the quite steep embankment and trying to see where there was a break in the fence at the bottom, beyond which there was a road which I hoped would lead us to our hotel. The descent was difficult, we slipped a couple of times and found ourselves fenced off from the road. We trudged along the side of the fence for a couple of hundred yards before we found what seemed to be a big enough hole in the netting. Both of us were getting exasperated - Jill with me, me with myself, the hole, the bags and the conference. But we did finally push ourselves and our bags through. By now it was past mid-day, and by Madras standards quite cool, but by any European standards the mid-day sunshine was strong and we now felt hot and exhausted.

'Well? Where do we go now? The man was right! Where do we go? Where is the bloody hotel?' Jill's mood was worsening. I had no real idea of where the hotel was, or how to reach it as we walked along the road in what I hoped was the right direction. After another twenty minutes of bad tempered silence, very slow progress and much consultation of the map, we did flag down a taxi driver who, when asked for the *Lodhi* Hotel, turned the car round, set off in the opposite direction and after another twenty minutes driving, delivered us. There was a small consolation: as we got into the taxi we could still see our train standing motionless on the embankment.

The water from the shower soon became black, and the conference suit - filthy and crumpled - lay on the floor. The hotel laundry would not return the clothes until next day, but in any case the temperature in Delhi was down to almost freezing at night and only pleasantly warm by day. We went to a market to buy warm clothes and I attended the conference, held in the newest, glitziest hotel in the capital (needlessly cooled by air conditioning, of course), in jeans, an itchy new sweater and swathed in a grey blanket. The Nigerian delegates, who seemed to be running things, resided in executive suites in the conference hotel. One wore flamboyant African dress, but the others wore three-piece dark suits, stiff white collars and immaculate silk ties. One asked me if it was true that there was a servant problem in the UK and had I difficulty in finding a post? Another asked me to fetch some luggage to his room. Security guards constantly asked me for my identity tag.

THREE DAYS & TWO NIGHTS: MADRAS TO UDAIPUR

Despite the discomfort and the length of time they took, our train journeys were always interesting, or rather, our fellow passengers were always interesting. One quite early expedition took us by train from Madras to Udaipur involving three nights and two days, with changes in Bombay and Ahmedabad. It had not started well as there had been a torrential unseasonal downpour before we reached the station. It was around 7 pm when we set off from the University Guest House, travelling in an auto-rickshaw that left a wake in the street like a small motor boat and sent waves over people standing ankle deep waiting for their buses. The usual Madras traffic continued to flow, but cyclists and cycle-rickshaw men wore brightly coloured capes, their passengers hidden under tarpaulins. Enterprising umbrella stalls had appeared, doing a brisk trade. Most people just trudged along, literally soaked to the skin, but apparently continuing to purchase their vegetables for the evening meal. Our driver demanded double payment (cheap at the price as we remained more or less dry while he was soaked in the few moments it took to unload our luggage).

Our fellow passengers had not been so lucky. During the usual long walk down the platform looking for our carriage (2nd Class A/C), passing the crowds of cheerful, smiling, but wet passengers and friends and relatives saying goodbye, we could see that the inside as well as the outside of the train resembled the *dhobi ghats* - the places where the washer-men communities bashed the clothing, broke the buttons and hung everything out to dry. From the barred windows of the 3rd Class hung *saris* (stretched along five or six metres of carriage), blouses, vests, shirts, underpants, *dhotis* (white) and *lungis* (checked or coloured). When we eventually found the 2nd Class A/C carriages, there were no bars on the windows - only un-openable dark glass. But we did find our names listed and pasted to the outside of the door of our carriage. We gestured to our porter - red-shirted, with a brass arm-band, carrying our bags on his head - and climbed aboard. Inside we found that our own berths were strewn with damp clothing. The family sitting in the berths opposite - he, relaxed in a vest and *lungi* with two small children on the lower, she in nightdress with another child above - had already spread out items of bedding on their own berths and had started on a meal being eaten from numerous metal and plastic containers. They smiled but made no move to remove their damp clothing from our berths as we struggled in with our porter and our quite modest luggage, indicating that we would like to occupy their laundry space.

The ticket inspector checked tickets; the carriage attendant came with our bedding; tea-sellers, biscuit sellers, tomato soup sellers, sandwich sellers and film-magazine sellers proffered their wares along the corridor. Passengers pushed past, porters hauled luggage. Outside on the platform came the calls for 'Cold drink, Limca, Goldspot' or 'Omelette, omelette' or 'Cigarette, cigarette' or '*Masala Dosa*.' Another couple settled into their corridor berths opposite our compartment - those berths located actually in the corridor, which we came to dread. There was no door on compartments to separate them from the corridor, just a pair of curtains that could be held together if the Velcro fastening was still intact.

When our bedding appeared, the attendant holding our bundle unceremoniously swept some of the drying clothing to one side to place the sheets, blankets, pillows on the upper bunk. Our immediate neighbour smiled and got up from his meal to take some of his damp clothes down. He then returned to his array of boxes, plastic bags, tiffin carriers and resumed his meal. His wife kindly leaned down from the top bunk offering us samples of the food - delicious *parathas*, different spicy vegetable dishes, sweets. It was, of course, difficult to refuse and it was also difficult to eat. To this day I have never acquired the skills of eating quite wet Indian food with a *chappati* or rice and the fingers of one hand. The train started and the family became more generous and more talkative. More food was offered and questions began: Where were we going? Where were we from? How did we like this place? What is your opinion of India? Of Tamil Nadu? Of Madras? The children were told to ask us 'What is your name? What is your native place? What is your age?' - and continued to do so, interrupted by sleep or more meals, until our arrival in Bombay next day. Hearing the conversation, other passengers called in to visit, some bringing snacks, drinks, but mostly just curious, friendly and helpful:

'Kindly allow me to help you with your bedroll. We are much experienced in making up bed-on-train.'

When it became obvious that we would like sleep - Jill reappeared from the toilet at the end of the corridor in her night-dress, carrying a tooth-brush - our visitors departed with smiles and 'See you...'

Two nights and the intervening day were spent, chatting, eating, reading but not sleeping much, as we slowly made our way to Ahmedbad (with a change in Bombay), arriving very early in the morning. There was to be a long wait until another overnight train would take us to our destination at Udaipur, but in the interval we discovered another drawback to train travel:

stations are seldom in very interesting parts of a city. Ahmedbad has much to recommend it - some beautiful mosques and other buildings, a famous museum of textiles… but finding them on a hot day when tired from lack of sleep was difficult and unrewarding, and we had another night on the train to look forward to. This time it was to be in a 1st Class (non A/C) carriage, but on an ancient rattling train over the hills to Udaipur.

Let me just say that the berths on 2nd Class A/C are narrower than 1st Class and those in the corridor are very undesirable. There is less space and less privacy than 1st Class, and there is much less dust and no need for fans to blow it about. We had certainly built up our experience of train travel, so when it came to planning a tour for our group, I had a number of factors to consider. Whether to travel by train at all? Which routes should be by train? Which class of travel? The discomforts of rail travel had rather faded from my memory, but I had been reminded quite forcibly by Jill.

'Just one night?' I had pleaded.

'One too many if you ask me. Why can't we fly?'

'Well the schedule isn't so good and the flights are so often late…'

'And can you see half of them getting up to the top bunks?'

'But I'm sure they can put up with one night - it's all part of the experience.'

'It certainly is.'

RAILWAY PORTERS

Railway porters, we had discovered, were an important part of rail travel, and if we were to take our groups - with all their luggage - by train, they would be indispensable; necessary, but also intimidating.

Our first encounter with a railway porter was at the cinema. My very affectionate students at Madras University invited us to a Tamil movie - to 'see if you can understand any Tamil!' was the ostensible reason, but really they wanted to ask us out for the evening and to take 'their teacher' along to see a rather daring film. It was called '*Railway Porter*' and, among the many set pieces of song and dance so common in Indian films, was the tragic love story of a lower-caste boy - the railway porter - and higher-caste girl. This was the daring aspect of the film - a non-arranged love match that was doomed. Very daring and very exciting; all the students knew their marriages would be arranged. The students, I may say, rightly guessed that our Tamil was pretty well non-existent, so, during one scene in a violent rain-storm they leaned across, helpfully whispering the explanation,

'Now it is raining.'

In another, when the all the villagers were being driven from their village, their belongings packed up on bullock carts, another loud whisper offered,

'Now they are leaving.'

As a result of the film visit we had quite useful discussions about love-matches and arranged marriages, inter-caste relations, the low pay, insecurity and low status of railway porters, but I had forgotten all about them when planning the train journeys for our first group tour. Now, as our coach pulled into the forecourt of Hyderabad railway station, we were met by what the group took to be a band of brigands. All had dirty red shirts and brass plates bearing their licence numbers, worn as armbands tied round the upper arm like a piece of body-armour; most had red bandanas tied around their heads; some wore trousers, most wore *lungis*, folded up to the knee and tied around the waist, giving them the appearance of thin, grubby kilts over thin legs with feet mostly in flip-flop sandals. Our guide got down, asking us to remain on board, and he was immediately surrounded by a clamouring, shouting mob. They shouted at each other, at someone who was presumably their leader, but mostly at the guide, who stayed on the lowest step of the coach to give him some height and some mastery of the situation. But he was also arguing and gesticulating as loudly as any of them. The language was *Telegu,* of which I understood not one word. This went on for some time and occasionally dissolved into heated outbursts and even some pushing and shoving. Our group in the coach was becoming anxious.

'What on earth is happening?'

'Who are these people?'

'This looks very dangerous.'

I tried to explain that they were the porters and Saddam would be selecting which ones would work and how much they would be paid. I climbed down to stand just behind him on the steps. As I did so the shouting grew louder - some directed at me.

'Sahib, sahib, baksheesh' I could certainly make out. But there were long shouted sentences, ribald laughter and more sentences.

'They are uttering filthy and disrespectful utterances,' said Saddam quietly to me, speaking from the corner of his mouth.'

'Tell them I understand every word and the baksheesh will grow smaller if I hear more.' He called out and the shouting subsided.

'They are demanding three thousand rupees and I am authorised to pay them one thousand only. That is fair price.' One thousand seemed quite a lot to me.

'They seem quite angry?'

'That is for show only, they will agree. But now you have said 'baksheesh', they will want some tip also.'

'Yes, yes, tip, tip!' - the cry was taken up.

'How many porters are you hiring?' I whispered to Saddam.

'No, I fix price only. How many porters only they are fixing among themselves only.'

'Tip, tip, more tip!' The noise was growing and the mood darkening. Mutterings came from the group inside the coach.

'What if you offered them a little more?' I asked. I had no experience of group prices or group tips. I was aware of the alarm behind me.

'But I am authorised to pay one thousand rupees only.' Saddam protested.

'What if you offered to pay them 1200?'

'But...'

'I'll pay the difference' I tried to whisper.

Saddam shouted some more rapid Telegu. Another howl of protest. I tried another ruse I'd used before.

'Tell them you'll pay 1250 and if they agree they may get another small additional tip from the group.'

He spoke again. Now smiles began to break out and there was some nodding and back-slapping.

'Make sure you said a small tip'

'I told them you are in-charge of group and will give good tip.'

Now the luggage was spilling out of the hold, off the roof and a great pile building up on the pavement. Our driver's assistant was on the roof, handing down bags to the porters below. The group members climbed down from the coach clutching their very assorted hand luggage. One small thin and rather elderly porter, his red shirt in shreds and a filthy dhoti, tied a small ragged towel into a ring and put it on his head. He bent both knees sideways as two other younger men heaved one of the heaviest suitcases up on top of his head. His thin legs seemed to flex under the strain.

'Oh my god, they're putting another on top' said someone from the group. And sure enough, the thin man stood grinning at us with two heavy cases on his head.

'And another. I don't believe…'

'Hey, that's mine. Make sure…'

The porter, now balancing three large cases on his head, momentarily let go with one hand and first one bag, then another was slipped over his arm and the straps hung on his shoulder. The process was repeated with the other arm. Three suitcases and four bags.

'Oh the poor man, it's too much…'

'Tell him to turn round, I must have a photo of this…'

'Can he go over there? I can't get him in from here…'

The same loading process was going on with the other cases and bags. In each case it was the puniest porters being loaded by the burliest.

'Good tip, sahib,' said one of the laden men.

'Very good tip,' muttered a porter who I knew had merely stood and watched.

There were about six heavily laden men who suddenly turned and trotted off at almost a jogging pace towards a railway bridge over the platforms. They were followed by another 15 or so completely unladen porters. We had difficulty in keeping up, some of our group pulling, some carrying their hand luggage. We passed a sign that said:

'*Licensed Porters Only. Maximum Rupees 5 per Headload*'

FIRST CLASS & SECOND CLASS, UPPER AND LOWER

To tell you the truth, I did know about the 1st Class and the 2nd Class. I had received a fax from the agents warning me about it months before, but I had kept quiet, keeping the unwelcome news from Jill and from the group, hoping that it would not happen. Now we were about to board the train - *our first train journey with a group* - it was going to happen. There was the group struggling with hand luggage; ahead of us was a bridge, and we could see our luggage towering above the heads of the porters, swaying as they rapidly ascended the stairs.

'Which platform?'

'Have we got to climb up there?'

'I can't go all up there.'

'They're going far too fast.'

I caught up with Saddam, our guide. 'Please tell me which platform we are on - the group is strung out a long way back'

'Platform 3. It is platform 3. We will join *Tamil Nadu Night Mail*. Hurry please. We must load all baggages and allocate seat numbers. Group is in two bogies only - 1st Class and 2nd Class A/C also'

Although I knew this, I was as dismayed as if learning it for the first time. It felt that I *was* learning it for the first time. I certainly needed to *behave* as if learning it for the first time.

'What? Are we in *two carriages*?'

'Yes, Yes. In two bogies only, very close. I think you already…'

'Do you mean we are not *together*?' I had to keep up the pretence.

'Very near. Please hurry as we have much to arrange - luggages, seat numbers, bedrolls. Dinner also can be bookable in advance'

We had experienced dinner, luggages, seat numbers, bed-rolls, upper berths and lower berths, on many earlier trips. But then there were only two of us. Now we were 27 and were to be split between 1st Class and 2nd Class.

'These bogies - are you saying that we have to *divide into two? Some in 1st and some in 2nd*?'

'Yes, yes, we have taken full allocation. Cost is same, so group can accommodate.'

Jill was listening and watching me closely; she addressed Saddam, 'How many berths are in 1st Class?' she spoke slowly, deliberately and quite firmly.

'There are 12 seats in 1st Class, others are in 2nd only,' He sounded defensive.

'I see.' She turned to me 'Did you know about this? (A pause) And how do you propose to divide them?'

'Er, well, I could ask who would prefer…'

'Ask? How will you ask? They are ambling about all over the place - look!'

I had already seen: some were buying water from a stall, others biscuits, bananas, others browsing at *Higginbottom's* magazine stall, some standing in knots, fending off beggars.

'Look' said Jill decisively, 'Much better to simply divide. Mr Saddam, do you have the seat numbers?'

'Yes, certainly, I have.' He handed me an envelope and inside were the complex tickets - each ticket had 8 or 10 names printed by a computer but designed to confuse the most seasoned rail traveller. Bogie numbers, code numbers, what may have been berth numbers. There were even numbers giving the ages of the travellers alongside an approximation of some names I recognized. The numbers were seldom consecutive, husbands and wives appeared on different sheets, unknown names appeared between them.

'Also, names are pasted on the bogie' said Saddam, helpfully, 'There will be no confusion.'

A diesel engine chugged towards us and pulled a long train of grimy carriages slowly past us. Most had barred windows, some labelled '2nd 2 Tier,' others '3rd 3 tier,' and one 'Pantry Car.' Now one painted a dark blue with black, opaque windows came to a halt just beyond us, '2nd Class A/C', and immediately behind it another dark red carriage - again with bars over the windows - labelled '1st Class Sleeper.'

'Is this our train?' People gathered together.

'Do we get in?'

'What's happening with the luggage?'

'Hang on,' I tried to shout above the noise - the hissing and grunting of the train, the vendors desperate to sell more wares, the whistles and bangs and general chatter all grew to a crescendo. 'It is our train, but we can't board yet, we need to sort out who will...'

'Can you all come nearer?' This was from Jill, for once calling quite loudly. The group obeyed, quite unused to commands from my wife. She looked at me. It meant *You've got into this mess, so do something.*

'Er, yes,' I started, 'It seems we will be in two carriages, so we need to divide you. Some will be in 1st Class and the others in 2nd Class, just next door... '

'We will travel 1st Class', said Jacky.

'Good,' said Jill, 'Who else would prefer 1st?' I recognised the steel in her voice, and hoped the others did not. Almost every hand shot up.

'I don't think we have so many 1st Class berths' I said anxiously, 'The 2nd is quite OK.'

'Oh, yes,' said Saddam, '2nd A/C is very comfortable. Also it is having A/C.'

'What has the 1st Class got?' asked several.

'1st Class is also very comfortable, but is not having A/C. Is having fan only. But now is the winter season, so A/C is not necessary.'

It was around two in the afternoon. The temperature on the railway platform was around 30 degrees. The raised hands withdrew.

Meanwhile, Jill had been busy with the lists and tickets.

'Here,' she hissed, 'I've made a list for the 1st Class. Just tell them where they'll be. I've put the older couples together and they'll just have to sort out who has which berths. There are more in the 2nd, but they are closer together. But, as I suspected, you and I will be in the corridor!'

'Oh, hell. Have they given us some in the corridor?'

'Yes, five, just to be awkward, but three are lower - one of them better be yours.'

We knew the corridor berths: narrower, distinctly less comfortable and vulnerable. The upper was simply a narrow shelf that folded down, with a meagre amount of padding under the grey plastic. The lower was a more complicated affair, made up from the backs of facing seats folding down to meet in the middle like a lowering bridge, making a narrow bed of no more than 20 inches wide and less than 6 feet long, normally with an unfortunate gap in the middle where the backs failed to meet. My experience was that this could vary from *actually overlapping*, occasionally meeting, to a gap of one or two inches. Sometimes one seat back lowered more than the other and sometimes the angle of the two ends varied, resulting in a twisted spine for the journey. As for vulnerability, on previous journeys the trips to the loo had so often meant stumbling into the projecting knee, or arm, or backside of a lower corridor passenger in the middle of the night. This had not appeared to disturb their sleep, whereas I seldom slept and was buffeted by the movements of fellow passengers along the corridor.

'Right,' I said, 'We've sorted it out …' and read out a list of mainly couples and sharing ladies and a series of berth numbers.

'You can go in the 1st Class carriage - there - and the rest of us will be next door in the 2nd - here. I had better keep all the tickets with me for the inspector. The thing is, you'll have to decide who goes in the lower berths and who goes in the upper.'

'I can't possibly go in…'

'Does it mean climbing up?'

'I have to get up in the night...'

'You mean down?'

'So do I. Quite often. I can't go climbing down…'

'Where are the loos, anyway?'

Crowds of people were now gathered around the doors at both ends of each carriage, struggling to read the name-lists pasted to the outside.

'What's that number? Are you number 74?'

'No I'm 27U, whatever that is. What's this 74?'

'You can identify by name and age also' said Saddam, helpfully.

'Heavens! I do hope they've not put up my age for all to see…'

'Molly, this is your one, 17L'

'Is that up or down?'

'Down. L is down.'

'Oh I don't mind going up, if someone needs to be down' said Molly kindly, 'but who is this Chatterjee M K 53 in 17U? Is there an Indian gentleman above me?'

'I think you are in the First Class,' said Jill, rather firmly, 'Molly, do you mind…'

'Well, there's an adventure,' cried Ingrid. 'I don't mind having an Indian gentleman above me…'

VEG AND NON-VEG

'Yes, yes, dinner will be available. Veg and non-veg, both. You can place order.' Our 2nd class bogie attendant's figure-of-eight head-movement confirmed his confidence.

'Oh good, and can you tell me, the people in First Class, can they also place order? More of my group is there and the door is locked - I wanted to speak with them.'

'Oh yes, they can place order in 1st Class with 1st Class Car Attendant only. 1st Class is having 1st Class Car Attendant. He will do the needful. Door is locked and only at station can you get down, but many stations are halting for only two minutes only. So you must not detrain except at big stations for 5 / 6 minute halt. Other halts are too short. At Suriyapet you may get down.'

'And when do we get to wherever you said? Can we order dinner there?'

'At Suriyapet. We will reach before one hour. But I am taking order. You want veg or non-veg.'

'I'll ask' I replied, calling out 'How many of you would like to order dinner? There's veg or non-veg.'

'What is non-veg?' someone asked.

'Non-veg is 25 rupees only: veg is 15 rupees only,' said our attendant helpfully.

'Yes, but what *is* non-veg?'

'Non-veg is also coming with veg,' came the reply, 'but veg is veg only.'

'Yes, but is the non-veg mutton or chicken or fish, or what?'

'May be *yeg* also. Not chicken. Not fish. Chicken is extra order.'

'Yeg?' I had forgotten that a South Indian Tamil pronunciation of English put a Y in front of as many words as possible. Visiting primary schools years before, I had heard the English alphabet being learned this way- Yey, B,C,D,Yee, Yef, G, H, Yi - and culminating in a flurry of Yel, Yem, Yen, Yo, P - all delivered to a punchy, tuneless but rhythmic chant and head-rolling.

'Yes, yeg curry, or maybe meat'

'What is he saying' asked several voices.

'Non-veg may be yeg, or may be meat' I explained.

'What about chicken?'

The attendant was starting to panic, 'No, no, for chicken special order is there. For chicken they must telegraph special order.'

'I'd like chicken.'

'Me too.'

'Catherine's got that packed lunch; we're sharing with her,' said Val.

Catherine had gone out for dinner with a Hyderabad family during our stay. They had been so horrified to learn that she would be on a train journey and expected to eat railway food, they had ordered a picnic for her from a caterer. Several cake boxes, all tied with pink ribbon had been delivered and stacked in the corner of her upper berth.

'OK' I said. 'Let's have a count-up. How many for the veg meal?'

'What about an omelette? Can I get an omelette?' someone asked.

'Yes, yes, omelette is there, but omelette is with omelette man only, he will be coming later. But that is not meal. For meal we must take order. Veg or non-veg.'

'Or chicken'

'Oh yes, for chicken special order.'

I repeated this as best I could and ended with a count of 7 veg, 3 non-veg, and 3 special order chicken. Jill said no - maybe an omelette man would come along…

'Suriyapet is coming,' called the attendant as the train slowed. 'Here is Suriyapet. Train is standing for 4 minutes only.' I quickly climbed down to the platform. Some of our 1st Class group were looking out through their open barred windows.

'What happens about dinner?'called Jacky

'Haven't you given your order to the car attendant?'

'I haven't seen one.'

'What about the others?' Others appeared at the next windows, but Jacky continued,

'Anyway, David won't eat any foreign food. Just an omelette will do.'

'Ah, there's supposed to be an omelette man coming round, you'll have to try to catch him. This station has omelettes, but I don't think there will be time… What about all of you? There are veg and non-veg meals.'

'Yes, I'll have some. I'm jolly hungry - veg will be all right for me,' said Jacky.

'We've shared some food we brought,' said Molly, 'Some biscuits and bananas; I don't think Jean would like to eat railway food…'

'Well I certainly would,' said Alwyn. 'I'm jolly hungry and I'm sure Hugo is too.'

'Certainly am,' joined in Hugo. 'I was quite looking forward to a proper train meal. Used to have them on the trains all the time when we were out here.' Hugo was an old India-hand.

Back in our 2nd Class I accosted the attendant,

'What about the people in First Class?' I demanded. 'No-one has taken an order for dinner. They have not seen any attendant. Can you contact him?'

'There is 1st Class attendant only. He is the in-charge and must take order and will do the needful.'

But *no*, at the next short stop when I should not have got down to enquire, I learned there had been no attendant and no order for dinner had been taken. No vendors had visited the carriage which, it now seems was not only locked at both ends from the rest of the train, but was also locked to the platforms except at major stations. The 1st Class passengers clearly had super security, but no access to food or drink.

At Vadorada, a big city with a slightly longer stop, while the 1st Class people were still calling out that no orders had been taken, our 2nd class meals were delivered by a waiter wearing a shirt, waistcoat, paper bow tie (askew and grubby) and a paper hat, pointed back and front. I asked him about the 1st class carriage, but he merely smiled and rolled his head. People's reaction to the food varied from 'Christ! It's so hot! It's uneatable!' to 'Delicious, if a little spicy.' Offers of 'try this one' resulted in veg being exchanged for non-veg, and chicken - distinguishable from the other by a piece of splintered chicken-bone protruding from one of the yellowish sauces - being exchanged for veg. The outcome was that not a lot was eaten. Cynthia was more positive,

'It *is* rather good, but there's far more here than I can eat. Richard are those poor people in the first class really not to have any dinner? Do you think they would appreciate some food parcels?'

'Here,' said Catherine, 'those people sent an enormous picnic. There's a mountain left over - sandwiches, cakes, some kind of cutlet things - salad and pickle…'

So a Famine Relief committee prepared parcels: some wrapped in foil, some in plastic. There did seem a lot of food. The contents of Catherine's boxes were divided up, the left-over train meals repacked. I went in search of our attendant.

'When is the next stop?' I demanded.

'No sir, next stop is not stopping. Two minutes only, sir'

'Two minutes or not, I must give my group members some food. It's now nearly 10 o'clock and some of them haven't eaten since morning.'

I was ready. Jill opened the door and held it open as the train slowed. I jumped down and the parcels were handed down. Two fell to the platform, but I didn't stop to pick them up.

'Food parcels' I shouted. 'Food parcels'

Hands began to appear, pushed through the bars of 1st Class. At each pair of out-thrust hands I deposited one or two parcels, but there were more hands than parcels, so I ran back to find those I had dropped. It occurred to me that some of the hands were quite dark in colour, but I had no time to find out who had received our gifts. I raced back to the hands - thrust the last squashy foil packs into the nearest - and ran back to my door, held open by Jill.

At Madras station the next morning I met a rather sullen lot of 1st Class travellers.

'We've been here for several minutes, and it's rather hot,' said Jacky, firmly.

Indeed the heat struck us as we climbed down from the train from our 2nd Class A/C.

'In fact, it's been hot the whole journey,' said someone else.

'So much for First Class.'

'Thank God you brought those food parcels. Whatever it was, it was very welcome.'

'I had a delicious sandwich - it may have been tomato and cucumber but…'

'Poor Jackie only got a packet of tomato ketchup!'

'What?' I cried, '*Tomato ketchup*!'

'Yes,' said Jacky, 'Those food parcels you sent were OK *for some*, but I got a foil packet that was *only tomato ketchup*! I spread it on some Marie Biscuits.'

Our attendant was hovering on the platform for his tip. I asked him why there was no attendant for 1st Class.

'I am only 2nd Class in charge, sir. 1st Class is out of station.'

CHARPOYS AND WHEELCHAIRS

That evening we were to leave Jodhpur by train for Jaisalmer - a romantic and picturesque city in the desert a few hundred miles away. The roads in those days were not at all good, and to save a very rough journey, I had plannd the group's journey by train. We had done it before - just the two of us - and while not at all comfortable, it had proved the most convenient way of getting to what was, after all, a wonderful destination.

But earlier in the day there had been two rather strange events. The first was while visiting the market in the centre of the city: it was here that, unknown to us at the time, we would meet an unfortunate character who we would see later under very different circumstances. Norman, one of our travelling companions, was a big, jolly and gregarious dentist - recently retired - who was intrigued by the out-door dentistry that was going on in the market square. Perhaps a dozen local dentists had set out their stalls in the market; mostly small wooden boxes, perhaps one foot square (which served as the dentist chair - or stool - when occupied), on which were displayed dental tools and several sets of false teeth. One enterprising dentist even had a sophisticated drill - the power supply coming from a small boy pedalling a bicycle with the rear wheel lifted off the ground. A cable was ingeniously linked to the gearing of the wheel, which powered the drill the dentist held in his hand as he attended to his patient. Everywhere there were queues of people, squatting in line, waiting their turn, watching the unfortunate undergoing treatment. More prominent than most was a poor man with an enormous bandage under his chin and his beard, tied with a huge bow on the top of his head, reminiscent of a scene from a *Dandy* or *Beano* comic. He rocked from side to side, one hand clamped to his cheek, uttering a long, low, continuous moan. Strolling among this scene, Norman stooped and picked up a large and powerful looking wrench from among the dental tools.
'My god! Look at this! These were in the dental museum when I was a student!' He squatted down beside the puzzled looking dentist and faced the queue of patients, brandishing the wrench and beckoning for the next in line to join him for treatment! Without a word the whole queue, including the bandaged rocking man, rapidly stood up and made their escape.

Later in the day we passed near the railway station and I was puzzled by a number of *charpoy* shops - perhaps 5 or 6 of them - with their *charpoys* lined up, stacked against the walls. *Charpoys*, I should explain, are those Indian beds with a wooden frame on four short legs, with cord, or nowadays even plastic webbing, interwoven between the frame to make the base for the bed. We had sometimes tried to sleep on these, without much success. I am not tall, but they were always too short, even for me. But why were shops selling *charpoys*? They were easy enough to make, and I had often seen shops selling just the legs for part of a home assembly kit. But why sell the whole, ready-made *charpoy*? So cumbersome to carry home…

The answer came later in the evening, when we arrived at the station for our train to Jaisalmer. Now the whole street where we had seen the *charpoys* was transformed into an open air series of hotels: the *charpoys* were laid out as beds onto the pavements and into the street. There must have been 40 or 50 of them. Each hotel had their *charpoys* laid out in a tightly packed block, with hardly an inch of space between. What I thought were *charpoy* shops were in fact hotels, providing accommodation, tea, snacks - even meals - for passengers waiting for trains. The *charpoys* now had lumpy-looking mattresses, and shrouded under blankets we could see there were many occupants sleeping. There were newer arrivals, clambering over the *charpoys* and their occupants to reach the vacant places. There were couples, even whole families, sitting up, but also wrapped in blankets, sipping tea or eating from tiffin-carriers.

I was certainly intrigued by this scene and, thinking perhaps of future tours, enquired the cost of a bed in this outdoor hotel. It was five rupees plus one rupee per blanket, inclusive of morning tea. Sadly, one figure was not sleeping or eating: he was our friend from the dentist surgery. We recognised him at once, now sitting cross-legged and disconsolate, on a charpoy in the centre of the street; the bandage still tied under his chin with the bow on top of his head, and still gently rocking side to side and to and fro, his hand still clamped to his cheek, and still uttering his low, sad moans - clearly audible to us who stared at the scene, and to his neighbours. We never knew if he had received treatment, or whether he would be travelling on our train.

But we had our own patient to worry about. Rosie, a most resilient and enthusiastic member of our group had not been well for some days. She had been OK in Jaipur, seemed unwell in Udaipur, a bit better in Jhodpur. But her stomach problems had not gone away despite, or perhaps because of the various remedies she had been given by several well-intentioned others. She had become quite weak, but was determined to carry on, and said she was not going to miss any part of the tour and certainly not Jaisalmer. I was quite worried about her; a night train - especially the rattling old rolling-stock of the Jaisalmer train - wasn't going to help her, but someone suggested I ask if the station had a wheelchair. This would help her to the platform and provide a seat while we waited and installed ourselves. I didn't hold out much hope: a wheelchair? At Jodhpur station? But to my surprise, our guide thought a wheel chair may be possible, and he said so in the hearing of Ingrid. Ingrid was a large, forthright lady, who so far had not exhibited any symptoms or even outward signs of illness, but when the wheelchair was mentioned she spoke up immediately.

'Oh, if there's a wheelchair, I've not been feeling at all well, and I should certainly have one…'

One wheelchair was most unlikely; two wheelchairs would be out of the question. But to my great surprise, after our guide went into the station to enquire, we saw two wheelchairs being pushed towards our coach. Ingrid was almost the first off the coach and rapidly installed herself in the first wheelchair, clutching her bits of hand-luggage around her. Rather like the driver of a husky team, she called out instructions to her pusher, pointed to the station entrance and set off. Several people helped Rosie down, two holding her arms, others with her hand-luggage, and they gently settled her down in the second chair, with the charming and smiling chair-pusher helping too. When we were all down, and the luggage had been attended to, we all set off for the station.

I was a little way behind Rosie's wheelchair and at first thought it was just a play of the light. The lighting was quite dim in the station fore-court, but it looked from behind as if one of the big wheels of the wheel-chair was not running true. It was not a play of the light: as they made their way over the fairly rough ground, the wobbling wheel became worse. I ran forward, but too late; the wheel fell sideways, and the chair followed, depositing Rosie in a heap in the dust, surrounded by her small bags. As she lay there, with others trying to get her to her feet she muttered quite loudly,

'I'm OK, really… I'm all-right… And don't worry, I'm saving up for the next trip. Just don't take me to any places ending in '*pur*'.'

CONSUMPTION OF ALCOHOL IS TOTALLY PROHIBITED

In the 19th century, the British parliament spent more time talking about *drink* than any other topic. Taxes, you may think? War? Industry? Empire? No! It was *drink*. Hardly surprising, then, that it should feature so prominently among our travellers to India. Except that parliament - torn between the temperance movement and the brewers and distillers - was talking about 'whether to drink', whereas our travellers were absorbed with 'when' or 'what' and sometimes with 'what' to drink 'with what'. Before leaving for a tour, questions were asked about what drink to take, how much to take, what we could buy there and what mixers could be found; when we were on tour, people were worried about finding *more* drink, and ensuring supplies lasted to the day of return. The fact that *tonic* was much more difficult to find, and often more expensive than *gin*, remains a major concern even to the present day.

Friendships have been forged and destroyed by drink. Two lovely elderly ladies, who had decided to share a room on more than one tour, came to me, slightly tipsy one day, saying,
'How could you know we would have so much in common?' What they really had in common was a reluctance to waste money on single rooms, but the practicality of sharing was bonded in liquid lunches and red-cheeked evenings. On the other hand, two men - also sharing a room to save money - one of whom consumed a lot and was always looking for the next supplies, the other who reeled about drunk after a mere sip, asked for separate rooms after a few days - their incompatibility reinforced by alcohol.

However, when travelling by train the following sign was often prominently displayed:

INDIAN RAILWAYS

THE CONSUMPTION OF ALCOHOLIC BEVERAGES IS TOTALLY PROHIBITED

OFFENDERS WILL BE FINED NOT LESS THAN Rs 3000 OR A PERIOD OF...

This was not taken too seriously by our travellers, and was, I regret to say, not so much ignored as evaded. Preparations for train travel often involved ensuring that supplies were to hand -

'I've got my Scotch in that other bag…' 'Thank God I've got the gin…' 'Have we got enough paper cups?'

And so that they wouldn't be immediately detected -

'I've got mine in a brown paper bag…' 'I've poured mine into this water bottle, they'll think it's apple juice…'

For some years we avoided clashes with the law. Our very first train journey - after sorting out the traumas of who was in which compartment and who would have upper or lower berths - although only a little after three in the afternoon, set the scene for many journeys to follow. Cynthia, raising a paper cup from her upper berth, said,

'Cheers! Isn't this exciting. Do have a little of this, it will lift the spirits. We shall be frightfully comfortable here.'

Catherine and Val climbed up on to the opposite bunk while the paper cups were being handed around. Others from neighbouring compartments came to visit, bringing more bottles, crisps and some *Bombay Mix*. Although the age profile was a little different, the scene started to resemble the train journey in that wonderful film *Some Like it Hot*, and the mood was indeed soon lifted.

Cups were held out and the mysterious bottle shaped brown paper bags were thrust out from the compartments. An Indian couple, sitting cross-legged and eating their fresh-from-home food in the corridor berths nearby smiled and nodded, but did not accept the offers made to them, and the Car Attendant also smiled knowingly as he made his way past us.

He was watching closely; the eating couple looking on, wide-eyed.

'Would your friend like some?' called Betty. She called over to him, rather familiarly, 'Here, I know you are very busy, but would you like a little drink?' There was a pause, a smile and the enigmatic figure-of-eight waggle of the head,

Of course: the penny dropped. Why else was he here? But no:

'Just one minute Sahib, I am coming,' and he shot off at speed, out of sight along the corridor.

'Oh God, now we're for it,' I said to Jill, 'he's gone to report…'

'I very much doubt it,' said Jill.

Within two minutes our man was back, but now accompanied by two disreputable looking colleagues - all three grinning in anticipation and not at all hostile.

'Just one tot,' said our man. 'My colleagues also are taking small tot,'

'Just one tot,' said his friend, another head waggle to confirm appreciation.

'One small tot only,' said the third.

So rather large tots were poured and with much gesturing which would have meant clinking, if only the paper cups would clink, our party increased. By now, the eating man, quite evidently against his wife's wishes, was holding a paper cup, and remarkably soon all four cups were thrust forward to be replenished.

I seem to be unable to learn from experience, and perhaps should not have been so worried when, on a journey years later, the train party having become a little loud and careless, the brown paper bags discarded and the paper cups replenished, I really did think we would be in trouble. It was Melanie, 90 years of age, and well known for both her capacity and her generosity, who was quite loudly offering drink to all those near her - a bottle in one hand, her cup in the other - who we nearly lost to the forces of law and order. Our railway attendant, who had brought round the bedding for the night - a signal that we should retire - was making unusually frequent appearances along the compartment. Although only about eight o'clock, some Indian passengers had indeed retired and I suspect had, not unreasonably, complained about the noise coming from the compartments we occupied. The attendant, a serious middle-aged gentleman with a gingerish beard that may have indicated he was a *Haji* - one who had been to Mecca - took me to one side and pointed out the prohibition notice.

'Please, sir, you are the in-charge. See - there is notice. It is not allowed…'

'Oh dear, I am so sorry. I'll see what I can do…' But what could I do? The group was clearly in no mood to stop or go to bed. Melanie was tottering towards us along the corridor, bottle outstretched. The attendant looked at her, opened the door at the end of the corridor and fled.

'I think we may be in trouble, Melanie. That chap just said we're not supposed to drink.'

'Not drink? Nonsense! Here, let me top you up.'

'No, hang on. I think he was serious. Did you notice his red beard?'

Sure enough, a few minutes later our *Haji* reappeared but now *accompanied by two armed guards*. They were in khaki uniform and each held a rifle.

'Oh Christ!' I looked at Jill, 'We're for it now.' I turned to the guards:

'I'm so sorry, but this lady has a heart condition, so you see, this is her medicine…' The guards had little or no English, but the attendant was remarkably considerate.

'Please, lady, sit. Please take a seat. Do not worry.'

'Would you like a drink?' asked Melanie quite loudly. 'How about these chaps?' She held up the bottle and several cups. The *Haji* smiled. One of the guards waggled his head in appreciation, the other stacked the rifles in the corner and passed round the cups.

RAILWAY TRACKS AND A RAILWAY KITCHEN

We left Madras Egmore station - a late Victorian extravaganza - more or less on time. It was not *very* early in the morning, but as the train slowly pulled out of the platform, a sight, familiar to me, but quite unfamiliar to the rest of the group, came into view. It was the rear view of several dozen men and boys and small children, all with naked bottoms, squatting, balanced on the complex of converging railway tracks. Each of them, though not far apart from one another, had found a certain distance from his neighbour. Each had a small brass or aluminium water pot for cleansing and squatted in a trance-like state, gazing unseeing into the distance. It seemed that the elevation of the metal track a few inches above the shingle, although offering only a narrow foot-place for squatting, provided a favourite and convenient lavatory for the residents of the shanties and other dwellings visible beyond the railway.

Jill and I had become used to this railway experience on earlier visits to India, having frequently pulled out of or into railway stations in the early mornings. Our only train journey with this group had departed in the afternoon (not an hour for group squatting), and arrived into Madras while still dark - before the others could be aware of this particular aspect of railway travel. Now they very soon became aware.

'What are all those people doing?'

'Good heavens, surely..?'

'Are they really…?'

'How frightful!'

'Thank goodness there's a hot sun.'

'It's a good job they can balance so well.'

'I must get a shot of this. No-one will believe… David, do you have your video handy?'

The train rumbled slowly through the suburbs - concrete houses, flats, sheds, warehouses, suburban stations. The buildings were interspersed with shanties and some waste grounds. We passed level crossings where queues of traffic - trucks, buses, motorbikes, bullock-carts, carts, bicycles - completely blocked both lanes while waiting for our train to cross. There were cows and bullocks munching from piles of garbage, then some fields and palm trees, and slowly we moved out into the countryside.

'*Chai, chai*, coffee, coffee, *chai*,' was heard approaching along the corridor, followed by a uniformed drinks man in smart 'Ghandi' cap, who slid open the door of the compartment.

'*Chai, chai*' he shouted at us. 'Coffee, *chai*.' Somehow he carried a large shiny tea-urn, paper cups, sachets of coffee, tea bags, sugar, and when some of the people said 'yes' to tea or coffee, he was able to deftly grip the urn between his knees while he held a paper cup below the tap which was turned to allow a pale milky liquid to flow into the coffee powder or tea bag. Several of these were passed to us.

'May I have black coffee, please,' asked Molly.

'Black coffee after,' said the man, who set down his urn and collected the few rupees per cup. People proffered 10 or 20 rupee notes.

'No change, you pay,' said our man abruptly, snatching a 20 rupee note, and he was gone.

Within a few minutes he was followed by a man offering 'Sandwich, sandwich', which, we learned, was 'Bread-butter sandwich', then another with 'Omelette, omelette,' 'Tomato soup,' '*Wadai, wadai*,' (a tough dough-nut like object, not sweet, but not tasting of anything else).

'Book, book,' was a magazine seller with the latest film magazines - stories of the stars of Bollywood and Tamil movies, and he was soon followed by others offering 'Chips' (crisps), 'Peanuts' and a host of other delicacies, but no black coffee.

I wondered along the corridor to look in on the others. Some, to my surprise were eating 'Omelette' and 'Sandwich' liberally dotted with tomato ketchup. Others were sipping the hot, but indistinguishable tea-cum-coffee.

'Have you seen the kitchen?' asked Ian, distastefully. He was eating a very western looking pastry, evidently taken from the hotel breakfast. 'It's in the next carriage, next to the pantry car. How any of you can eat anything made in there is beyond me. We never…'

'I don't suppose you'd much like the place your bun was made,' said Betty, rather cruelly, tucking into an omelette. 'This is delicious, it's got onion and tomato and quite a lot of green chilli.'

It was only nine o'clock, but we had eaten breakfast at six, the omelette did smell good and I went to have a look. Beyond the lavatory at the end of our compartment, I could cross over into the next: here was the pantry car and the first section was a small cafeteria with several Indian gentlemen sitting eating and drinking at the plastic topped tables, smiling and nodding as I passed through.

From the cafeteria, the corridor went on alongside the kitchen. I peered through a hatch, and grinning men inside waved to me to join them. It was a dramatic sight: at either end of the kitchen was a large, black, iron, coal-fired range, and beside each, a pile of coal on the floor. Both ranges had flames roaring out of the top, while cooks stood over them wielding huge frying pans, tossing the food to and fro; sometimes one of them would lean across and stir one of the big cauldrons of indistinguishable yellowish mixtures bubbling away, and above all this was the steam and smoke rising from the ranges. Another man was loading pieces of coal into the top of one of the stoves, not with a shovel, but with his hands. Against the far wall, between the windows in the middle of the kitchen was a *tandoor* oven, a tall cylinder of clay, with a man hooking out freshly cooked *rotis* with a long handled metal hook and throwing them into small baskets. As he did so another man was placing the newly made *roti* dough on to a cloth pad and leaning over the *tandoor* to stick them to the inside wall of the oven. He took them from a stack prepared by the third man of the *roti* team who stood in the centre of the space at a long aluminium topped table. He was deftly scooping up fistfulls of dough, dipping it in flour and patting it against the palm of the other hand to make a *roti* about the size of a side plate. This three man team worked so fast that there was a constant supply thrown into baskets that were whisked away by the waiters. At the same table there were another 4 or 5 men standing, chopping vegetables and stirring strange mixtures in huge metal bowls. All the men were wearing vests, *lungis* tied round their waists and white cloths tied round their heads, and some were bare-foot. They were glistening with sweat - the outside temperature was certainly very warm when we boarded the train - perhaps 30 degrees, but in this fiery kitchen it must have been at least 45.

'Taste, taste,' called one of the men, grinning. 'Cutlet' called one, '*Pakora*' called another, '*Wadai*,' a third, and soon I was tasting everything on offer. Piping hot in every sense, and some rather delicious. A hot, sizzling cheerfulness emanated from the place. The men grinned, sweated, wiped their foreheads with their arms, or with grey cloths slung over the shoulder. All this was too good to be true; surely this was a film opportunity? I watched and tasted for several minutes and in a kind of sign language interspersed with a few words of English - Hindi - Tamil we all seemed to get on very well together.

'I have friends with film camera' I said, miming a 'cameraman' by holding one hand with thumb and middle finger making a frame to one eye and winding an imaginary handle by my ear.

'OK to film?' Film camera they certainly understood; who we were they did not. Perhaps we were Movie Film Makers? For that moment I imagined we were and scurried back to find the Movie Film Makers within our group.

'David, do you have the video camera ready? There's a wonderful scene down at the pantry car.' I quickly told him about it.

'Oh, rather, that sounds very good, but Tom's taken the camera down to the open door - he's taking the passing scene.'

'I think you'll find the pantry car very much more interesting. And they think you are making a film, so they are very keen to take part… I'll be back.'

I left him to find our camera man sitting on the floor of the corridor at an open door, filming the passing rural scene of relatively dull patch of scrub land, palm trees, fields and occasional cows. He was very soon persuaded to bring the camera to the pantry car. By the time we had collected David there were seven or eight of us squashing into the pantry car, soon joined by several of the Indian gentlemen who had been eating 'Meals' in the café. The animated scene I had left became even more animated. Our rather large old-fashioned video camera could, with a stretch of imagination, be that of a team of 'Movie Makers'. The large crowd of foreigners and Indians I had brought with me could pass for the Movie team. Certainly our cook-actors responded magnificently, posing extravagantly, whirling the *rotis* in the air, shouting instructions to one another, tossing the fried items, causing huge flames to leap from their pans and all the time shouting 'Taste, taste' to us and pushing fingerfuls of food into mouths and hands. We had to act our part, too. With thumbs and fingers made into rectangles and held to eyes David and I shouted directorial instructions to Tom, others joining in:

'Here, here, we need this shot.'

'Pan over here.'

'Get this chap in.'

'Tracking shot.'

'Cut. Take 47.'

'Action,' and much more nonsense.

The cooks redoubled their efforts, shouting 'Me also' and copying our 'Here, here.' It was no pretence; at last we were on the edge of making a major Movie. We had action, we had colour, we had emotion, we had stars.

HOLY PLACES

A FEW WORDS ABOUT INDIA'S HOLY PLACES

The great majority of Indians are very devout, and like all devout people, they have lots of places to be devout in. As we all know, if they are Moslem this can be wherever they happen to be at prayer time: all that's needed is to know which way to face towards Mecca. If they are Hindu, or Jain, or Buddhist, or Sikh (all of which started off in India), or Christian, the place for devotion can also be very simple and close to home: a poor family may just have a postcard or other picture of their favourite deity or spiritual leader stuck on the wall of their home, or they may have a little shelf on which they may light a candle or an incense stick in front of some small clay or brass or plastic images. If a bit better off, they may have a cupboard containing a shrine, and if really well off, even a room for daily worship. But all the religions also like to build special holy places, whether for communal worship, ceremonies, instruction or just to get a sight of their god. Like most religious people the world over, they build a lot. We have all built a lot - we have our churches and cathedrals and chapels dotted about. It's just that Indians build so very many. The Jains didn't build just one or two temples at Palitana - just one of their holy places - they covered the hillside there with them; there are nearly 900 together in a big job-lot. And whereas we have lots of denominations all requiring a separate place to worship, so do the Indian religions, and in addition the Hindus have hundreds, some claim millions, of gods and goddesses who all need somewhere to be. The hugely wealthy Mr Birla of the great Birla global industrial empire apparently received warnings from on high that if he stopped building temples his empire would collapse, so he keeps on building them. And very grand and lavish and beautiful they are too; he even employs Group 4 Security to guard some of them and turn away any really scruffy improperly dressed people who want to go inside.

We are fortunate that man's religious zeal for Holy Places has produced all this art and architecture - and music too - for it has given us most of the man-made wonders of the world and leads us to travel about to look at them. It's certainly why many people go to India. Yes, there are the mighty Himalayas to look at, and we might go about hoping to see a tiger, and certainly there are some pretty impressive other buildings - forts and palaces, for example - to admire, But when we think of going there, surely it's the Taj Mahal we think of (a tomb, I know, but a pretty religious one, which is also a shrine), or the great mosques, mostly built when the Moghuls ruled India. Or those exotic and mysterious temples, religious caves, or the holy bathing ghats at Varanasi, where we can watch bathers and cremations and fire ceremonies.

India is not content with just holy buildings, but also has sacred cities, sacred rivers, sacred hills and mountains. Those old sages certainly knew a thing or two about the geography of the whole sub-continent because all their mythological stories are firmly located in these holy places: gods and goddesses got married here, were born there, vanquished a demon on that hill, performed a miracle in this river, resided in that mountain abode. And while Christians have mainly stopped going off on pilgrimage - apart from a trip to the Holy Land, perhaps - Indians are great pilgrims, setting off individually or in great throngs to visit their holy places. Eventually the very devout would like to end their days by being sprinkled into a very special holy place - the Holy Mother Ganges or one of her substitutes.

India's holy places and the fascination of her mysterious religious practices are among the attractions that draw us there. Sadly, though, we tourists don't have the stamina of the pilgrims. All over the orient one hears the phrase, 'Oh no, not another temple!' or 'Oh, no, not another mosque,' or, 'Sorry, I'm templed out.' Mind you, nearer home, the cultured traveller to the Italian Renaisance can easily overhear similar phrases: 'I won't mind if I don't see another Madonna and Child as long as I live'. And in the east a whole range of pernicious, sometimes painful, and often contagious diseases has developed among travellers - *templitis* and its side-effect *temple-groin* are not uncommon - the latter brought on by the frequent necessity to *climb*; people succumb quite rapidly to *mosque-fatigue*, *tombitis*, and in some areas even *fortitis*. Sadly, the main antidote, often prescribed by unscrupulous guides as they lure the unwary patients into a 'co-operative' of a thousand delights, has resulted in the rapid advance of yet another incurable disease of tourists - *shopaholicism*. It is not always the fault of the guides. A cultured Indian friend of ours told us how, as a student, she had tried to earn a little spare cash as a part-time guide in Delhi. Showing an American group the history and wonders of that city - the Qutub Minar, the Friday Mosque, the Tomb of Emperor Humayun, the Birla Temple, they would respond,

'OK, baby, that's enough! When do we get to the shops?' At the shops they would demand,

'Huh! We saw the same thing cheaper! How much is your cut?'

A BLESSING AT RANAKPUR

Let me say straight away that the Jain temple at Ranakpur is one of the great sights of India. It is just wonderful: a complex, beautiful and intricately carved pearly-white marble jewel box, and, unusual in Indian temples, suffused with light: a lovely, soft, marble-reflecting light. It is tucked away into the edge of the Aravali Hills, in what was a remote spot, but is on a major highway and so very accessible to pilgrims and tourists. Everyone who goes to Rajasthan visits this place, or if they don't, they should. We have been so many times and have known the chief priest and watch his family grow up over many years. There is always something new to discover here - another carving, another dome - for while it may be a jewel box, it is a very large one, and therein lie some of the problems we have encountered. The main temple is built with more than 1400 huge carved columns supporting numerous domes; there are stairs up and there are stairs down, there are balconies and terraces, quiet corners... And while the main temple - the one dedicated to the Jain spiritual saviour *Adinath* - is the big one, there are two more Jain temples and a Hindu Sun Temple all very close by, and a whole complex of buildings for pilgrims - lodges, kitchens, baths and toilets. If one were not careful, one could easily get lost.

When it came for the time to depart (we'd been there for well over an hour), Jean was missing. Jean, as you know, had a delicate constitution: her poor legs, her delicate stomach, her susceptibility to bites and stings all made her very anxious about travelling in the India that she loved so much. As a child she had played with her father's army memorabilia - his cap badge, his medals, his photographs - and she had stored up a well of affectionate nostalgia for a place where her distant father had lived. So she was here with her medicines and her fears. And now, in the Ranakpur temple, she was missing. She walked slowly and with a stick, so she couldn't have gone too far. Perhaps she had not heard my request that we meet at the bottom of the steep entrance steps, but she was certainly not there. Perhaps she had strolled to the Sun Temple or one of the other temples? Some of the other members of our group, Ingrid, Catherine and a few more, on learning that there were more explicit *erotic* carvings to be found there, had drifted away. Was Jean with them? But the erotic-seekers re-joined us - a little late - without Jean. No, she had not been with them. Tom, Betty, Molly (Jean's room-mate) and I decided we had better go back inside and find her; Jill would stay outside with the rest of the group to see if she turned up there; a few braved the toilets and would look for her there.

Back inside, the enormity of our task struck the three of us. More than 1400 columns! Each one wide enough to conceal her; she could be behind any of them. Was she in the crypt? Or on one of the upper balconies? - back then we were allowed to go up for the wonderful views down into the temple and across the hills. For half an hour or more the three of us criss-crossed the complex, sometimes even losing one another. Tom attempted some calculations about how many people it would take to search behind each column… I was not the only one beginning to panic. Had she fallen down or collapsed somewhere? Molly, usually so brave and caring, was close to tears. And then, at last, I saw Jill under the dome of the main entrance, looking for us. Jean had been found. She hadn't been to the temple *at all*. Faced with the flight of steps at the entrance, the heat, she had decided she could not attempt this most wonderful of Indian places. She had found her way back to the coach.

The complexity of the temple and the difficulty of finding someone in it possibly contributed to another incident in the Ranakpur Temple. Earlier, as we explored the place in one ones or twos, we met several of the group who had been adorned with a smudge of yellow in the centre of their foreheads. Cynthia and Betty were among those who had been so blessed.

'Yes,' said Betty, 'There's one of the priests who's grinding up this yellow paste. He's putting it on people's heads. He said it was for good luck.'

'We did not know whether to offer him a gratuity,' said Cynthia. 'He had such a spiritual air, we felt it rather inappropriate.'

'What is it he's put on your head?' asked someone.

'I believe it is sandal-wood paste,' said Cynthia. 'It does have a rather delicate scent, and he assured us we would be blessed. He had a kind of marble rolling-pin and was sitting down, rolling, rather like pastry…'

'Where is this fellow?' asked Jacky, 'I could do with a bit of blessing. Come along David, you could do with a bit of blessing yourself.'

'Oh really? Oh, must I?' David had not been noticeably enthusiastic about a number of Indian practices. 'Where do we have to go for that?'

'He's behind one of those columns… I think it was over that way…' Betty pointed vaguely across the temple complex. 'But be careful, because he had a whole lot of other stuff with him which didn't smell at all good. Make sure you get the sandal-wood paste.'

A few of the others joined Jacky and David in search of the anointing priest while the rest of us split up and continued to wander about to photograph or just gaze in awe at the architecture. A few of us stood to watch a Jain family worshipping before one of the idols. This, too, was a curious and moving sight. A father and son had evidently changed their clothes and now, wearing a pale yellow silk shawl over the torso, and a pure white *dhoti* from the waist, were kneeling with the wife and daughter dressed in *sarees* before some low tables. On the tables they were arranging little piles of rice-grains into various auspicious shapes - swastikas, scripts and other shapes - and from time to time they would prostate themselves completely before the idol. Other worshippers arrived and would ring one of the large brass bells hanging from the decorated marble to announce to their god that they needed his attention. It was all very fascinating and difficult to tear ourselves away, but time is always an enemy and we had to meet the others and make our way to our next destination.

Before we realised that Jean was missing and the anxiety set in, several of the sandal-wood paste seekers were talking about their experience. They seemed disappointed, and there were hardly any more adorned with the yellow smears.

'We couldn't find the fellow you were talking about,' said Jacky. 'We looked where you said, but we must have got it wrong.'

'Well, we found a man sitting behind a column,' said Val, 'but he couldn't understand what we wanted. He was sitting there with quite a few little dishes that were yellow, but it didn't look the same as yours, and we couldn't see any rolling pin. There were six or seven of us, and I asked him,

"Are you the man with the sandal-wood paste? We want you to put - it - on - our - fore-heads." He just smiled and shook his head, you know, in that side to side, up and down way.'

'Yes,' said Tom, 'I was with them as well. He just looked up and smiled. He had all these dishes with stuff in them. I asked him as well,

"Is that the sandal-wood? Are you the priest who does the blessing?" Well we were pointing to his dishes, and pointing to our heads, but he didn't cotton on. He just sat there, shaking his head. In the end, with us all standing around and pointing and asking, he handed up this dish with different kinds of yellowish stuff in little piles in it.'

'Yes, he handed it to me,' said Jacky, 'And I sniffed at it, but it didn't smell like sandal-wood at all. We passed it round and we all had a sniff. It smelt rather horrid and stale, and a bit spicy. It took a few moments before we realised: it wasn't sandal-wood; this wasn't the blessing priest. I've no idea who he was, but whoever he was, it was his lunch.'

ON THE HOLY HILL OF PALITANA

The first time we went there they warned us that we should make a very early start. It would be hot climbing the hill when the sun got high, and we should be at the top before then. Yes, certainly, we were assured, it was a most wonderful sight - all those temples, especially at sunrise - and the most sacred place for the Jain religion. Yes there were many steps but we should not miss it. Jill and I didn't have a group with us on this occasion- we were there to have a look to see if a tour to Gujerat, including the holy Palitana Hill, would be a good idea for a group. So we did set off early - not four-thirty as the guide suggested, but still leaving the hotel in the dark. Even this, we realised, did not bode well for a group tour; early starts were never popular. We were also warned that no leather items could be worn, and we may not eat or carry any food.

Arriving at Palitana we came across a notice that said

HOLY HILL
Ladies in their periodicals must not climb on Holy Hill
THANKING YOU
Anandji Kalyanji Trust

Luckily Jill was not in her periodicals, so we could proceed. Another notice said

NOTICE
It is advisable not to climb on Holy Hill before 'Sun Rise' & Come Down before "Sun Set" most valuable ornament, cash. Etc should not be with them. Gaurds staying on each rest venue as two gaurds are ever concurrent in foot moblie duty to relax from arised trouble
THANKING YOU
Sheth
Anandji Kalyanji Trust

This was also OK, as we had left our most valuables back at the hotel, and it was reassuring to know about the guards as we had no idea what trouble may arise.

Now, our guide, who had been quite active and helpful up to now, asked us if we would like to be *carried* up the hill, and would we also pay for *him* to be carried up? We declined, thinking we should certainly walk, so he said *he would wait* at the bottom of the hill for us. It was only now that we really understood that there were indeed *more than 3,800 steps* up this hill, and we could see that some of them were quite steep. But we had said we would walk… There were lots of porters, men and a few ladies, waiting near the first steps with chairs attached to long poles (for the heavy-weights), to be carried by four men, and also little platforms, or sling-chairs, that were swung by four ropes from a single long pole (for the lighter-weights) that could be carried by only two men, or, we found, *two women*. There was a party of French tourists getting ready to mount the hill in this way: all the men and some of the bigger women were getting in to chairs, a few of the lighter women were having difficulty sitting cross-legged on the little square platforms of the sling chairs, and there was much squealing and giggling, and some ignominious falling off. A little while later, while we were puffing and struggling up, we were astonished to be *overtaken*, yes overtaken by two ladies carrying an elderly Jain nun in one of these contraptions, the seat swinging to and fro as the two carrying ladies, one in front, the other behind, positively trotted up the steps. We learned later that whereas every Jain believer should ascend Palitana Hill at least once in his life-time, a Jain Nun should go up many more times - some said 999 times - but I found no confirmation of that. Anyway, they are supposed to keep going up, but when too elderly or frail they may be carried, *but not by men*. They must never be touched by a male, and who knows, with the swaying of the swing chair, anything may happen. So a community of lady swing-chair carriers were there who would also offer their services to any lady, nun or not, who preferred to be carried by women. Among the many people we met both overtaking us on the way up, and much, much later, on the way down, were many more Jain Nuns, some very young, some not so young, scampering along with joy, their white masks across their mouths and sweeping the path before them with whispy brooms for fear they may swallow or tread on an insect.

All this was most fascinating, but by golly it was tough going. The sun was up, it was getting hotter and hotter and the steps loomed ahead of us. We stood, or in my case, sat down to let another tour group overtake, the carrying men shouting for us to get out of the way as they went up at speed. A few pilgrims were also being carried up - fat men in the big wicker chairs, fat ladies swinging on swing-chairs, even one swing chair with two small children while the fat father and mother, in their seats, laughed encouragingly to us.

'Why are you walking? It is too much. You can take chair. Are you Jain also?'

Why were we walking? It was too much. And as we weren't Jain also, why were we there at all?

As we had got this far it seemed ridiculous to turn back, so with many stops for breath and a certain amount of grumbling, we did make it to the 'top'. But was it the top? We could see lots of temples spread out for what seemed like miles over the hillsides. Some were a long way away, some seemed further up; were we supposed to make our way over to them? Our guide was not with us to explain either what we should do or what exactly we were looking at. They all looked similar and, to be frank, *en-masse* and although many were ornately carved, they were a little disappointing in comparison with other very beautiful temples we had seen at Ranakpur or Mt Abu. I expect it was our exhaustion and our uncertainty about what we were looking at that made us a bit jaded. Curious and astonishing, certainly, but not being Jain also made us wonder why? Why so many? Why at the top of 3800 steps? Another feature of the journey up were the caravans of donkeys, laden with building materials also making their way up. The process of temple building and temple renovation was going on apace; no wonder that no-one could actually tell us how many temples there were, or how much of the Jain community's wealth was being poured onto Palitana Hill, or rather poured into donkey panniers to be carried up.

It's a prosaic thing to say, but there was a wonderful thing to be found at the top. In the place where all the chair carriers were relaxing, we were offered pots of the most delicious yoghurt in the world. Quite large earthen-ware dishes of thick white yoghurt, about the size of a large soup plate were on offer to refresh us. The chair carriers were consuming several each, chattering and laughing, before setting off down in the hope of finding some more passengers to bring up. It occurred to us that some of the donkeys must have carried these yoghurt pots up the hill. They were lovely and we ate two each - yoghurts, I mean, not donkeys. That was just before Jill tried to stand up and found that she had twisted or sprained a knee. She was in quite a lot of pain and could only move with difficulty, but refused absolutely to let me hire a chair carrying team to take her down. No, she would not be carried down, she would make her own way, at her own pace. So down we went, Jill gingerly taking two steps for every step: 3,800 steps up; 7,600 steps down.

The knee got a little easier after the first few thousand steps and when nearly at the bottom we met a joyous gentleman and his family who had just started their walk up.

'Good morning!' he greeted us (it was almost the afternoon and so, so hot). 'You have been to our Holy Hill. That is wonderful. Did you enjoy?'

'Well, it certainly was an amazing sight. Have you seen it?'

'No, no, we are from the USA. We are a Jain family living there these many years, but we have pined to visit to this place. We are so pleased to see you foreigners also visiting. But your poor wife? Has she hurt herself?'

'Yes, I'm afraid she has. We found it very hard work climbing the hill, and she seems to have strained her knee. I see you are going by foot. Some others are being carried. I rather regret not being carried.'

'No, no, that is not so proper. If we are capable we should certainly walk. You have walked; that is good. I am sure God has lifted your footsteps to carry you up?'

'Well, we are nearly down, but you are just starting up, and it's much hotter now. I hope he will lift your footsteps.'

A year or two later, when we returned to Gujerat with our group and were staying in the comforts of Bhavnager Palace, the nearest jumping-off point to Palitana, the group was ambivalent about the visit, so I decided to make the trip up the hill optional. The guide was enthusiastic and encouraging as he had been before.

'Oh, it is a must. Mr Richard and Mrs Jill were there before. Was it not a most wonderful visit?'

'Oh yes, it was, but may I remind you that you did not accompany us up the hill? You stayed at the bottom.'

'Yes, but that was…'

'It was because we walked up and you stayed down.' Jill was joining in.

'How many steps did you say it was?' asked Betty. 'You don't mean 3000-odd? Surely you mean 300?'

'Er, no Madam, in fact it is…'

'You said we'd have to start really early. How early is early?'

'Well, we ought to leave really early. We should leave by five…'

'*FIVE?*' There was an outburst from most of the group, '*Five?* How long is it…'

'Well I'm going to give it a miss,' said someone,

'Yes, so will I. I'm looking forward to those lions in the forest', said Betty (Asiatic lions in the Gir Forest, I should explain, were our next stop after Palitana). 'We'd be exhausted after going up that hill to see a temple.'

'Er, it's not just one temple,' I began, 'there are rather a lot, you see the Holy Hill…'

'A lot! Christ! Not another temple,' David was getting rather worked up. The group took a vote; no-one voted for the Holy Hill.

LORD BAHUBALI AT SHRAVANABELAGOLA

I'm sure you will know, even if you haven't been there, that going to see Holy Places in India quite often involves climbing up hills. Hindu and Jain places sometimes involve a stiff climb and the same idea has spread across Asia with Buddhism. Evidently we can gain quite a lot of merit by putting in the effort. In comparison with climbing up to see the temples on Palitana Hill (you may recall that this involves a climb of nearly *4000 steps*, and our group lost merit in declining to do it), going up to see the famous statue of Lord Bahubali is not so strenuous and most of our group members *do* make it. He is only 500 steps up a hill, so it is easy to take him in our stride. Mind you, the hill is not so easy to get to if you are in a bit of a hurry, as we always are, trying to get from Mysore to our next stop. He is quite a detour, and although you can see him looking very tiny from a very long way away, that's not really the point. There's not much merit earned by looking out of the windows of a coach.

The reason we can see him from so far off is that he wasn't *put* there; they could never have *taken* such a huge statue anywhere, let alone to the top of the hill. No, he is carved from the solid rock, starting at his head, from the top of the hill, and working away down to his feet; a big task force must have got rid of the hill on all sides as the sculptors worked on the image. As he stands very nearly *60 feet tall*, there he is silhouetted against the sky, visible for miles and miles. But who on earth is he, you will be getting impatient to know. No doubt the question *why* will be in your mind too, why is he up there and why we should go to see him? Well, we know who he was: Bahubali is a short name for Bhagavan Gomateshwara Bahubali, and he was a son of the first of the twenty-four Jain religious teachers, called *Tirthankaras*, who helped others to achieve enlightenment and are the main object of Jain worship. Bahubali was also a king who gave up his kingdom to become an ascetic, achieved enlightenment and is worshipped as a saint throughout the Jain world. We know all this because there is an inscription, put there by the donor, that tells us all about him and that he was carved in 983AD. We go to see him mainly because he is there, the biggest monolith statue in the world, and his statue is so astonishing that, although most of us have never heard of him, he was recently ranked first in the seven wonders of India! There are quite a few other statues of him dotted about and even some still being built, but this is number one.

It so happens that whereas we could see him from far off, as we drew nearer, driving through the hills, he was mainly lost to sight; just occasionally we could see his torso, or just the top of his head. And from the bottom of the hill where the steps start we couldn't see him at all. I have to say that our first group were not so keen on the idea of the 500 steps, and were not especially encouraged by seeing a group of Jain monks before we set off on the climb. These monks were of the *Digambara* branch of Jainism which, like most religions, is broken up into sects. As the writer Garrison Keillor so profoundly said of American religious groups, but could apply to many, 'They couldn't agree and broke up, and after they broke up they kept on breaking up.' The Jains didn't go that far, but in addition to doctrinal differences the *Digambara* monks have absolutely no possessions - no begging bowls, no shoes, no clothes - whereas the other main sect (the *Svetambaras*, who are the majority) - do allow their monks to wear a robe. Both sects worship Bahubali, but he is specially venerated by the *Digambaras*, so it was walking past a group of naked monks at the bottom of the hill that was our group's introduction to this Holy Place.

After much puffing and panting, we all got up there to look at the statue. Bahubali is also naked. He stands there, stock still, deep in meditation. Despite the difficulties he's not distracted by anything at all, not the ants in the ant-hill that grew up beside him while he meditated, not the snakes who took shelter in the ant-hill, nor even the crowds of devotees who climb up the hill to worship, or tourists who gape in awe. He stands there, so deep in meditation, so still and for so long that creepers (sculpted creepers, I should say, not real ones) have grown up his legs and even twisted up his arms. Our guide led us to the platform immediately in front of Bahubali's feet where offerings should be placed; it was rather beautiful with fresh flowers left by devotees. Without wishing to be at all indelicate one cannot help but notice that as one stands at his enormous feet, each foot being larger than a human figure, and looks up trying to see his peaceful face, a rather prominent feature gets in the way, generously proportioned to fit his sixty foot stature. It hangs there, as it were, poised thirty feet above us. Being so close is not the best vantage point to appreciate the art of the whole figure and the guide's commentary did not help elevate the mood.

'This is definitely the biggest single stone sculpture,' he said unnecessarily and for the umpteenth time. 'It is made out of one piece of stone, carved from the solid rock. It is very much venerated by all Jains and many others also.'

'So it is,' said someone.

'Oh dear,' said Tom, 'And I was led to believe size isn't everything.'

'Well, as you can see,' said Ingrid, 'It's pretty important round here. You can see why he's venerated.'

Once every twelve years there is a huge festival here to especially venerate the guru, a tradition which has been going on since the 10th century. At our second or third visit to this Holy Place, we were lucky enough to be there in the right year at the right time. In fact these huge religious gatherings are both an attraction and also an anxiety for our group visits: it is certainly interesting to see what is going on, but what with the crowds and the crush and the inevitable delays, not everyone wants to go. However, I had put it on the itinerary long before we knew we'd coincide with the festival, so we went. We only learned that it was on a few days before, but if we hadn't known about it we would have heard it long before we arrived. From several miles away we could hear the festival in full swing: echoing around the hills the powerful loudspeakers were broadcasting the jubilation of the priests chanting and preaching and the sacred music. We were also told that a good deal of the shouting was about crowd control. So, despite my forebodings about people getting lost in the crowd, or worse, we arrived, managed to park our coach and joined the crowds climbing up the steps.

It was certainly worth it. As we neared the top we could see above the excited crowds, and even above the statue, that an enormous scaffolding structure had been built behind him. Climbing up the special steps on to the platforms above him was a pretty constant procession of priests carrying large vessels which, when they reached the very top, they poured as a libation over Bahubali. At the time of our visit they were pouring milk or curd, and the white liquid was pouring down the head and the arms and torso of the figure. At each pouring the crowds roared their appreciation. Many of them were gathered near his feet and were attempting to have the holy liquid land on them. Once again, at the risk of being a little indelicate, we all know that when a man has a shower, although some of the water will flow down the arms and legs, a good deal of it is channlled down the chest and stomach and pours off the member. So it was with Bahubali, and the more fervent devotees, now soaking wet, were joyously welcoming the blessings raining down on them.

At other times during the 30 day festival he is anointed with *ghee* (butter), rice-flour, turmeric, honey and other holy substances, so by the end he is pretty striped and discoloured. All the time the loudspeakers call out the holy good news, the music blares, the crowds cheer and chatter excitedly. Some of us were able to get closer to the statue, although not too close for fear of a spattering, and there, between his feet was a large notice, written in several languages. In English it simply said,

SILENCE MUST BE MAINTAINED AT ALL TIMES

A PUJA AT MADURAI

In complete contrast to the luminosity of the Ranakpur Jain temple, the interiors of most Hindu temples are dark and secretive. There are good reasons for this: gods and goddesses, when not on the move saving the universe, live in caves deep inside the Himalayan Mountains. It is only natural, then, that the holy of holy - the place where devotees hope to see a glimpse of their god - is inside such a dark cave, reproduced in thousands of temples all over India. To reach there, the worshipper may have to pass through several outer courtyards and dark passage-ways, and of course there will be ancillary shrines on the way, the occupants of which will all deserve the attention and the offerings of the devotees. The outside of many temples is also symbolic, representing the Holy Mount Kailash in the soaring Himalayas - temples often have a towering peak or several peaks, often cut with deep channls so that in the monsoons the rains pour down in river torrents - the river being the Holy Ganges. In parts of south India the temples have grown into huge complex structures and these towering peaks have become the gateways to the courtyards of the great temples. These *gopurams* as they are called, are multi-story entrances reaching up, often covered in a myriad of mythological figures - gods, goddesses, demons, angels, musicians, dancers…

Madurai, in the south part of Tamil Nadu, has such a temple and after our first visit there, we felt we just had to bring our groups to look at this place. Not only was it a wonderful example of Indian architecture and sculpture, it is so busy with Indian life it must not be missed. If we wanted to see Hinduism going on at a break-neck pace, this was the place to see it. Every day the place was and is thronged with visitors - family groups, bus-loads of pilgrims, business men dropping in for a quick blessing, tourists galore. The Hindu religion is usually very happy and the temple a place to be happy in; people chatter and applaud, eat picnics, read, do school homework, sing hymns, hold business meetings, do some shopping. Every day a variety of ceremonies go on, some arranged on a regular basis, others arranged for a particular family, village or women's group. So we knew we could visit the evening *puja* with the group, and if we were lucky there may also be a day-time procession, or even a floating ceremony when one or other of the idols would be paraded around or floated in the sacred temple pond. This pond, by the way, is another cause of anxiety for me: it is a judge of literature - I mustn't let this piece of writing anywhere near, as if it doesn't float but sinks in the water, the judgement is that it is worthless. Good job it's not written in *Tamil*.

We visited the temple first in the day time. As I say, it is just enormous - if one wants facts and figures it covers over 40 acres and many of the *gopurams* soar over 150 feet high. If I said that it was easy to get lost in Ranakpur, Madurai is very much bigger and has four main entrances leading the unwary into different parts of town. But fear not, no-one did get lost partly because a little man gets his living there by being a tourist mopper-up and finder. He attaches himself to tourist groups and is very skilled at keeping an eye on everyone and rounding them up to rejoin the flock when led astray. The difficulty is that there is quite a long way to walk after leaving our shoes at the shoes-off place, and some people have great difficulty in walking without shoes. Poor Lydia, of the Raj Quartet was such a person. She had quite a lot of problems *with* shoes, and wore very sensible sporty 'trainers' to be able to get by. *Without* shoes her arthritic feet caused her agonies. We'd not been inside for more than a few minutes when Ann asked me to halt the group and return to Lydia. She was leaning against a pillar, obviously in great discomfort.

'I fear, Richard, that fascinating as I find this place, I shall not be able to continue,' she told me.

'Oh dear, would you like me to see you back to the coach.' I didn't tell her, but this would be difficult; the coach could not park where it had dropped us, it would have to be summoned.

'That is extremely kind of you, but I could not allow that to happen. No, I shall be perfectly content if I can find a seat. I shall remain there and should you *happen* to remember me on your return, I will be so obliged.'

We did find a seat; in the next large courtyard was the temple pond and we installed Lydia on the stone steps and in the shade. Ann and Cynthia offered to stay with her, but Lydia would not hear of it.

'Certainly not. You must continue with the others, and I shall look forward to hearing about your discoveries when you return. No, this place is perfectly delightful. In fact it is heaven. Which reminds me, do not concern yourselves if, on your return, you find me lying here dead. I may well have died, but I will be perfectly content to have died in heaven.'

When we returned Lydia had not died. Instead, she had been busy and was surrounded by a crowd of admirers - men, women and children - watching her work as she produced a very competent drawing of the Madurai sacred pond. When she struggled to her feet for the painful walk back, her admirers broke into applause.

Sadly, though wisely, Lydia did not join us for our evening excursion to the temple. The Madurai temple is unusual in that it has two major shrines, for this is the place which celebrates the marriage of Lord Shiva to his consort

Parvati - except that in Madurai she is called Meenakshi. Indeed it is called the Meenakshi Temple and it is dedicated to her - not her husband. Each morning both the deities, who have spent the night together in *her* shrine, are woken up, bathed, given their breakfast, and Shiva is conveyed back to his own shrine for the day. Every evening, after he has been fed by the temple priests, Shiva is taken in a little procession from his own shrine, where he has spent the day, round a few corridors and passages back to Meenakshi's shrine, where he spends the night with her. These processions have taken place every day for hundreds, some say thousands of years. We chose to go to the evening ceremony partly because the morning was far too early for our group - around six am - but mainly because the evening ceremony is more exciting - the temple lighting is minimal, dark and mysterious (although a growing number of fluorescent tubes are brightening things up), and the brief and hectic procession is accompanied by torch bearers. We were told to get there early to secure good positions for viewing and photographing; the procession would start at nine sharp.

We did get there early - far too early, but there was a good deal to see. In the semi-gloom, with many fewer people present, the place looked entirely different. The hundreds of tiny oil lamps which devotees had lit before many of the minor deities sparkled more brightly, the shadows cast by the many carved figures, the huge granite carved columns and the people moving about gave the whole place a feeling of mystery and exoticism. Some of us had torches to shine on the faces of the gods and demons that stared down from every facet. And there was also the smell - a curious, musty, rather sickly smell. Quite apart from the air of expectancy that hung over the place as we waited, there was another curious activity going on. As you know, it is usual to make offerings to Hindu gods: money, certainly, but also food - *Prasad* which may be sweets or rice, or bananas or coconuts or other fruits - which is blessed by the priest, offered and then returned to the donor as holy food. Well, all this does happen at Madurai, but there is another practice here too. Several Hindu gods had a fondness for butter, and a tradition has grown here of adorning large images of them, very close to the entrance to Shiva's *sanctorum*, by *throwing* small butter balls at them, hoping they stick on. A lot miss, but very often they score a direct hit, and with thousands doing this - of course there are 'butter-ball stalls' handy to supply the worshippers - the images and surrounding area get caked in butter and have to be cleaned off from time to time. Here we were in the semi-light, the little oil-lamps lighting up the scene, watching families having a lovely time hurling the small blobs of butter at the impassive, more-than-life-size figures, black with old butter, but splodged with recent missiles. I didn't hear it myself, but a good friend who travels to India a lot told me she had come across an Indian family from Yorkshire; the children had been born and bred there and hadn't been to India before. They had brought the traditional offerings but were having a high old time at the butter throwing game. One little boy of perhaps seven was rather confused by what was expected. She heard him, in his rich Yorkshire accent, say to his mother,

'Ey-up, our Mam, is this where we chuck fruit salad at god?'

In all honesty, the procession was a bit of an anti-climax after all this. It was not nine sharp; it was more like nine thirty before it began and not only our group, but other foreign tourists were looking a bit weary of waiting. Not being Hindus we were not allowed inside Shiva's shrine, but all the time we had been waiting, and watching, a steady stream of Indian devotees had been filing in and filing out, making their offerings, catching a glimpse of their Lord and leaving - they were certainly not hanging about to see any procession. We could hear a good deal of cymbal banging, drumming and snatches of loud music from inside, and eventually the waiting crowd perked up. A small palanquin covered in rich green cloth was carried out of the shrine, the elaborate silver doors banged shut and the music - drums, cymbals and piercing *shenais* (a kind of reeded clarinet) - reached a crescendo. The priests all had bare torsos with holy threads over one shoulder and wore white dhotis. Half a dozen were musicians, there were four to carry the palanquin and more to carry fans and long elegant fly-whisks, which were whirled above the palanquin to keep Shiva cool and free of flies. A bit of frantic fanning and whisking and *something* - it turned out to be Shiva's tiny gold shoe or was it a pair of shoes? - was put into the palanquin and it was off, and at what a pace! We had to run to keep up! Every few minutes the procession stopped outside another shrine or before an image, and there was more frantic fanning and whirling while the music brayed, and then we were off again at top speed. This went on for about ten minutes and finally we were outside Meenakshi's place. There was more rummaging about, the *something* (shoes again) was rushed into Meenakshi, her doors slammed shut, and that was the end.

We retrieved our own shoes and made our way back to the hotel. Next day I heard some of the group telling Lydia what had been going on.

'How interesting,' she said, 'How interesting that their Lord could have shoes in the temple. Do you think that if I, too, achieve divinity, I will be allowed shoes? I do so hope so.'

THE TAJ MAHAL IS ONLY WHITE

Certainly we should go to the Taj Mahal. People often say that they would like to see the *real* India, the India *off the beaten track*, but we would hardly drive so near and not see the Taj Mahal. It is, as you know, in Agra, not too far from either Delhi or from Jaipur, and these three cities comprise what the Indian tourist industry call the Golden Triangle. And it is a golden triangle, containing not just the Taj, but many more wonderful monuments - more tombs, more forts, more palaces, more gardens. It also contains more tourists and, most important, more tourist shopping than the rest of India together. Here is the real gold of the Golden Triangle - the gold that flows into the pockets of the shop-keepers, middle men and commission agents as people struggle home with their carpets, jewellery, marble inlaid tables, clothing, illustrated *Kama Sutras* and the rest. Trying, not altogether successfully, to avoid some of this, we have sometimes called our tours just that - *Off the Beaten Track.* Unfortunately I have been caught out; the Indian agents printed their own very verbose and elaborate version of the itinerary devised by me and presented to each of our group members, a document headed:

Itinereay specially prepared for Travellers Club
RAJASTHAN & MOGHUL INDIA BEATEN OFF THE TRACK

This turned out to be mildly prophetic as we were not infrequently beaten off the track into the shops by wily guides and coach drivers. The Moghul India bit was, of course, going to Agra and ending up in Delhi, two of the capitals of the great Moghul Emperors.

I've lost track of the times we have been to the Taj - several dozen, I suppose - but can truthfully say that it is just wonderful every time. That first stunning view, seeing it framed in the archway of the entrance gate, pale and slightly misty against the blue sky, is overwhelming *every time*. I remember when Jill and I took poor Rosina there, who had been so ill that she couldn't go earlier with the group that day, and she was so weak and thought she wouldn't get to see it. She just burst into tears. I think we all burst into tears. Over the very many years of our visits the conditions for visiting have changed a lot. There are lots more visitors and more queuing. It's now closed on Fridays (whereas it was *free* on Fridays, the day of Muslim collective prayer), now quite expensive and there's all that changing into electric buses for the last few hundred yards to reduce pollution. Never mind; it's still a marvel. And if you're wondering why the Taj Mahal is in this section about Holy Places, it is a holy place; it is in the Garden of Paradise, the resting place of The Empress Mumtaz Mahal and, later, her grieving husband, Shah Jehan, who was buried there by his wicked son Aurangzeb. He was the one who deposed and imprisoned his father and murdered his brothers. Moslems regard this place as a holy shrine and flock here during pilgrimages to even holier places. At such times it is very difficult to see, so crowded does it become.

In the old days, when it cost so little to go in, and when security was not so strict, we often went several times during a visit to Agra; sometimes without a guide to just gaze and soak up the atmosphere, sometimes at dawn, or at full moon. Just ambling about was and still is such a pleasure. Of course there were the very Indian aspects of it: at one time the lawns (a British introduction, by the way, from the time the Taj was *closed to Indians* and became a sort of British Club. The Moghuls had filled the gardens with fruit trees, not lawns, and they had become very neglected and overgrown when the Brits took over) were mowed by bullock-powered lawn-mowers. We have watched as the skilled gardener driving his pair of bullocks, each with a bag tied under the tails hoping to catch the shit, knowing their animals so well, would dive forward as one or other of the bullocks was about to deposit a pile, and catch any that didn't go onto the bag with two hands, deftly depositing the handfuls that otherwise may have fallen onto the pristine lawn, into the rose beds. Nowadays petrol-driven lawn-mowers have replaced this diverting scene.

We shouldn't have been so easily diverted for there is so much to see. The approach alone is a masterpiece of design, with places for pilgrims to stay: the remains of the old artisan quarters of the thousands of workers who built the place, the caravanserai. Then there is the great gateway and the walled gardens, with a huge red sandstone and marble inlaid mosque on one side of the garden, and a matching building just for symmetry on the other, all divided up with water channls. And facing us, at the end of the garden, with just the river and the sky behind, is the white marble tomb itself, high up on a white platform and flanked by the minarets. And this is without stopping to look at the wonderful detail - all that exquisite carving and inlay work and calligraphy. Oh my goodness, if you haven't yet been to the Taj, you must go, and if you have been, please go again. And when you go, try to imagine the river as a wonderful waterway, lined with gardens and tombs and palaces of the courtiers, the Red Fort in the distance. Not much of all this survives, but some does and the Taj is the most wonderful of all.

Which is why it is sometimes a little disappointing if people's reactions are not quite as enthusiastic as our own. Jean couldn't help it, I suppose, as it was quite hot and she was obviously a bit overcome with the glare of the white marble when she had struggled up the steps, barefoot, to the great platform where the Taj stands. It was Jill who found her slumped against one of the minarets in the corner.

'What's the matter Jean?' Jill demanded. She could be quite brusque, though it was kindly meant. She had been kind to Jean a good deal during the long tour, and this was nearly the end.

'I think I'm having a heart attack,' cried Jean plaintively.

'No you're not. Look around you,' said Jill, 'This is the Taj Mahal! It's just wonderful. Have a rest and then have a look at it.' Jean did have a rest and a look and recovered remarkably.

June and Olly, however, took an odd attitude towards it. To be fair, June and Olly took an odd attitude to quite a lot of things. June had even been accused by a guide (not to her face) earlier in the trip - a trip dogged with some bad luck - of having the '*Evil Eye*'. A few days before, after we had made our way by elephant all the way up to the top of the great Amber Fort near Jaipur, a long ascent after queuing for our elephants for quite some time at the bottom, June had turned to the devoted Olly and said,

'Oh, Olly, I've left my drink on the coach. Just run down and get it for me will you?' I couldn't believe what she was saying; we were just about to set off on a longish walking tour of this most wonderful palace with our guide who was most anxious to tell us all about it.

'But June,' I said, 'You don't have to worry about that! There's a café up here if you need a drink.'

'Oh, no,' said June, 'It's my special drink. I have to have it. Olly won't mind, will you Olly?'

'No, I won't mind, June. Did you leave it in that bag?'

'Yes, that's right, Olly, it's on the seat, I think. Can you just run down…'

'But the coach has gone to a coach park,' I broke in gazing across the landscape we had just climbed up on our elephants. 'It's about a mile away from where we started off. And how will we find Olly, if he does go? How will he find you to give you this drink? And he'll miss seeing this place - we've only just got up here…'

'No,' said Olly, 'I'd better get it. June won't be happy if she doesn't have…' And he was gone. Much later, *two hours later*, after we had finished the tour some of the group, including June, had told the guide that they didn't want to walk down and would go down by jeep. The rest of us started to walk and met Olly on his way up just too late, looking hot and flustered.

'Where's June? I've got her drink. I had to walk up and I couldn't find the way...'

I met June and Olly in the garden of the Taj. I had suggested to everyone that we went down there at dusk for a quiet time to soak it all in, unmolested by a guide's information.

'Oh there you are; are you enjoying it?' I asked.

'Well,' said Olly, 'It's all right.'

'Oh dear, only all right?'

'Well it's not as good as Tamburlaine's.'

'Tamburlaine's?' I was mystified.

'Yes, in Samarkand. I think it was in Samarkand. Wasn't it in Samarkand, June? His was green. *And* it's older.'

'Green? What was green?'

'His tomb, I think it was his tomb. Wasn't it his tomb, June? It was green, this one's only white.'

'Only white? I'm sorry, I'm afraid you have the advantage of me, I haven't been to Samarkand.'

'Well you should. His was green.'

'Oh, no Olly, this one is beautiful.' June was on my side. 'I like this one. He said it was beautiful and it is beautiful. But what I want to know, Richard, is, who lived in this palace?'

'Who lived in this palace?'

'Yes, you know, you've been going on about all those emperors and Moghul Akbars Mumtazes and that. Which of them was living in this one?'

SHOW ME THE EROTICS

A very dear friend of ours, Wendy, who had frequently been a guest lecturer with a very erudite travel company, not a mere tour leader like me, and who led several of our own tours to India, had once told me that an American client had taken her to one side at the start of a tour (not one of ours, I hasten to say) and said,

'Listen, baby. I've joined this tour to see the erotics. I'm not interested in all that other crap. Just show me the erotics.' As her tour was called 'Art Treasures', in this case the art treasures of central India, she was a bit non-plussed as to how this gentleman would fill his time between the rather sparse diet of erotics. There would be a few places, some very famous, displaying something to interest him from time to time, but very few and not very often.

At least this gentleman knew what he was signing up for, even if he was only interested in one aspect of it. There are people who join tours, or indeed many other activities under what can only be misapprehensions. I remember *at the end* of the first two hour meeting of a longish 20 week adult education course I was teaching - it was on the Victorian Age and that evening involved a bit of film, a number of documents and some discussion all about Queen Victoria - a man came up and asked if the course was on astronomy. He had joined up, sat for two hours on Monday only to find much later that Astronomy was on Tuesday. Even in our tours people did not always get what they hoped for. One lady rang me - she got my number from an article in The Daily Telegraph - and we spoke for over an hour about the tour. I sent her detailed descriptions and she and her husband even came to a pre-departure lunch and briefing. At our first stop - on the beach near Madras - he declined to join any of the expeditions to see temples, farming, villages, the city. No, he would stay on the beach. On our long coach journeys he declined to get off for photographs or any sightseeing. The tour lasted well over three weeks, and the last few days would again be on a beach in Goa. Every day he asked me when we would reach what he called The Promised Land, rather like a child asking 'Are we there yet?' He was perfectly behaved and undemanding, but took not the slightest interest in anything Indian, not even the erotics. He was only interested in sunshine and, in the unlikely event of finding it, a secluded bit of beach. India is not much given to seclusion. His wife was not so different and usually stayed back with him beside hotel pools.

It has always been a mystery to me as to just why there are erotic images on some of the temples of India. Nowadays we may think of India as perhaps guarded, even prudish, certainly in comparison with the west, when it comes to matters of the public display of sex and moral behaviour. Films and magazines don't show much in the way of overt sexual material; the behaviour of young people and choice of marriage partners is still strictly controlled by parents; dress is almost always modest - if ladies swim at all their costumes are figure-concealing, and they often bathe fully dressed. Even holding hands is still commonly frowned upon (apart from between young male friends). And yet, carved on the sides of medieval temples, female dancers and musicians reveal their sensual, full and often bare-breasted bodies. At a few, and it is only a few, of the well-known sites the medieval carvers have gone further and shown a pretty extensive catalogue of sexual activity. These, no doubt, are what the American gentlemen travelling with our friend was after. Various explanations have been offered by theologians, art-historians, sociologists, but I've never come across any that I find totally convincing. One view suggests the carvings are up there as instruction - what to do and how to do it - following the instruction manual found in a small part of the Kama Sutra, but does this sound convincing to you? Another explanation is that sex is a normal pleasurable part of human and divine life, all of which is considered a proper goal of life in Hindu philosophy. Well, yes, but why depict it on temples? A few suggest there is a connection with esoteric tantric rites, but I think this is not only incorrect, but descends into the area of mumbo-jumbo and hocus-pocus.

However, leaving the 'why' on one side, there are erotics dotted about at some Holy Places. Many are well known in the west and have been for a very long time. I am always intrigued by what Victorian wives and missionaries may have made of them after they began to accompany their husbands to India. I came across an entry in Murrays Guide to India, Burma & Ceylon (1924) describing the temple of Konarak in the state of Orissa in Eastern India - not one of the places that was on Wendy's itinerary with the American gentleman.

> *'Kanarak... celebrated for its Black Pagoda (c.1250-60), which everyone should visit in spite of the discomforts of a night journey through heavy sand in a palanquin. (Cost about Rs.25). A relay of bearers should be sent on half-way: provisions and drinking water must be taken. One should leave Puri at 10pm; arrive at Kanarak at 4.30am (20 miles).*
>
> *The shrine at the w. end of the temple has been cleared of the mass of superincumbent ruins, and it is now possible to realise the splendid carvings on it, including the grand wheels and horses, which indicate the fact that the temple was the chariot of the Sun-god, to whom it*

was dedicated. There is a number of very fine carved figures of green chlorite on the walls, but, unhappily much of the decoration is of a licentious character...'

A visit was evidently thought worthwhile back in those days despite the discomforts of a night journey and despite the licentious character of the art. We travelled there rather more comfortably and found that all mannr of imaginative sexual activity is displayed as decoration on those grand wheels, but its matter-of-fact open acceptance was brought home to me when I saw some Catholic Nuns leading their teenage school-girls on a tour of the Konarak temple. They strolled past, stopping to look without comment, and the girls demurely looking, too.

Of course there are the prurient, and I may have appeared to be one, as a helpful would-be guide, lurking around a corner, hissed at me,

'Pssst! You want to see group sex? I show you group sex.'

'Er, no thank you.'

'You want to see mabsturation?'

'Mabsturation?'

'You don't know mabsturation?'

'Thank you. I can see all I want without your help.'

Rather more well-known than Konarak are the very famous temples of Khajuraho, where quite a few of the many remarkably beautiful temples have some erotic carvings. They have become so famed, not for the erotics I trust, but for the quality of the art and architecture. It is, after all, a World Heritage Site. The Indian tourist industry has built an airport and several hotels to attract visitors to what otherwise would be a remote and inaccessible spot. It must have been pretty inaccessible as the temples were spared the destruction of the invading Moslem armies that defaced so many of the Hindu temples in other places, and, although the region was abandoned and many temples fell down, those that remain are mostly in a wonderful state of preservation.

'Every detail can be seen,' as our guide, Mr Singh, pointed out.

Actually, he was a pretty good guide, thorough, knowledgeable, with excellent clear English. He led us around and inside several of the temples, explaining the history, architectural styles and many of the mythological stories of the Hindu gods depicted inside and outside. At last he began on the topic that had been hanging in the air.

'It now remains to say something of the erotic carvings for which Khajuraho is justly famed,' he began. 'They are very much in a minority among all the other wonders that are here,' and then went off into a bit of the mystical mumbo-jumbo area which left us all mystified. Luckily, he returned to the carvings, and he was eloquent about the beauty of the poses, facial expressions and tenderness of so much of the work.

'And here you will see that this young couple is attempting a most difficult position for their love-making. To achieve this, you will observe that they have obtained the help of two assistants - that lady and that man. Actually, they are probably servants, but it is difficult to be sure as they are naked. Anyway, as you can see these two helpers are also very much enjoying, although the lady is looking so sweetly bashful …'

A little further on he pointed out another coupling;

'Ah, here you will find this position is not only difficult, it is quite impossible, as the gentleman is standing on his head…'

'I don't think he's standing on his head at all,' said Debby, who evidently knew about these things, 'They're lying down, surely, and if they are lying down it's not impossible.'

'But,' said Mr Singh, slightly cross at the interruption, 'If it is not impossible, I can assure you it is very inadvisable. I had a German tour leader here last year who took the same view as this lady, but the following day he could not continue his tour as he had severely damaged his back.' He was interrupted again by a loud peal of laughter.

'Now,' he went on, leading us to another vantage point, 'If you will all come to this point here, and look to that point there (he pointed above our heads with his long bamboo cane), yes, that couple in standing pose, there; you will see that the artist has left nothing whatsoever to the imagination.'

'Where?' came a cry from several.

'I don't see what you are looking at,' came from others.

'Ah,' said Mr Singh, 'If that gentleman there, with the binoculars, will raise them to this point here (he again pointed above us), I am sure that you will see that the artist had a most perfect knowledge of anatomical detail.'

It was David who had the binoculars. He stood rather embarrassed in his smart sun-hat, elegant shirt, neatly pressed long shorts, with long cream-coloured socks neatly turned over below the knees. Rather reluctantly he raised the binoculars to the pointing cane,

'Oh… I say…'

'What is it? What can you see?' called the group.

'Come along David,' called Betty, 'Hand over those glasses.'

A HOLI FESTIVAL

May I mention not so much a Holy Place as a Holy Festival that goes on in most places, not just Holy ones? It had better be just one festival, as there are so very many belonging to all the many religions of India. This one is a Hindu festival, but it is so popular that many of the others join in too: you can see Sikhs and Moslems having a great time. It goes on during February or March, the period of Spring in most places in India. To confuse matters, although it is a *Holy* Festival is called *Holi*. People enjoy this festival a lot. It is quite messy as people throw coloured water or powders at each other (and in the process ruin their own clothes, so they put on old ones, quite often those of passers-by, who don't have on their old clothes, and sometimes throw their powders at cars that are passing or parked nearby). The whole affair can get quite boisterous. The people who probably enjoy the festival most are young men, who drink, shout, dance and roar about in gangs making fun with their elders and sometimes even tourists. Some of these tourists also *appear* to enjoy Holi. We've seen them in the smartest places - the foyer of The Imperial Hotel for instance - their faces, hair, clothing, cameras caked in the bright pinks and blues and greens of Holi colours after going into the street to 'participate'. They smile, a little wanly, a little embarrassed, but I'm not sure they have enjoyed the experience; what I do know is that we have come to fear, loathe and avoid it.

The background to the festival is not altogether joyous, either. Holi, or Holikar as she was really called, was a demoness, who was burned to death in an episode in a long and complicated story involving Lord Vishnu vanquishing evil. She was the sister of an unspeakable King of the Demons who got too big for his boots, went about oppressing the world and even tried to kill his own son because he worshiped Vishnu. Luckily Vishnu saved the boy, but in the process Holikar perished in the fire, and Vishnu went on to destroy the Demon King by putting him over his knee (belly up - he wasn't there for a spanking), and tearing out his entrails with his big claws. Claws? Well may you ask! Well yes, Vishnu, had, for this purpose become a 'half-man half-lion' - just one of the incarnations he needed to do his job of preserving the universe - so he had some fearsome claws. This happy ending to a happy tale brings a sense of peace after oppression and also ushers in spring, with its vibrant colours. So fires are lit commemorating Holikar's demise, the colours of spring are thrown about and there's a general sense of celebration.

Although we try to avoid Holi, it takes place at a time when we are quite often in India. It lasts for a couple of days (except in Mathura, near Agra, where it lasts for sixteen days - mind you Mathura is the birthplace of Lord Krishna, who is another of Vishnu's incarnations, so they have a good deal to celebrate) and those two days can be a bit tense. Some members of our group, who know about it, don't respond too well to the news that it will happen while we are there.

'Oh Christ! That again? Can't we keep out of the way?'

Our own first experience of Holi, when Jill and I were alone in Jaipur, was rather unexpected. We had been warned all about the dangers and difficulties of the festival from friends - a very respectable and hospitable family. They had invited us for the day, to keep out of the way, we thought. So we bought some gifts and had them beautifully wrapped, put on our best clothes, paid our cycle rickshaw man a lot extra to warn the marauding crowds to NOT daub us with colours, and arrived at our host's door unmolested. When it opened our friend's welcoming wife threw a tin bath full of pink dye over us. How they laughed. They dressed Jill in a saree (saying that she could give the ruined clothes to the poor), but I had to go out, soaking wet, with the men-folk to have the coloured powders added to face, hair and wet pink clothing.

Our first time of Holi with a group was no better. The agents had sent a message,

'As you will arrive in Delhi on day of Holi, all monuments and shops will be closed. Therefore we have arranged a special Holi party for your group. You are invited to our GM's home for Holi.'

I expressed some concern about this, remembering the tin bath episode, but they were reassuring. Another fax arrived:

'Do not worry, there may be a little colour, but it is definitely washable, and we will make sure your guests are not inconvenienced in any way. There will be eats and you will enjoy very much.'

There were eats, in fact there was a very generous and sumptuous buffet lunch for us, family friends, all the employees of the agency, together with all their children. Perhaps it was the children that led to things going wrong. They didn't have just water pistols and water cannons to fire the dye, and it wasn't even the stirrup-pumps in big buckets of dye that was the main problem, it was the sticky silver paint they daubed on our faces, and the powder dyes they threw at our wet clothes. Quite a lot of fat little over-excited boys of about twelve ran around the party firing, daubing, throwing, while the adults shrieked with laughter and joined in. Before long the whole garden and everyone in it looked like a war zone. Back at the hotel, I heard Jill sobbing in the shower. Her hair was streaked purple and green; her clothes and underclothes lay discarded on the floor; pink dye had run into the blue dye. It was some weeks before the hair grew out…

But it wasn't all misery. At Mandawa Castle - one of those big Rajasthan palace hotels - some of us really did enjoy at least parts of the Holi Festival. I say some of us as Jill and some others kept very much out of sight. But at Mandawa it is a big affair, with a fun-fair, musicians and a big climax in the courtyard of the palace when villagers come to pay homage, and play Holi with the noble family. Quite a number of us decided to join in this jolly occasion and went into the town to see what was going on. Pretty soon youngsters were coming up to us, quite politely asking if they may daub our faces with a little of the powder. How could we refuse? And some young men were generously offering us sweet-meats. I remember that one of our group - Dick, who had not been with us before - was saying how delicious these sweets were, while his anxious wife Mary was telling him not to eat them - who knows where they may have been? After a while Dick disappeared and Mary was getting quite anxious, not least because the daubing had become a little more forceful and there were clear signs of smallish, brightly coloured hand prints over her bosom. We went off in search of Dick and eventually saw him being led into the distance by a group of teen-age boys. We ran after them calling, but Dick seemed very unresponsive. Two of the boys who had hold of him were curiously dressed as girls, with heavy make-up - not Holi colours, but eye make-up, rouge and bright lip-stick. All was well as we soon realised that these young men were not what we feared, but were the dancers. It was, we learned, very inappropriate for *girls* to dance in this conservative town, so *boys* did the dancing. All was not well with Dick, however. His voice, when we got him to speak, was slurred and he was unsteady on his feet. He had been eating more of the delicious sweets which we learned were laced with hashish. Quite what his fate would have been if we hadn't spotted him, we never knew. Mary, already disconcerted, led him back to the hotel in disgrace.

Back in the courtyard of our palace-hotel we watched the climax of the proceedings: each of the bands had male dancers dressed as girls and one of these was lifted up on to the large drums of the bands that were competing for a prize. There they danced, held aloft, swaying and circling over the heads of the bands while the drumming and trumpeting became quite frenzied. After the prize-giving the bands made their way back into the town and a few of us (not Jill, nor Mary and Dick) followed them, still daubed with our colours. By now quite a lot of drink had been consumed and the young men were a good deal less restrained than earlier in the day. Our friend Norman's wife, Val, was quite a shy, smiling, but big lady, with a very ample bosom. Indeed the bosom was so ample as to require special dispensation on our coach journeys - she needed to sit quite near the front to avoid too much bouncing about on the uneven pot-holed Rajasthani roads. Now young men were coming up to Val and calling,

'Kissy, kissy, touchy, touchy…' and already, like Mary earlier, Val had clear evidence of a good deal of touchy, touchy, with much Holi colour applied to her breasts. Norman was not taking this lightly. He too was a very big person, with huge forearms and fists the size of water-melons. He responded by thrusting his fists under the noses of the offenders, saying,

'Watch it! I'll give you kissy, kissy, touchy, touchy… I'll give you a good…'

'Oh, hang on!' I interrupted. 'You're frightening them to death. They've never seen anything so enormous!' I was, of course referring to his huge fists. Unfortunately Val thought I was addressing her,

'You horrible man!' she said, 'How rude!'

MASSAGE

A FEW WORDS ABOUT MASSAGE

Let me say straight away that I am not at all keen on massage. I have tried it, rather reluctantly, two or three times and each time found it either a painful or humiliating process, or both, and have not found the after-effects in any way beneficial. Perhaps this is because, as one may say about other matters, I never *paid* for it: as a tour leader it was sometimes offered to me free-of-charge in the hope that I may encourage members of our groups to take part. After those early disappointments, I have avoided massage and declined any 'on the house' offers that were made, however apparently tempting. On the other hand, there have been many of those who travelled with us, and we have met many others too, who find massage to be both pleasurable and beneficial, and who go out of their way to look for it and often pay very high prices for their choice of the various treatments on offer.

We all know that massage is very ancient: Greeks did it, Romans did it, no doubt ancient Chinese too, and it is found in many cultures, and comes in many forms. So, despite my personal antipathy, I haven't doubted its efficacy for others. I have always assumed it is broadly used as a therapy for fatigue or aching, or damaged or ageing muscles. Offers of massage have been available from our very earliest travels - on beaches, at swimming pools, in hotels, airports, even sometimes in street-side booths. No doubt the services have been genuine, but just occasionally the offers, and perhaps even the acceptance of such offers have been a little suspect. When we returned to a hotel in Aurangabad after an interval of a year or two I enquired whether the massage man we had encountered earlier was still there.

'He is no longer with us, sir. We had to let him go.' I had a pretty good idea of why they had to let him go when some of the revelations about his massage filtered through to me - mostly, I should add, from appreciative ladies. Debbie was one who went rather further than she intended, when, on our last evening of the tour, having taken a drink or two too many, she mentioned that her massage had been rather more than expected. To my surprise she went on to say that her massage man had lightly brushed her pubic area and enquired 'Here also?'

'Well,' she said, 'I thought, why not? But after he brought me to orgasm, he asked if I wanted a bit more, and I said no, that was enough…'

We went on to talk about other matters, and I was gratified to learn how much she had really appreciated several aspects of the tour that she had not anticipated. She said she hadn't been much interested in the art and architecture before we got there, but was just amazed by what she'd seen. Later, at the farewell dinner I had to respond to a request for a little speech, and I was about to mention Debbie's reminder of our wonder at the cave temples of Ajanta and Ellora, not far from Aurangabad.

'Oh yes,' I said, 'Debbie just reminded me of how much…'

'*Don't tell them that!*' shouted Debbie, horrified, from the other end of the table…

Presumably, after our departure from the Aurangabad hotel, a less appreciative lady spilled the beans.

Ayurveda massage, an ancient speciality of South India, is part of a mainly herbal medical system, often making use of quantities of oil. In the last 20 or 30 years it has become one of the most widespread forms of massage to be found all over India and far beyond. We once visited an *Ayurveda* hospital in South India where massage was offered for many conditions including even broken bones and stroke victims. A poor old man who had had a stroke was brought in to be shown to us. The energetic *Ayurveda* doctor seized him and whirled his arm around with great vigour.

'See, see. When this man came to us he was paralysed. Now look… he can move.'

I knew a bit about stroke victims; my father had lain paralysed for months in hospital, so I asked.

'Maybe he did not have a very bad stroke? He seems to have made a good recovery?'

'Yes, certainly, it was mild stroke only. But we have patient with worse stroke. You wish to see worse? Shall I bring another?'

We all protested that another patient would not be necessary, and were led to a massage room. To our surprise we came across a Western visitor there. On one of the wooden massage tables lay a bronzed and fit-looking middle-aged German gentleman who was not suffering from any discernible medical condition, and who, we were told, came every year for *two weeks* of massage, while spending a month or two on the beaches of Goa. He was modestly clad in a wisp of cloth for the benefit of the visitors, with the traditional *two* young Indian male *masseurs* on *each side* of his body, massaging in the healing oils. We were puzzled at the time, but was he, I now ask myself, simply an early *massage tourist*?

This is just part of changing times. Whereas in the early period of our visits to India and other places a few hotels may have offered massage as an ancillary service, now massage tourism has become a major industry in its own right and there are hotels - many that were just called hotels but now add the words '*-and spa*' - where massage and all mannr of holistic treatments are the main reason to go. Some of these places are beautifully located - on beaches or in the mountains - but few are related to the curative powers of mineral waters, which is what spas *used to be* all about - think of Baden-Baden or Bath, Aix-les Bains or Cheltenham. Mind you, the word has changed its meaning and 'spa resorts' can be found everywhere - central London, country house retreats… They are concerned with health, well-being, beauty, relaxation, exercise and diet, offering to 'de-tox' or 'de-stress' their clients and proudly offering 'pampering products' in their tempting shops. Who knows what our simple *Ayurveda* hospital may have become in the meantime? In India or the other places we visit the spa hotels are sometimes so well-placed on our tourist trail and in such lovely places that we would like to stay there *en route* to the next destination. But no! Their remarkably high prices often include a number of therapies which we (or at least I) don't want, and in any case they are often *full* - filled with clients who have gone on a spa 'holiday' precisely for the pampering. These are the new 'high-end' clients that the high-end tourist industry aims at. And there seem to be plenty of them - well-to-do Russians, Chinese, Westerners (including our antipodean cousins) and of course a growing number of Indians - happy to spend a lot but *not to see* what we used to think of as the 'real India', let alone the slightly less real, but spectacular and beautiful things to be seen in that wonderful country. Perhaps for the high-end few this has become the real India?

A MASSAGE IN MYSORE

It was early the next morning that I encountered Rajan. I was on my way back from a swim before breakfast.

'Excuse me, sir, are you the group leader of the British group?' The voice was deep and confident. The speaker was a tall, thick-set, portly but powerful and handsome Indian, with a proud moustache.

'I am.'

'We are having an excellent new facility in the hotel. We have all kind of massage facility.' The voice was now confidential, almost hushed.

'Oh, do you?'

'Yes, sir. Allow me to introduce myself? My name is Rajan and I have introduced this facility. Do you think your group will be interested?'

'Well, I really don't know…'

'If you will recommend to your group it will be very much appreciated. I have introduced Indian massage in Canada, where I am working. But in Canada the winter is too cold, so now I have introduced in this hotel also. All kind of massage: *Ayurveda* from South India is a very much appreciated speciality, and we have many…'

'Well, yes, but I don't know if…'

'And for you it will totally complimentary.'

'Well, thank you but I am not much interested in massage…'

'But sir, for you we have two very beautiful Thai girls. With them you will enjoy very much.' As he enthused over his massage facility, his voice had grown louder and more insistent. At the mention of the complimentary Thai girls his voice had dropped and once again became hushed - almost a whisper in my ear.

'The Thai girls are very much appreciated.'

'I'm sure they are. Thank you, but I'll mention it anyhow.'

'That will be most kind. For your wife - I believe your wife is here also? - for her also the facility will be complimentary. It is there, near the swimming pool.' He indicated the changing rooms from where I had emerged when he first accosted me. 'Also they can inform at the reception.'

'Yes, thank you. Most kind…' and I made my way to breakfast, meeting Cynthia and Betty on the way. I started to tell them about Mr Rajan's massage facility.

'Oh, we know about that,' said Betty, 'We've already met the man, and he's told us all about it. We met him yesterday. Ingrid said she's interested and Val's already booked.'

'Yes,' I replied, 'He told me about the Thai girls.'

'Oh? He didn't say anything about Thai girls. He told us about how he worked as a masseur in Canada, but it's too cold there in winter and that he comes back to India to work here.'

Rajan had evidently spread the word himself and I forgot about it. Certainly I saw no sign of any Thai girls in or around the hotel during our entire stay.

It was not until towards the end of our last day in Mysore that the matter of Rajan the massage man came up again. We'd had a busy time visiting the lovely carved temple of *Somnathpur* and *Tipu Sultan's* palace the day before, but on this last day we were having a day of 'leisure' when those who wished to return to the city could do so, and others could choose to relax in the garden. Our only gathering was to have a short expedition that evening to see the famous illuminations of the palace, which happens only for one hour on Sundays and public holidays. Leaving the pool at about four in the afternoon I met Betty, shaking with laughter as she walked up the staircase that led from the garden to the hotel.

'What's been happening?' I asked, cautiously. Betty's laughter, I had learned, was often a cause for concern.

'Yes, I can't help laughing. She *is* a *hoot*! You see, I booked a massage for myself and one for Cynthia. She's been such a lovely room companion that I thought I would buy her a massage as a present. She said she's never had one before, and I did rather have to persuade her.'

'Was that all-right?' I was becoming apprehensive. Cynthia had come on this trip not knowing anybody and I felt a special duty of care.

'Well, mine was fine. He was a bit suggestive at first, but I didn't play along with any of that…'

'*He*?' I exclaimed. '*He*? I thought he had Thai girls who gave the massage? Er, for the ladies,' I added rather hastily, 'I mean he has ladies to massage ladies?' This was a question.

'Thai girls? I don't know anything about Thai girls. No, he does it himself.'

'What? Do you mean that great big strong chap - what was his name?'

'Yes, him, Rajan. He's jolly good. The others said he is, and he is.'

'*Others*? What others? Anyway…I'm sure he is. But what do you mean '*a bit suggestive*'?' I was now alarmed.

'Best you don't know. Anyway, I was telling you about Cynthia…'

‘I hope he wasn’t suggestive to Cynthia!’ My alarm was growing.

‘Well, I wouldn’t know about that. That’s what I’m trying to tell you. She’s with him now. I did warn her, so I don’t think you need worry. But even so, she is a hoot!’

‘What do you mean, “needn’t worry”? What do you mean “she’s a hoot”? What’s happened?’

‘Well nothing really. It’s just that I had my massage first, and Cynthia was next, so I waited a bit to see that she was happy about it.’

‘And was she?’

‘Well, I suppose she was. But I had to leave; I just couldn’t stop laughing. It’s just that the last thing I heard her say to Rajan - in that lovely voice of hers - was “What? Everything *orrf*?”

A rumour circulated a little later that Cynthia had booked another massage from the massage man, though when I tried to confirm whether this was the case, she vehemently denied it. I don’t think it can have been true as we left Mysore next morning and there would scarcely have been time, but I became more concerned as to just what had been going on when, during our coach journey over the Nilgiri Hills up to the hill station of Ooty, I overheard more than once the phrase ‘Rajan, Rajan the massage man,’ repeated as a slightly hushed refrain from some of the ladies of our group sitting behind me. Then Ingrid, always forthright in her comments, could be heard quite plainly from half-way down the coach, apropos of nothing that I could hear, saying,

‘Well, I can understand having to strip off if they’re going to use all that oil all over you, but I’ve never heard of him having to strip off as well…’ The rest was drowned in roars of laughter and I never learned the aftermath of Ingrid’s encounter.

RAJAN RAJAN THE MASSAGE MAN

But there was more to follow. A couple of days later we arrived in Cochin (nowadays called Kochi) and drew up at the Taj Malabar Hotel at around five in the afternoon after a very long drive down from the hills. Once again the hotel was overbooked; once again I had to ask for volunteers to share a grand suite - this time the Chinese suite - and once again it was Cynthia and Betty who volunteered to share with Catherine and Val. But in the middle of this long negotiation, while others waited for keys and identified baggage, the reception clerk held out the 'phone and called,'

'Tour leader, tour leader, phone, phone. A call for you.'

'Me, are you sure? I'm not expecting…'

'Yes, he is asking for tour leader of British group.'

'Perhaps another British group?' I was thinking of the Lady B.B. group, the rather fierce lot we had encountered in Mysore. Were they following us here? Were they here already, taking our rooms? Nonetheless, I put my ear to the receiver.

'Hello, hello, yes, who is speaking?' There was a lot of noise in the lobby and it was difficult to hear.

'Hello, is that Mr Richard?'

'Yes it is. Who is there?

'Can I speak to Mrs Val?'

'Mrs Val? Who is speaking?'

'This is (crackle voice)…'

'Who is speaking?'

'Can I speak with Mrs Val. This is Rajan here.'

I couldn't think who it could be.

'Rajan, (pause) it is Rajan, from Mysore.' The repetition of 'Rajan, Rajan' brought him back. What had happened? Had Val left something behind and he was phoning to arrange to return it? Had she not paid for a massage? Why would he phone her? She was standing not far away and I held out the phone for her.

'Val, there's a call for you. It's that fellow Rajan from Mysore…' There were some rather unlady-like whoops of delight from some other members of the group and cries of,

'There you are!'

'It's true, then. He said he would…'

Val rather sheepishly took the phone from me and I carried on with my lists, keys, luggage identification but also trying to field the usual queries.

'I need a room on the ground floor,' from Jean.

'We've decided we need a twin room and ours is a double,' from a different Betty with a grumpy husband.

A half-whispered voice was close to my elbow.

'Richard, can I have a word?' It was Val. She was still holding the phone.

'Is everything all-right? Have you left something back in…'

'No, no, everything is OK. I just wanted to ask you - how long are we stopping here? I can't remember; is it three days or maybe four?'

'Er, it's three days, or four nights, rather. We leave early on the last morning. Why?'

'I see. Thanks, I'll be back to you.' And she went back to the phone. A few minutes later she was back. The lobby was now nearly empty as luggage was being carried, followed by people going off to find their rooms. Even so, Val was half-whispering and almost apologetic.

'Can I have another word? Would it be all-right if I left the group and re-joined you before you set off on the last morning?' There was a pause.

'Er, leave? Er um, yes, of course… er, but can I ask..?'

'Yes, well, you see, he's asked me out to his place. It seems they have a small farm somewhere near here…'

'Really? Do you mean the massage man. It was him on the 'phone wasn't it?'

'Yes, yes, of course. Yes, he's come down here from Mysore. I just happened to mention that we were coming this way.'

'Did you? Yes, well. Er… Will you be all-right? I mean, is he…'

'Oh yes, I'll be perfectly OK. He's a Prince, you know. Did I tell you that? Yes, he's some kind of prince, and they have a plantation down here.'

'Really?'

'Yes, you needn't worry. It seems they have this rubber plantation. I'll just sort out some of…'

'A rubber plantation?'

'Yes, if it's OK with you I'll just sort out my things. I'll leave my big case with Catherine if you don't mind. She said she'll look after it.'

'Oh, Catherine knows about this? Do the others know..? It'll mean one less in the shared suite…'

'I must go. He'll be here in a few minutes.'

'Well, OK. But… we'll be leaving at 7.30 on Thursday - in the morning - to catch a train so you'll have to…'

She had gone.

There is a brief addendum to the scene. Some years later a reunion of this group and some other Indian travelling groups was held in Val's house as an evening party. Val was by now married to George, a fit and active chap, but not at all in the first flush of youth, to whom she had become engaged on one of our trips to Nepal a year or two after the massage in Mysore (George, you may recall, had bought the ring at a bazaar stall for a very small sum). She and George had then become disengaged on yet another tour, during a major row on the steps of Siena cathedral. But they made it up and were married, continuing a passionate but stormy relationship. At the reunion party someone started to reminisce about a very grand elephant ceremony we had all visited in Cochin. Val had gone there with Rajan, and we had seen her in the crowd.

'Wasn't it wonderful?'

'Oh, it was fantastic!'

'The colours and that music.'

'Marvellous.'

'I'm just sorry we missed the fireworks,' said someone (I should explain that the group had decided to miss the firework display as it wasn't due to begin until three in the morning).

'Um…' mused Val. 'I didn't…'

Fortunately George was quite hard of hearing. He did not hear the reminiscences, though he did ask the reason for the great outbreak of laughter that no-one would explain.

CYNTHIA BY THE SEA

I was reminded of Cynthia's wary approach to massage when, years later, on a tour in Eastern India, she was approached by another massage man. We were in the state of Orissa, staying close to the sea, and a group of us had made our way down to the beach on bicycles borrowed from the hotel. It was an extremely hot day and cycling along the sandy track was very hard work - making us so much hotter - and I was keen to get into the sea to cool off. Our little group included Cynthia and her sister-in-law Lucy. The other two members of the Raj Quartet had stayed at the hotel as they were not fond of beaches and had no wish to bathe in the sea. In the light of what happened it was as well they stayed behind: it was not a very salubrious beach, frequented by fishermen, a few local youths and even fewer foreign tourists. But, as always, there were ladies to greet us selling sarongs and bead jewellery, men selling postcards and necklaces, and there was a massage man. He was a complete contrast to Rajan, the massage man from Mysore. This one was small and very thin, dressed in a *dhoti* and rather grubby vest, and with a rather cringing mannr. Like some of us, he had also arrived by bicycle, which advertised his trade with a small wooden box on the rear carrier, labelled in crude painted lettering *Very Good Masag Man*.

'Massage, massage, very good massage, Madam,' he called as he wobbled over the sand towards us on his bike. Cynthia and Lucy were standing near us in a small knot of our group members.

'See, Ladies, here! You can have very good massage. Gents also. Tourists have written…' and he produced a dog eared notebook for our inspection. 'See, Germany people, French people…' He seemed to be directing his attention to Cynthia.

'No English people?' I enquired as I thumbed through his book. But it was more of a firm statement, made in Cynthia's direction.

'Yes, yes, many people from England also. See, here is my friend, she is from Barnet, you know Barnet? She is giving 'photo. See, she is having massage…'

A page in the notebook had an old crumbling photograph of a young girl with the massage man -rather younger than today - both grinning at the camera.

'You will take massage, Madam? Very good massage. See, you can lie on towel.' The towel he produced was a small, thin, rather greasy cloth, about the size of a tea towel, which he proudly spread on the sand at Cynthia's feet. He squatted down beside it and patted the towel in a welcoming gesture.

'You don't want a massage do you?' I directed my question to Cynthia, remembering the Mysore Incident, but meaning the whole group. To my relief she was quite decisive,

sweeping aside the massage man's attempts:

'No thank you. It's frightfully kind of you, but no, I do *not* want a massage.'

'But head massage, Madam. Head massage is very good. I give very good head massage. You will see. Feel very good, look very good…'

Lucy joined in. Lucy's voice was lighter, but equally grand and very determined.

'No thank you,' to the massage man. And then to Cynthia, 'Cynthia, darling, do say no to this man. I think you should say once more and make it very clear indeed that you do *not wish* for a massage.'

Evidently both Lucy and the massage man had discerned some slight hesitation in Cynthia's reply, and now a conversation began between Lucy and Cynthia, meant to be *sotto voce*, but heard by everyone.

'Well, a *head* massage, Lucy dear, may be rather nice. It has been rather an exhausting morning, and it may smooth away the fatigue...'

'Cynthia darling, you did say that you would not take a massage.'

'But a head massage, Lucy dear, just a head massage… it may…'

Other members of the group had slipped away towards the sea, and I could see them pulling off trousers and skirts to reveal swimming costumes before paddling in the very low surf. Torn between staying to protect Cynthia and the need to cool down, I went to join them. Before going in to the water I turned round to see Cynthia sitting down, with the massage man squatting behind her. I waded in very slowly; a few of the others were jumping up and down as the surf reached their knees.

'Look! I think they want you,' said someone. 'Lucy's waving. I think they want you.' I turned round and Lucy was waving a scarf rather agitatedly. I walked back up the beach and could hear Lucy saying slowly and very deliberately,

'No, please stop. No! That will be quite enough.' I speeded up as matters had clearly reached some kind of crisis.

'Richard' called Cynthia, who had caught sight of me. 'Thank goodness! Do stop this man.' The massage man was now kneeling in front of Cynthia, pushing down on one outstretched leg while she seemed to be trying to get to her feet. She was turning on to her side on one knee and pushing up with one arm. The massage man was almost in tears.

'No problem Madam. Yes, yes, head massage only…'

'Oh dear, what's happened? Are you all-right?'

'I am perfectly all-right, Richard dear,' replied Cynthia, rather breathlessly. She seemed quite composed, but went on, 'But I have had quite enough. I fear the head massage has reached the inner thigh!'

A TURKISH ASIDE

While on the subject of massage, may I take you to Turkey for a few moments? We went there from time to time; in fact, we still go there, but not necessarily for the massage. We were led to Turkey in those days by my good friend Godfrey, an expert on Ottoman culture, and he was the one who suggested that a Turkish bath, followed by a massage in the bowels of the hotel would be a good idea.

Now these matters are usually strictly segregated - ladies and men at different times, different days, sometimes different premises. So I joined Godfrey and a friend, George - the only males in the changing rooms. This alone was a curious experience, as Godfrey, quite a neat, dapper man, if a bit crumpled, began to undress. Removing his rather dusty jacket, he revealed a pullover in a very disreputable state. There were holes in the elbows and the arm-pits seemed to be badly torn. The shirt was not too bad, and only a little frayed around around the collar, but the underwear was not attractive: both vest and pants were sagging, yellowing items for which Godfrey felt he needed to apologise.

'I am sorry about the state of these clothes,' said Godfrey, 'But I always take my oldest clothes away on tour and throw them away before I return home.'

We were joined after our time in the steam bath by the in-house *masseur*. He was an enormous man, dressed only in baggy Turkish trousers and cummerbund, but it was his shape that was so extraordinary. His big bald head was egg-shaped, almost pointed at the top, and the outline of this shape flowed down and outwards, past his cheeks and out to his very wide sloping shoulders in one continuous sweep. There was no apparent neck, but his torso was muscular and, together with his huge arms and prodigious stomach, covered in luxuriant hair. As he approached George - first in line for the massage, and lying on the table wearing just his towel - he bent over him with great intensity, his hands reaching out. I was reminded of a lurid illustrated paper-back cover of Dennis Wheatley's '*The Eunuch of Stamboul*'. Godrey and I retreated from the scene, and I confess I did not return. George's report on his massage was enigmatic -

'All right. Bit rough and ready.'

How was it then that David and Jackie had taken their Turkish bath together? I didn't see a set of rules about the bath, and this was a hotel rather than a public bath-house, but it was certainly against all convention, and Godfrey was deeply shocked when he learned about it. And even more astonishing, how was it that the masseur had provided massage services to *ladies*? I didn't know that he had until two ladies, who did not know each other well but were sharing a room on this tour, told us about it during dinner. One, Helen, was almost elderly, a gentle and kindly lady; the other, Julia, was much younger - perhaps half her age - but a rather shy, even timid young lady. It was Helen who brought up the subject.

'Well, we went and had a massage after the Turkish bath,' she said. 'It was jolly good, but I've never had a massage by a man before.' The room fell silent, knives and forks were put down.

'Which man?' I was a bit startled. Surely it wasn't the man we had left with George?

'Oh, a great big chap. He was wondering about in the steam room, which was a bit strange, so I asked him about how we could get a massage. He said he was the hotel massage man.'

'Did he have big baggy black trousers? Er… rather hairy?' I couldn't help asking.

'Yes, that's him. Julia wasn't too keen, but I persuaded her to stay and have one.'

'Oh… and was it OK? I mean…'

'Oh yes, it was. He was jolly good.' I must say Helen looked quite radiant and relaxed as she told us. Julia was not looking relaxed; she was looking quite wide-eyed and startled.

'And what about you? Was it OK for you?' I asked.

'I haven't had a massage before. Is that what they're like?'

Jacky broke in to the conversation. She and David and some others were sitting at the next table, but everyone around us was focussed on Helen and Julia.

'I had him,' she said. 'You're quite right. He was the one. He was hanging about in the steam room when David and I had finished.'

'David and you?' asked Godfrey. 'It is not usual for the sexes to mix…'

'Well, we did. There was no-one else there, so we both got in the hot bath and then went in the steam room together. This fellow was in there and asked if we wanted a massage. David didn't, of course, but after all that banging about on the coach to get here I decided I did.'

'He was good, wasn't he?' said Helen.

'Well, I don't know about that,' said Jacky, rather sharply. 'He was all-right at first, but after a while I had to ask him “What kind of massage do you call this?”

He said, in that great deep voice of his, “This is the deep muscle massage, Madam.”

And I said, “Oh is it? Is it indeed? Well, let me tell you this, you won’t find any muscles in there!”’

EPILOGUE

'Well, I'm sorry to hear that,' I said. 'We'll miss you; but surely, we must have been doing *something* right; after all these years together?' Sir A and Lady B had just announced, as we were returning from a tour, that *anno domini* was catching up and they wouldn't be doing any more long-haul trips. They had been reminiscing and couldn't recall whether it was *eight* or even *nine* trips they had done with us; several to India, to Sri Lanka, to Indo-China and to other places.

'Yes, you have,' cut in Sir A, shortly. 'You charged rather less.'

Deflated, I felt, to quote one of our Indian guides, that I was being 'sent home with a flea between my knees.' Of course I should have known better. He was, after all, a very high ranking officer and a bit abrupt in mannr. His wife had been a bit stand-offish towards us at first, but had mellowed over the years. Mind you, they were both extremely cross when their luggage failed to travel with us on one flight - I was not to blame this time, ours was missing too - and we had to ask the group if anyone had spare knickers to lend lady B till it arrived. Though kind to us, her reputation remained intact: years later, standing on the battlements of an Indian fort-hotel, I could hear the ringing clipped voices of a British group far below in the courtyard. Standing near me was an Englishman, looking down. He called to his wife,

'Bloody Hell! There's a bloody *Brit* lot down there.'

'I'm afraid I'm partly responsible,' I murmured to him, apologetically. 'Some of them are travelling with me…'

'Are they? Are they just? Christ, look, that one- is he one of yours? I know his voice; I know him.'

'Er, yes, that one? Yes, he was in the army…'

'I know he was; he was my commanding officer… Hang on! Isn't that his wife with him? I was wrong; *she* was my commanding officer. Oh Christ!'

Eight or nine trips was unusual; once or twice or three times was more common, but there are others who came even more often. Everyone knows how big India is and many see that it is unwise to try to see 'it' in one go, although there are people who want to include everything: the Himalayas, beaches, palaces, tigers, the Taj Mahal, Kerala backwaters…. Over the years our tours went beyond the Indian sub-continent, and, together with friends and colleagues who led many of them, have extended all over Europe, the Middle East and Indo-China. Our travellers loyally tried out new destinations with us and come back again and again. And we have often met up with many in between trips, sometimes in advance, and also afterwards at the summer reunion parties we arrange in the garden. These, too have had their ups and downs. At one pre-departure lunch party, involving cooking curry for 20 or more people, a couple came, ate huge portions, drank copiously and then cancelled their booking, thereby proving that there is such a thing as a free lunch. As we have no idea of the number who will turn up at our summer barbecue, we normally ask people to bring contributions to share, food to cook on the barbecues, photographs to astonish but not alarm potential travellers. Some, like David, who likes to sit down at a proper table with a proper knife and fork, come suitably equipped.

'Barbecue? Certainly not,' he replies to people watching him tuck in with a napkin around his neck. 'I bring my own lunch.' Another couple, who I had never seen before, turned up at the summer party one year but clearly hadn't read the invitation or brought anything at all.

'Bring food and drink!' she said, outraged. It was not a question. 'How astonishing!'

'Don't worry,' I said, 'I'm sure there'll be something you can have, there's lots of food over at that buffet table. Do have a glass of wine meantime.'

After several glasses of wine; I saw her looking down at the barbecue where someone was cooking some enormous prawn kebabs for a party of eight. I heard her say to her husband,

'I say, darling, look at these; they look frightfully good!' with which she swept them all up and carried them off, hotly pursued by the owner, calling,

'I say, I say, excuse me…'

They did not show any interest in our tours; we never saw them again. Strangely, if I ever had it, I must have mislaid their address.

You will know, dear reader, that these little incidents have been drawn, rather at random, from several of our tours over a long period. Rather like the tours themselves, the stories flit from place to place and time to time, and during all this time we have seen much of India changing dramatically before our eyes. Shopping malls have arrived in the cities; I recall seeing, some years back, one of the first JCB earth-movers replacing an army of mainly women earth-movers with little metal dishes on their heads, shifting rubble at a building site. A cartoon of a similar scene appeared in England during the depression years of the 1930s, with a new-fangled mechanical shovel and unemployed men looking on,

'By heck, there's work there for a hundred men wi' shovels.'

'Aye, there is, or a thousand wi' tea-spoons.'

But not everywhere; I say 'much' of India as on many journeys, if we choose to be beaten off the track, we can still see scenes that have not apparently changed at all. Bullock carts still trundle about, women still carry water or huge loads of firewood on their heads, harvests are often gathered by hand. Even here, though, if we look carefully we may see changes - the bullock cart has old lorry wheels, not wooden ones; the water pots carried by the women are often brightly coloured plastic, not clay; a fisherman dressed in a tiny loin-cloth, carrying a huge net from his flimsy thatched home to his primitive boat, has a mobile-phone to his ear. In the hut, his son is glued to the Premier League on the generator-powered TV, or flicking channls on his iPad. I wonder what happened to the little shops and street vendors in the area of the shopping mall? To the lady earth-movers (there are JCB's everywhere)? To the wheelwright and the potter? I wonder what we will see next time?

What has been rather more constant, and what has been so very gratifying, are the people travelling with us. Of course the most recent of these people are not those who came on the first few tours. The university department that spawned the first Indian travellers no longer exists, and sadly, a number of those who came are no longer with us either. Others from those earlier days plead frailty, or seek a 'proper holiday' rather than a challenging experience. My dear wife has pointed out for several years that I am in the same situation: whereas we used to lead groups of mainly elderly people, we are now the elderly people. Well not quite; we still go, remain very gullible travellers, and accumulate more fond memories to fall back on.